DISCOVERING THE FIRST CENTURY CHURCH

The Acts of the Apostles, Letters of Paul and the Book of Revelation

MARGARET NUTTING RALPH

Second Volume of the New Testament
in the Series
DISCOVERING THE LIVING WORD

PAULIST PRESS
New York/Mahwah

Library of Congress Cataloging-in-Publication Data

Ralph, Margaret Nutting.
    Discovering the first century church: the Acts of the Apostles, Letters of Paul, and the book of Revelation/Margaret Nutting Ralph.
    p. cm.—(Discovering the Living Word; v. 2)
    Includes index.
    ISBN 0-8091-3254-0
    1. Bible. N.T. Acts—Textbooks. 2. Bible. N.T. Epistles of Paul—Textbooks. 3. Bible. N.T. Revelation—Textbooks. I. Title. II. Series: Ralph, Margaret Nutting. Discovering the Living Word; v. 2.
BS2625.5.R34   1991
225.6'1—dc20
                91-15112
                CIP

Published by Paulist Press
997 Macarthur Boulevard
Mahwah, New Jersey 07430

Printed and bound in the
United States of America

Contents

Paul's Letters

Selected Letters

The Book of Revelation

* * *

List of Maps

To my father and mother,
Charles and Mary Agnes Nutting,
in gratitude for a life "planted in love and built on love."
(Eph. 3:18)

Preface

Since you are reading the Preface to a book entitled *Discovering the First Century Church: The Acts of the Apostles, Letters of Paul and the Book of Revelation,* I think I can safely assume that you are beginning a study of the Acts of the Apostles, of selected epistles, and of the book of Revelation.

The book which you now hold is based on the premise that the first thing you should do to begin such a study is to read the selected biblical text first *before* you read about it. Do not start with this book. Start with that book of the Bible which you are interested in studying. Let your first impression be that New Testament text and not what someone else has to say about it.

If you wish to begin with the Acts of the Apostles, read the text through quickly the way you would a novel. As you read, jot down every question which comes to mind. Do not stop to read footnotes or commentaries. Allow your first impression to be an impression of the whole.

Obviously, each New Testament author's intent was that his work would be read as a whole, not chopped up—a paragraph here and a paragraph there—read in random order and out of context. There is no book on earth with a plot which you could possibly understand with such a haphazard method. The books of the New Testament are no exception.

Over the years I have collected the questions which students ask when reading Acts, a selection of letters, and the book of Revelation for the first time. This book is a collection of short articles written in response to those questions.

It is my experience that the content of these articles is appropriate and useful for juniors in high school and anyone older. I do not recommend this book for most younger students. I have found that one must have developed beyond the very "literal" way of thinking which is normal in the early teen years before one is able to understand the points made in these articles.

The quantity of material is appropriate for a variety of religious education settings. If two articles were discussed every class meeting, this book would be a one-quarter course for an in-school class that meets every day, a semester course for an in-school class that meets two to three times a week, and a year-long course for an out-of-school class that meets once a week. One may, of course, go faster or slower, depending on how much time is spent on the review and discussion questions. The material is also appropriate for adult education groups.

The format of question and response may tempt the students to skip responses to questions which have not occurred to them. This would be a mistake. One question often leads to related questions which do not appear in the heading but which are addressed in the articles.

Despite the question and answer format the short articles written in response to specific questions are not pat answers. I have tried to respond to the questions in such a way as to teach a methodology, so as to enable students to think. The goal is to equip students with the tools they will need to search out answers to questions which do not appear in these articles.

The fact that the responses deal with methodology is an additional reason to read the articles in order. Methodological points made in early articles are usually not repeated in subsequent articles.

It may be that a student will be unfamiliar with a word or concept in a given article which has been presumed known and so is not explained. The glossary in the back of the book has been designed to help the student in such a situation. Students should remember to use the glossary if unfamiliar words appear or to review concepts which were explained in earlier articles.

In addition to a glossary, the book contains an index of biblical passages. This will help both teacher and student locate comments on given passages.

Both teacher and student may expect, and even want, to read more introductory material before reading the specific New Testament texts. This desire is purposely thwarted in this book in an attempt to let the texts themselves have the first word. Some background information is provided in various articles as the need arises. However, the student is urged to read the biblical text first so that questions are not explained away before the student has had an opportunity to ask them. All commentary is secondary to actually reading the New Testament text.

Of course not all questions which students raise will be addressed in this book. This is all to the good. To grow in one's ability to raise the questions, to explore answers and to live with mystery are goals in themselves. While it is wonderful to reach a degree of understanding as we read the New Testament, not one of us will ever succeed in completely understanding the truth and wisdom which are to be found in the Acts of the Apostles, in the letters, and in the book of Revelation.

■ THE ACTS OF THE ■
■ APOSTLES ■

ARTICLE 1

What Kind of Writing Is Acts?

Question: "What is the earlier work referred to in the opening sentence of Acts?" (Acts 1:1; Lk 1:1–4 also discussed)

The earlier work is the gospel according to Luke. Luke's gospel and the Acts of the Apostles are really two parts of the same whole.

The gospel according to Luke begins: "Inasmuch as many have undertaken to compile a narrative of the things which have been accomplished among us, just as they were delivered to us by those who from the beginning were eyewitnesses and ministers of the word, it seemed good to me also, having followed all things closely for some time past, to write an orderly account for you, most excellent Theophilus, that you may know the truth concerning the things of which you have been informed" (Lk 1:1–4).

Since Luke and Acts are one work with one method and purpose, a careful look at this introduction to Luke's gospel will help us better understand the Acts of the Apostles.

The author of Luke/Acts addresses his method when he says that he has edited ("an ordered account") inherited oral and written sources which told of events which had occurred. Let us look at the steps referred to in this passage carefully because an understanding of how the work came into existence will help us understand the kind of writing we are reading.

The process started with events. In the gospel these events surround Jesus' life on earth, his death, and the period immediately after his resurrection. In Acts the events start with Jesus' post-resurrection appearance and continue with the birth and growth of the church.

The author of Luke/Acts is not claiming to be an eyewitness of

---

GROWTH PROCESS WHICH PRECEDED ACTS

Events: God reveals himself through events (i.e. Pentecost, Peter's dream, Paul's conversion, etc.).

Oral Tradition: People talk about these events as faith experiences.

Written Tradition: Parts of oral tradition are gradually written down (i.e. sermons, miracle stories, diaries, etc.).

Edited Tradition: Luke edits the inherited traditions: "It seemed good to me also, having followed all things closely for some time past, to write an orderly account . . ." (Lk 1:3).

Canonical: The worshiping community recognizes Luke's word as inspired and accepts it as a vehicle of revelation because it faithfully reflects the experience and beliefs of the community.

---

these events. Rather he is basing his work on accounts which have been drawn up by others "exactly as these were handed down to us by those who from the outset were eyewitnesses and ministers of the word" (Lk 1:2).

Notice that the author's sources were not historians but "ministers of the word." They were passing on the good news not to answer the question, "Tell us exactly what happened," but to answer the question, "What is the significance of the Christ event in our lives?"

So in both the gospel and in Acts the author's purpose is to teach "how well founded the teaching is that you have received." While his teaching is about events, his goal is not to accurately describe those events for his audience but to help his audience understand the significance of these events in their own lives.

CHARACTERISTICS OF LUKE'S EDITED WORK: ACTS

1. Not exact quotations. (Speeches and dialogues are composed by Luke to teach the audience.)

2. Only crucial events are included; others are omitted.

3. Summary transitions emphasize the role of the Holy Spirit as they connect episodes.

4. Individual components may represent a variety of literary forms which existed independently of Acts.

Also notice that the audience has already received the teaching. Luke/Acts is not written to evangelize those who do not believe but to help those who already believe to understand more deeply the course of events in which they are now involved.

It is very important to understand that Luke/Acts is an edited arrangement of inherited oral and written traditions because this knowledge can protect us from bringing false expectations to the text and so misunderstanding the author's intent.

For instance, if we know that we are reading an account based on oral tradition, we know that we should not expect the account to contain exact quotations. In fact, the speeches which you will read in Acts are composed by the author to teach his audience the significance of events. The main audience of the speeches is not the listener pictured in the text as present at the event but the reading audience represented in the prologue by Theophilus, the person to whom Luke addresses Acts. The speeches are teaching devices.

Many speeches appear in the context of an event that had great significance in the life of the early church. Events have been selected as important by the editor and are thus emphasized. No attempt is made to be all-inclusive, to tell of less significant events in order to make the account more complete.

To link one event with another, the author composes summary transitions which encapsulate what is significant about an episode and move the reader on to the next event. The summaries connect episodes so that the reader can clearly see the growth of the church under the guidance of the Holy Spirit.

A knowledge of the kind of writing we are reading when we read Acts is not simply background information which may be interesting but is not crucial. Rather, a knowledge of literary form is essential to our understanding of Acts. If we misunderstand the kind of writing, we misunderstand the intent of the author. In the case of scripture, if we misunderstand the intent of the author we misunderstand the revelation which the book contains.

Since the Acts of the Apostles is made up of a variety of sources, it contains a number of different kinds of writing, just as the gospel does. We will need to recognize this variety as we encounter various stories in order to correctly interpret them.

Who is the editor of Luke/Acts? The work is traditionally attributed to Luke, a companion of Paul's, who wrote to a largely Gentile audience, possibly in Ephesus, around 85 B.C. In the combined volumes Luke traces Christianity from its source, the person of Jesus, through its growth throughout the then known world.

Review Questions

1. What is the earlier work referred to in the first sentence of Acts?
2. Name four steps of the process which resulted in Luke/Acts.
3. What events lie at the core of the Acts of the Apostles?
4. What is the author's purpose in both Luke and Acts?
5. Who is the primary audience of the speeches in Acts?
6. Why does it matter whether or not we understand the kind of writing we are reading in Acts?

Discussion Questions

1. How does the motivation of the author of Acts differ from the motivation of an historian?
2. Did you presume that you would be reading exact historical quotations as you read speeches in Acts? Do you know why?

3. Does the fact that the speeches in Acts are composed by the author make them more or less valuable in your mind? Explain.
4. Did you presume that Luke was an eyewitness to the events he describes? Do you know why you had this presumption?
5. Which do you think is more likely to be accurate, the eyewitness of one person or the agreed upon witness of a community? Explain.

ARTICLE 2

The Power of the Spirit

Question: "What does Jesus mean when he says, 'John baptized with water but you, not many days from now, will be baptized with the Holy Spirit' (Acts 1:2–8)? Didn't the early church baptize with water too? Isn't that why we still baptize with water?" (Acts 2:41; Acts 8:12; 8:38; 9:18; 10:47–48; 16:15; 16:33; 19:2–7 also discussed)

This question rests on an important passage in the Acts of the Apostles but takes from the passage a different focus than Luke would have us take. Rather than focusing on the role of water in the church's baptismal ritual, we would do better to focus on the role of the Spirit in Acts. However, before we take this focus we will answer the original question.

John's baptism with water was a baptism of repentance. It did not confer the spiritual power which Acts describes as accompanying baptism with the Spirit. This distinction is made clear later in Acts when Paul speaks to John's disciples at Ephesus: "And he said to them, 'Did you receive the Holy Spirit when you believed?' And they said, 'No, we have never even heard that there is a Holy Spirit.' And he said, 'Into what then were you baptized?' They said, 'Into John's baptism.' And Paul said, 'John baptized with the baptism of repentance, telling the people to believe in the one who was to come after him, that is, Jesus.' On hearing this, they were baptized in the name of the Lord Jesus. And when Paul had laid his hands upon them, the Holy Spirit came on them, and they spoke with tongues and prophesied" (Acts 19:2–6).

This baptism of the Spirit was the initiation rite in the early church, and did use water (see Acts 2:41; 8:12; 8:38; 9:18; 10:47–48; 16:15; 16:33; 18:8).

In our present-day celebration of initiation we still celebrate with the pouring on of water (baptism) and the laying on of hands (confirmation), initiation rituals which have biblical roots.

The focus which we can more fruitfully find in this passage, however, is not the emphasis on water but on the role of the Holy Spirit.

The apostles are to receive the Holy Spirit, the same Spirit who had inspired Jesus to chose the apostles in the first place (Acts 1:2). Only by the power of the Spirit will the apostles be able to continue the work of Jesus through time and space. "But you will receive power when the Holy Spirit has come upon you, and you shall be my witnesses in Jerusalem and in all Judea and Samaria and to the ends of the earth" (Acts 1:8).

When Luke says that the apostles will be Jesus' witnesses "in Jerusalem," throughout "Judea and Samaria," and "to the ends of the earth," Luke is introducing his readers to the structure and plot of the Acts of the Apostles. In chapters 1–7 we will read of the witness in Jerusalem. Chapters 8–12 tell of the witness in Judea and Samaria. Chapters 13–28 tell of the spread of Christianity to Rome, "the ends of the earth."

The story of the birth and growth of the church will be told through a description of the "acts" of some of the church's greatest leaders. However, these leaders are not acting on their own. They are acting under the guidance of the Holy Spirit.

The role of the Spirit is all important both in Luke's gospel and in the Acts of the Apostles. The action of the Spirit accounts for all that had occurred from the conception of Jesus until the time when Luke is addressing his Gentile audience. The child was conceived through the power of the Spirit, the Spirit led Jesus to the desert in preparation for his ministry, and the Spirit was present at Jesus' baptism. As you read Acts you will see that the Spirit's role in the course of events becomes even more prominent than it was in Luke's gospel.

That the Spirit is responsible for the course of events is central to Luke's theme. After all, Luke's audience finds itself in a strange situation. How is it that Gentile Christians rest their belief on a

---

ORGANIZATION OF ACTS

"The apostles will be Jesus' witnesses . . ."

- "In Jerusalem"—chapters 1–7
- "Throughout Judea and Samaria"—chapters 8–12
- "To the ends of the earth"—chapters 13–28 (Paul's missionary journeys)

Jewish messiah who has been rejected by his own people? Who, one might ask, is responsible for such a strange turn of events?

Luke wants to make it clear to his audience that the Holy Spirit is the moving force behind all that has happened. Without the Spirit the church leaders would be nothing more than ignorant and frightened men, unable to speak or act as Christ's witnesses. After all, the apostles had not understood who Jesus was during his lifetime, and had deserted him at his death. As you will read, without the Spirit the apostles would not have known that Gentiles would be included in the covenant. The whole direction in which the church grew, in fact the very existence of the church, is all due to the action of the Holy Spirit.

So as the Christians in Luke's audience read his account they were reflecting on their own roots and on their own identity. Luke is constantly addressing his audience through the characters in his narrative, helping them to understand the story of which they have become a part. That story begins with baptism by water and the Spirit.

Review Questions

1. What was the difference between John's baptism and the baptism of initiation into the early church?
2. What is the structure and plot of the Acts of the Apostles?
3. Why is it central to Luke's theme to stress the role of the Holy Spirit?

4. Who is Luke's audience and why is Luke's story important to them?

Discussion Questions

1. When you hear the words "Holy Spirit," what do they mean to you? Explain.
2. Do you think the Holy Spirit is as active in the church today as the Spirit was active in the first century? Why or why not?
3. Are you aware of the power of the Holy Spirit in your own life? Explain.

ARTICLE 3

Legends about Judas

Question: "I thought Judas hanged himself. Why does Peter say that Judas fell? Isn't this a rather gruesome story?" (Acts 1:15–20; Mt 27:3–10; Acts 5:1–11; 12:20–23 also discussed)

The person who asked this question has read Matthew's gospel. In Matthew we read another story of Judas' death (Mt 27:3–10). We will compare Matthew's and Luke's accounts because, through the comparison, we can learn something about one literary form which is included in the Acts of the Apostles, and thus something about the intent of the author as he tells this story.

In each account, Judas is presented as the one who betrayed Jesus. In each Judas dies a gruesome death, although not the same death. In each a field is bought, known as the Field of Blood. However, in Matthew the chief priests purchase the field and the blood is a reference to Jesus' blood. In Acts Judas himself purchases the field and the blood is a reference to Judas' blood.

In each account Old Testament passages are used to show that events fulfilled the words of the prophets. However, in Matthew the prophet quoted is said to be Jeremiah even though it is actually Zechariah. In Acts the quotations are from the book of Psalms, attributed to David.

So in each story we have an identical core plot: Judas, Jesus' betrayer, came to a terrible end. This plot is told to illustrate the same theme: the fact that Jesus was betrayed does not mean that God had lost control of the course of events. Events fulfilled God's plan and evil was punished.

We see, then, that around the core story are woven different details and different quotations. What accounts for these similarities and differences?

16

COMPARISON OF JUDAS LEGENDS

Elements in common
1. Judas is the one who betrayed Jesus.
2. Judas dies a gruesome death (not same death).
3. The Field of Blood is bought (not by same person).
4. Events are shown to fulfill the words of the prophets (not the same prophet).

Details which differ
1. The kind of death: hanging or fall.
2. Who purchases the field: chief priests or Judas?
3. Whose "blood" is referred to in "Field of Blood": Jesus' or Judas'?
4. Which prophet is quoted: Psalms or Jeremiah (actually Zechariah)?

Lesson in each: Events fulfilled God's plan and evil was punished.

Remember that neither Matthew nor Luke is an author. Rather, each is an editor. Each organized inherited stories, stories which were already present in the community.

It seems evident that in the years since Judas' betrayal a variety of stories had developed about this nefarious character. The stories were told not to record historical fact but to use historical fact to illustrate theological truth: terrible deeds result in terrible ends. The end for those who do good and those who do evil is not the same. Evil is punished.

As the stories are told a variety of details are added. While those details differ from one account to another, the central plot and purpose of the stories remain the same.

Stories which have an historical core accompanied by imaginative details are called legends. When such stories account for the origins of names of people or places they are called etiologies. We have seen that both Matthew and Luke include a legend about Judas and an etiology about the Field of Blood in their edited accounts.

In the case of Acts, Luke places the legend and etiology on the lips of Peter. It is clear, however, that the speech which Peter gives is meant to teach Luke's readers rather than Peter's listeners. Otherwise Peter would not be pictured as explaining to his audience that the Field of Blood was "in their language Akeldama" (Acts 1:19). Peter's audience would not have needed such an explanation.

By emphasizing the gruesomeness of Judas' end the author's intent is to affirm the power and justice of God. Evil does not go unnoticed. As you read Acts you will notice other stories with the same gruesome emphasis—the deaths of Ananias and Sapphira (Acts 5:1–11) and the fate of Herod (Acts 12:20–23). While the stories definitely sound cruel to us, a first century audience would have understood that imaginative details were added to the story in order to teach the lesson that evil acts lead to evil ends.

A legend of Judas' death, then, has been appropriated by Luke to emphasize the fate of those who do evil. However, even human evil does not subvert God's justice or God's plan.

Review Questions

1. What do the two stories of Judas' death have in common?
2. How do the two accounts differ?
3. What is the core plot of the stories?
4. What is the theme of the stories?
5. What is a legend?
6. What is an etiology?
7. Why did Luke include this legend in Acts?

Discussion Questions

1. Does it bother you that the New Testament contains two different stories about Judas' death? Why or why not?
2. Can you think of any stories you know from your childhood that you would call legends? Etiologies? What are they?

3. Do you think Jesus made a mistake when he chose Judas? Why or why not?
4. Do you think the presence of evil on earth means that God has lost control of the course of events? Explain.

ARTICLE 4

The Gift of "Tongues" at Pentecost

Question: "What really happened at Pentecost? Could the apostles really speak languages they didn't know before?" (Acts 2:1–13; Acts 10:46; 19:6; 1 Cor 14:27–28 also discussed)

The person who asked this question will have a frustrating time in trying to understand the Acts of the Apostles (not to mention the gospels) because he is asking a question which the author is not addressing. The author of Acts is not trying to describe "what really happened." Rather, the author is trying to describe the significance of earlier events as they are understood in hindsight.

One can speculate about the actual experience but that is just what it is—speculation. Much more valuable is to try to understand what Luke intends to say to his audience.

Luke signals to his audience that he is about to describe a momentous event when he begins, "When the day of Pentecost had come . . ." (Acts 2:1). Luke pinpoints fulfillments with this wording. He used the same technique in describing the day of Jesus' birth (Lk 2:16).

Pentecost was already a day of celebration for the Jews. On the fiftieth day after Passover the Jews celebrated their covenant relationship with God as they commemorated Moses having received the law on Mount Sinai. Just as Luke described a reinterpretation of the Passover celebration in the light of the new covenant as he pictured the last supper, so does he describe a reinterpretation of Pentecost, showing that it has been given a new significance.

Luke makes it clear that in his description he is using images to describe a reality that is really indescribable as he says that the sound which came from heaven was "like" the rush of a mighty

20

wind (2:2) and that there appeared to them tongues "as of" fire (Acts 2:3). What exactly is Luke trying to communicate through these images?

Wind and fire have been images of God's presence throughout the Old Testament. The same or similar images were used to describe God's presence to Moses on Sinai (Ex 19:16–19). Isaiah uses these images when he says, "For behold the Lord will come in fire, and his chariots like the storm wind . . ." (Is 66:15). In Acts, however, the fire is "distributed and resting on each one of them" (Acts 2:3). This is to signify that each member is filled with the Spirit.

The effect of this indwelling of the Spirit is that the disciples become missionaries, spreading the word of the gospel to all nations, including the Gentiles. Luke knows that this is the effect of the experience because he is writing from hindsight. So he describes the experience to make this effect clear to his audience.

Thus Luke describes the gift of tongues as one which makes it possible to spread the gospel to other lands. Scripture scholars speculate that the gift of tongues actually experienced by the disciples was the one referred to as *glossolalia,* a kind of prayer which was not understandable and needed to be interpreted by a person with the gift of interpretation. This phenomenon of "tongues," as you will see, appears elsewhere in Acts (see Acts 10:46; 19:6).

The purpose of this gift was to affirm the presence of the Spirit in the community. Because this charismatic gift could not always be understood, Paul, in his letter to the Corinthians, suggests that those with the gift of tongues should, in the absence of an interpreter, remain silent (see 1 Cor 14:27–28).

The gifts which Luke is describing in his account of Pentecost are the gifts which enabled the disciples to spread the good news of God's saving power to all nations, so that all nations would hear this good news in their own language, even Luke's Gentile audience.

Scholars suggest that Luke used the gift of tongues known to the community, *glossolalia,* and reinterpreted "tongues" as an ability to speak in foreign languages in order to symbolically stress the missionary effect of the gifts of the Spirit which the disciples received.

Through the image of "tongues," then, Luke shows the real significance of the Pentecost event. The separation of God from his people, pictured in the story of the tower of Babel (Gen 11:1–9) in which language is confused so people can no longer understand each other, is reversed. No longer are God and his people separated. The Spirit of God now dwells with his people.

What really happened at Pentecost? Luke describes the event in terms of its effect. At Pentecost the disciples received the wisdom, the courage and the power to become missionaries and to spread the good news to God's people in every land.

Review Questions

1. What is the author of Acts trying to describe?
2. Why did the Jews already celebrate Pentecost?
3. For what are fire and wind images?
4. What is signified by describing the fire as distributed and resting on each one?
5. What is "*glossolalia*"?
6. What is Luke stressing as he describes the apostles as able to speak in foreign languages?
7. What is the significance of the Pentecost event?

Discussion Questions

1. Does it bother you that Christianity has appropriated and redefined Jewish festivals? Why or why not?
2. Have you ever heard anyone speak in tongues? When and where? Do you speak in tongues yourself? If so, what does the gift have to do with prayer?
3. What do you think was the greatest gift which the apostles received at Pentecost?
4. Why will a person who keeps asking "What really happened?" find reading Acts frustrating?

ARTICLE 5

The Prophets' Words Are "Fulfilled"

Question: "In that Judas story (Acts 1:15–20) Peter said that the Holy Spirit, speaking through David, foretold the fate of Judas. Now, after Pentecost, Peter says that the prophet Joel was talking about Pentecost (Acts 2:16–21). How did the prophets know what was going to happen in the future? Is it just that the Holy Spirit told them?"

The gift which the Spirit gave the prophets was not the ability to know what would happen in the future. Rather the prophets' gift was an ability to see the ramifications of present behavior in the context of covenant love.

When Luke has Peter quote the psalms, as he did in the Judas legend, or quote Joel, as he does in the Pentecost speech, Luke is using the Old Testament passages to explain the significance of present events. He is giving the prophets' words a meaning which the prophets did not initially intend.

All of this will need further explanation. In order to understand how Luke is using the Old Testament let us first make sure that we understand the function of a prophet. A prophet was not a fortune-teller but one who spoke for God. The prophet was a person with spiritual insight. He had a keen understanding of God's love for his people as well as insight into what kind of behavior was appropriate for people who were God's people.

When the prophet saw God's people doing wrong he would warn them that trouble lay ahead because God was too holy to permit his people to continue a life of sin. When the people were suffering the prophet would encourage the people to hope. God's love is eternal and God would not forsake his people.

So the prophet's words pertained to the future in that they spoke of the ramifications of present behavior. However, this is far different from fortunetelling, a practice of the occult which was against Jewish law.

When Luke quotes scripture to support the point he is making, he is not claiming that the prophets intended to say what Luke is using the prophets' words to support. Rather he is saying that a new level of meaning can be found in the prophets' words, that the words are applicable to a setting different from the setting in which the prophets spoke. Thus the prophets' words are "fulfilled" in that they are given a fuller, a different meaning.

The truth of these statements can be illustrated by looking at the quotations which the questioner cited. The first is the quotation from the psalms attributed to David and applied to the fate of Judas. "Let his habitation become desolate, and let there be no one to live in it," and "His office let another take" (Acts 1:20). These lines are taken from Psalm 69 and are the lament of someone who is faithful to Yahweh yet persecuted. The psalmist is asking Yahweh to punish the persecutors. Since Judas persecuted Jesus, who was faithful to the Father, Judas is an example of the kind of person referred to in the psalm. So the words are applicable to Judas without the prophet having foreseen Judas' treachery.

The quotation from the prophet Joel which is included in Peter's speech dates back to the time in Jewish history known as the post-exilic period or the time after the exile in Babylon, probably around 400 B.C. This was a time when the Jews needed prophets of hope because they were recovering from the experience of having lost everything which they considered essential: their king, their land, and their temple. Joel's words of hope are encouraging his people that God has not deserted them. God will pour out his spirit on them. "And it shall be that whoever calls on the name of the Lord will be saved" (Acts 2:21; Joel 3:5).

The early church saw in Joel's words a hope that they experienced as having been fulfilled in them. Upon them God's Spirit had been poured out. So Joel's words are fulfilled at Pentecost as a hope is fulfilled, not as a prediction is fulfilled. Joel did not foresee Pentecost. He foresaw the ramifications of covenant love.

All through Acts, indeed through the whole New Testament, you

---

**SOME "FULFILL THE WORDS OF THE PROPHETS"
PASSAGES IN ACTS**

1:16	3:21
2:16–21	3:24
3:18	13:27
	13:33

---

will see passages from the Old Testament reinterpreted to cast light on the significance of recent events. The words of the prophets are shown to have been fulfilled not in the sense of a prediction coming true but in the sense of spiritual insights being accurate and hopes being fulfilled.

Review Questions

1. What is the gift which prophets receive?
2. What was a prophet's function?
3. In what sense are the prophet's words fulfilled?
4. In what way are Old Testament passages used in Acts?

Discussion Questions

1. Did you think that prophets were fortunetellers? Why or why not? Would you like to be able to see into the future? Why or why not?
2. Do you think anyone functions as a prophet in our society? Who? Why?
3. Do you think it is a legitimate use of the Old Testament to use it to cast light on the significance of later events? Why or why not?

ARTICLE 6

Preaching the "Kerygma"

Question: "Why did Peter insult his audience, accusing them of killing Jesus (Acts 2:23)? You'd think they would get mad rather than repent. This whole scene doesn't seem realistic." (Acts 2:14–39; Acts 3:12–26; 4:8–12; 5:29–32; 10:34–43 also discussed)

The person who asked this question is unaware of the kind of writing she is reading. There is an inaccurate presumption behind the question. The presumption is that Luke is writing as an historian, accurately recording exactly what was said on one particular occasion.

Remember, Luke is an editor, utilizing the inherited traditions of the early church—traditions which, by the time Luke is writing, had taken on a variety of forms to fulfill a variety of functions in the community.

One function which the apostles performed was that of preaching. Scripture scholars distinguish among the kind of preaching which was done in terms of its purpose. Was the preaching to proclaim the word? To explain the word? To exhort people to live by the word? Or to apply the word to daily life?

The earliest core of preaching was to proclaim the word. Scholars call this kind of preaching the basic "kerygma," the preaching which contained the basic core of beliefs as preached in missionary settings.

By the time Luke is arranging his inherited materials, the content of the basic kerygma was well established. Five facts are stressed in the kerygma. First, Jesus is named and certain details are given regarding Jesus' earthly ministry, his death, and his resurrection. Second, Jesus is shown to have "fulfilled" the words of the proph-

---

FOUR KINDS OF CHRISTIAN PREACHING

- Kerygma: Proclaiming the word
- Didache: Explaining the word
- Periklesis: Exhorting people to live by the word
- Homilia: Applying the word to daily life.

The kind of preaching found in Acts is primarily kerygma.

---

ets. Third, Jesus is declared to be the messiah. Fourth, Jesus is said to be exalted to the right hand of the Father. Fifth, people are called to repentance, for God is calling his people to himself.

Luke utilizes this basic kerygma in the speeches which he pictures Peter giving not only on the occasion of Pentecost but on other occasions as well (see Acts 2:14–39; 3:12–26; 4:8–12; 5:29–32; 10:34–43).

So when the questioner asks why Peter would insult his audience this way, the questioner is assuming that the speech is being addressed primarily to the people pictured as being physically present to Peter. In fact Luke is utilizing a traditional speech and is addressing it primarily to his reading audience.

In the speech Luke pictures Peter including all the elements of the kerygma. First he names Jesus and speaks of his ministry, death, and resurrection. "Jesus of Nazareth, a man attested to you

---

THE CONTENT OF THE KERYGMA

1. Jesus suffered, died and rose
2. Jesus fulfilled the words of the prophets
3. Jesus is the messiah
4. Jesus calls us to repentance
5. Jesus will come again

---

by God with mighty works and wonders and signs. . . . This Jesus you crucified and killed by the hands of lawless men. But God raised him up . . ." (Acts 2:22–24).

The blaming of the Jews which our questioner noted is laying the groundwork for the call to repentance which will come later.

Next Jesus is shown to have fulfilled the words of the prophets. Peter is shown quoting Psalm 16, attributed to David, in which the psalmist feels such total love and commitment to Yahweh that he is led to express a belief that he will escape death since his great love must be eternal. Peter points out that David couldn't have been speaking of himself since David did, in fact, die. David's words take on a fuller meaning when applied to Jesus who overcame death.

Peter then goes on to say that Jesus is "exalted at the right hand of God" (Acts 2:33). He then declares that Jesus is the messiah. "Let all the house of Israel therefore know assuredly that God has made him both Lord and Christ" (Acts 2:36). The word "Christ" is a synonym for the word "messiah." To say that Jesus is Christ is to say that Jesus is the messiah.

The people then ask what they should do. Peter admonishes them to repent and be baptized.

Luke is skillful in inserting the kerygmatic preaching into his narrative. While the reader is accurate in noting some lack of realism in the account, one must realize that "realism" is not one of Luke's main goals. This is obvious from the fact that the setting changes without notice from a place where the disciples receive the outpouring of the Spirit to a place from which Peter can address the crowds.

Luke is weaving together inherited sources of various literary forms in order to help his reading audience reflect on and more deeply understand the traditions and beliefs which they themselves have embraced. The kerygma is, of course, central to Luke's purpose in that it proclaims Jesus' role in salvation history.

Review Questions

1. What various purposes might preaching have?
2. What is the kerygma?

3. What five facts are stressed in the kerygma?
4. To whom is Peter's speech primarily addressed?
5. What significance does the speech have for the primary audience?

Discussion Questions

1. If you were going to tell someone who knew nothing about your beliefs a few facts which are central, what facts would you pick? Why?
2. Did you include in your short list the fact that we are called to repentance? Why or why not? Do you think this fact deserves a central place? Why or why not?

ARTICLE 7

The Political Setting for Persecution

Question: "Who were the Sadducees that they could arrest Peter and John without cause?" (Acts 4:1–3; Acts 4:13; 5:17; 23:6–10 also discussed)

The Sadducees were one of the main religious parties in Palestine during Jesus' lifetime and in the first Christian century. During the time Peter was an early missionary, the Sadducees were the party of the high priests.

The Sadducees were powerful in the sanhedrin, which was the highest governing body of the Jews. Under Roman rule, the sanhedrin regulated religious affairs completely. It regulated civil affairs within the limits set down by Rome.

The sanhedrin was made up of three divisions of elders, representing the lay aristocracy, the high priests (these would have been Sadducees) and the scribes (these would have been mainly Pharisees).

You may know that in the gospels the Pharisees appear as the main persecutors of Jesus. In Acts, however, the Sadducees appear as the main persecutors of the early church (see Acts 4:1–3; 5:17; 23:6–10).

As you already know, a basic tenant of the kerygma is the resurrection. After the healing of the lame man (Acts 3:1–10), Peter is pictured proclaiming the early kerygma to the crowds. This speech contains the same elements we have already noted in a previous article. Central to each of these kerygmatic discourses is the fact of the resurrection (see Acts 3:14–15).

Since the Sadducees do not believe in the possibility of resurrec-

---

THE APOSTLES' MINISTRY:
AN EXTENSION OF JESUS' MINISTRY

Both:

- Act under the guidance of the Spirit
- Proclaim the good news in words
- Proclaim the good news through healing
- Suffer persecution

---

tion from the dead, they are the ones who persecute the early church, and thus are the ones to arrest Peter and John.

Once more we must remember, though, that Luke is teaching his audience through editing and arranging inherited sources. Whenever we slip into treating his writing as purely historical in nature and intent we raise great difficulties for ourselves, and we miss Luke's point.

Notice, for instance, that when Peter defends himself before the rulers, the teaching of the resurrection is no longer the issue. Peter's speech is asserting the fact that it is in the name of Jesus, and in his power, that the lame man has been healed. The rulers' question "By what power or by what name did you do this?" (Acts 4:7) is a rhetorical device which allows Luke, through the person of Peter, to explain the significance of the healing.

With the healing and the beginning of persecution we can see that the ministry of the apostles is more and more becoming a mirror image of the ministry of Jesus. Both Jesus' ministry and the apostles' ministry is done under the guidance of the Holy Spirit. Both ministries consist primarily of preaching. In both ministries the message proclaimed in the preaching is confirmed in signs through healing. Peter uses the healing to reaffirm the power of the risen Christ in whose name the healing has been accomplished. "And his (Jesus') name, by faith in his name, has made this man strong whom you see and know; and the faith which is through Jesus has given the man this perfect health in the presence of you all" (Acts 3:16).

Finally, both ministries result in persecution. The persecution which begins here will, as you will read, lead to the believing community in Jerusalem having to disperse, and eventually will lead to the proclamation of the word to the Gentiles.

Review Questions

1. Who were the Sadducees?
2. What was the sanhedrin?
3. What about the kerygma caused the Sadducees to persecute the early church?
4. What significance does the healing of the lame man have?
5. How does the apostles' ministry resemble Jesus' ministry?
6. What is the result of persecution?

Discussion Questions

1. Do you believe in resurrection? What does it mean to you? How does this belief influence your life or your choices now? How should it influence your life or your choices?
2. Have you ever experienced persecution? Explain. Do you think persecution strengthens or stamps out belief? Explain.
3. Who do you think of as Christ's disciples today? Why? Do the lives of these people resemble Jesus' in any way? Explain.
4. Do you ever think of yourself as a disciple? Why or why not?

One Kind of Miracle Story

Question: "This story about Ananias and Sapphira (Acts 5:1–11) is awful. It makes both God and Peter seem cruel. Why would Luke include a story like this?" (Acts 2:43; Acts 4:32–35 also discussed)

This is a good question. Notice the questioner is assuming that the story had a life of its own in the community and that Luke chose to include the story in his narrative. Why would Luke do that? What is Luke teaching his audience through the story?

Notice that the story is one of two examples which follow a summary section (Acts 4:32–35). The summary section describes two ideals of the early community. Some renounced personal property for the sake of community property. Others sold personal property and distributed the proceeds from the sale to the poor. In both cases, the relinquishment of property was a matter of choice.

The summary passage is followed first by a good example. Barnabas, about whom we will hear more as we read Acts, sold a field and gave the money from the sale to the apostles.

Next comes a bad example. Ananias and Sapphira sell their property and then pretend to give the proceeds to the apostles when in fact they secretly hold back part of the money. Their sin is not that they didn't give all the money. As Peter points out, both the decision to sell and the decision to give the proceeds to the apostles was a matter of choice. Neither was required.

The sin was in the deceit, and not deceit just before men but before the Holy Spirit. By expecting to get away with such behavior Ananias and Sapphira were essentially denying the presence of the Holy Spirit in the community.

Notice the story does not explain how Peter knew that the couple was being deceitful. His knowledge appears to be a gift of the Spirit to the leader of the community. Peter himself names the sin as a "lie to the Holy Spirit" (Acts 5:3). "You have not lied to men but to God" (Acts 5:4).

The reaction of the crowd to both Ananias' death and that of his wife is fear. Fear is not simply a negative reaction, one of anxiety. Rather fear is an appropriate reaction to the presence and power of the Spirit in the community. Fear is a sense of awe at the ways of God and an accurate perception of human beings' proper place in the scheme of things. People react with fear because they realize that a Spirit-filled community is a community in which evil cannot comfortably remain.

Notice in the story of Ananias and Sapphira that Peter names the adversary as "Satan." "Ananias, why has Satan filled your heart to lie to the Holy Spirit?" (Acts 5:3). With this introduction of Satan into the narrative, the actions of the apostles once more mirror those of Jesus who also had to battle Satan.

The story of Ananias and Sapphira is an example of a kind of miracle story in which a person who violates a divine ordinance is swiftly and dramatically punished. Luke undoubtedly felt perfectly comfortable including this traditional story in his narrative. The purpose in telling the story is not to picture either God or Peter as cruel. Rather Luke's purpose, as his audience would have understood, is to affirm the power and presence of the Spirit in the early Christian community, in the church.

Review Questions

1. What two ideals are described in the summary section (Acts 4:32–35)?
2. What two example stories follow the summary?
3. What was the sin in the actions of Ananias and Sapphira?
4. Why is fear an appropriate reaction to the presence of the Spirit in the community?
5. What kind of story is the story of Ananias and Sapphira?
6. What is Luke's purpose in telling this story?

Discussion Questions

1. What do you think the phrase "fear of the Lord" means? Do you like or dislike this phrase? Why?
2. If we lived our beliefs, what would be our attitude toward material possessions? Explain.
3. Does our culture have any stories in which "the good guy" always wins? Do these stories ever contain an element of cruelty? Does this element ruin the story for you? Why or why not?

ARTICLE 9

Angels: God's Messengers

Question: "Did an angel really open the prison door and tell the apostles to go back to the temple and preach?" (Acts 5:19–20; Acts 4:18–20; 5:19–39 also discussed)

The person who asked this question, which is a "what really happened?" question, is in danger of missing the point Luke is stressing as he tells of this second period of persecution.

However, the way to help the questioner get focused onto the point of the passage seems to be to address the question first.

Luke is writing to a first century audience that believes in the existence of angels. A modern day reader who also believes in the existence of angels would have no problem with Luke's account. A modern day reader who doubts the existence of angels might well ask the question which this person asked.

When human beings come in contact with a force or power which we experience as "supernatural," or outside of what we understand as human beings ("supernatural" means beyond the natural from a human being's point of view), we personify the force, be it good or evil, and traditionally describe it as an angel or a demon.

However, what we are describing, while "it" exists, is beyond our perception. We are not using scientific language. Rather we are naming an element in an experience which we really don't understand.

In both the Old and New Testaments "angels" appear. In the narratives in which they appear they are serving as God's messengers. The word "angel" means "messenger." By using the word we are describing a function more than we are describing a being because the function is within our experience but the nature of the

---

**SOME PASSAGES IN WHICH ANGELS
PLAY A ROLE IN ACTS**

5:9	12:7–11
8:26	12:23
10:3	27:23

---

being is outside our experience. Nevertheless, we name the being "angel."

In addition, when a person of faith has an experience in which God's power and presence is felt in some dramatic and intervening way, the person uses words to describe the experience which make it clear to the listener that it really was a powerful faith experience. In such a description we often use the word "angel" to describe another human being whom we believe to have been God's instrument in aiding us.

Whether we use the word "angel" to describe a messenger of God who is a supernatural being and thus beyond our knowledge, or a messenger of God who is another person, we are nevertheless making a statement of faith that God intervened in the course of events. The experience of God's presence through his messenger, his "angel," is the important point.

So, did an angel really open the prison door and tell the apostles to go back to the temple and preach? One cannot answer the question with a simple "yes" or "no" because the kind of writing which we are reading does not directly address the question. Luke's motive is not to answer the question "What really happened?" but to answer the question "What was the significance of what really happened?" Luke is telling his audience that God intervened in a powerful way so that the apostles experienced their escape as the work of God through God's messenger, whom we call an angel.

God is behind events: This is the point of the whole second persecution narrative. That God is on the side of the apostles and that the word is being spread through God's express desire and power are said over and over again.

This point has already been emphasized by the apostles when

they explain why they cannot obey the sanhedrin's warning to no longer preach (see Acts 4:18–20). When the apostles ignore the warning and continue to preach they are again arrested. However, the angel's words make it clear that they are doing God's will. "Go and stand in the temple and speak to the people all the words of this life" (Acts 5:20).

After escaping, the apostles are again brought before the sanhedrin and asked why they have disobeyed and continue to teach in Jesus' name. The apostles' answer remains the same. "We must obey God rather than men" (Acts 5:29).

Finally, through the words of Gamaliel, Luke brings the point home. Gamaliel advises his fellow council members, "So in the present case I tell you, keep away from these men and let them alone; for if this plan or this undertaking is of men, it will fail; but if it is of God, you will not be able to overthrow them. You might even be found opposing God" (Acts 5:38–39).

The point being emphasized as Luke recounts the persecution faced by the apostles is that, like Jesus, the apostles were persecuted only for doing God's will. As with Jesus, God's messengers, God's "angels," assist the apostles who persevere in doing God's will even in the face of persecution.

Review Questions

1. What does "supernatural" mean?
2. What does "angel" mean?
3. In what two ways do we use the word "angel"?
4. What is Luke's point in saying that an angel was responsible for helping the apostles escape?
5. What is the main point in the second account of persecutions (Acts 5:19–39)?
6. Why were the apostles persecuted?

Discussion Questions

1. Do you believe in angels? Why or why not?
2. Do you believe that God is present and active in events? Why or why not?

3. Have you ever been in a situation in which Gamaliel's advice would be good advice? Explain.
4. Do you know anyone in today's world who is persecuted for doing God's will? Explain.
5. How do you think one should go about discerning God's will? Explain.

ARTICLE 10

The Birth of New, Formal Ministries

Question: "Is there some special significance to picking those men to wait on tables? Why is it such a big deal?" (Acts 6:1–6; Lk 6:12–16; 24:45–49; Acts 6:8–7:60; 8:5–8; 11:30; 14:23; 15:2; 16:4; 20:17; 21:18 also discussed)

There is more involved in the "appointment of the seven" (Acts 6:1–6) than finding someone to wait on tables. When Luke selects an individual episode to describe, it is usually because the episode has significance beyond itself. The episode becomes an example of something greater than itself.

So far in Acts, which we know is going to tell us about the spread of the gospel to the ends of the earth, missionary activity has been limited to Jews in Jerusalem who speak Aramaic.

However, there are other Jews, not only in Jerusalem, who have become Hellenized and speak Greek. These Greek-speaking Jews are called "Hellenists."

Luke tells us that there was friction between the "Hebrews," the Jews who spoke Aramaic, and the "Hellenists." The apostles, in responding to this problem, in deciding how to take care of the needs of these people, formally delegated and thus extended to others some of the authority and ministry which they had received from Christ.

Luke laid the groundwork for a hierarchical structure in the church in his gospel when he pictured Jesus selecting the twelve apostles (Lk 6:12–16) and later giving them authority and spiritual power. "You are witnesses to these things. And behold, I send the promise of my Father upon you, but stay in the city, until you are clothed with power from on high" (Lk 24:48–49).

40

THE BEGINNING OF STRUCTURES IN THE CHURCH

- Jesus chooses apostles (Lk 6:12–16; 24:45–49)
- Apostles choose deacons (Acts 6:16)
- Elders (overseers) are appointed to head local faith communities (Acts 11:30; 14:23; 15:2; 16:4; 20:17; 21:18)

Now, while the apostles are yet to leave Jerusalem, their ministry must expand to the Greek-speaking Jews. Seven men are chosen to fulfill this role.

The ministry of the seven will not be limited to waiting on tables. As you read Acts you will see two of the men who were picked preaching, debating, and working wonders in Jesus' name (see Stephen's activities in Acts 6:8–7:60 and Philip's in Acts 8:5–8).

In formally choosing the seven, the apostles pray and "lay on hands." This action is a way of ritualizing the passing on of power and dignity which is received by those who will share in the apostles' ministry.

Some scripture scholars see a foreshadowing of the universal spread of the church in the fact that "seven" were chosen to serve. The number seven represents perfection or completion. Perhaps in specifying that seven were originally chosen, Luke is suggesting that this spread of the church will eventually include all nations.

Those who serve, sometimes called "deacons," are not the only formal hierarchical structure in the church. As you read Acts you will begin to notice the appointment of "elders." Elders were appointed to be heads of local faith communities (see Acts 11:30; 14:23; 15:2; 16:4; 20:17; 21:18). The elders were also called "overseers."

As you continue to read Acts it will be important to notice that a formal structure is established. This structure is, as we see in the appointment of the seven, revised and expanded in response to need. Also, the roles of those in formal ministry positions grow as the ministers respond to the problems with which they are confronted. In time the gospel will be preached not just to Greek-speaking Jews, but to Greeks who are not Jews at all.

Acts shows us a church growing not only in its numbers and structures but even in its self-understanding and identity as God continues to reveal his will through events.

Review Questions

1. What are "Hellenists"?
2. What will the ministry of "the seven" involve?
3. What might be the significance in the fact that seven were chosen?
4. What are "elders"?
5. In what ways does Acts picture the church growing?

Discussion Questions

1. In today's church what formal ministries can you think of?
2. What role does a hierarchy of defined roles play in the church? Do you see this as a strength or a weakness? Explain.
3. The early church grew and changed in response to need. Can the church still do this? Does the church still do this? Explain.
4. Do you see some needs today which demand change? What are they? What changes do you think would be good?

ARTICLE 11

Reflections of Christ:
Before and After

Question: "Why doesn't Stephen answer the charges against him when he talks to the sanhedrin? Why does he get so completely off the subject?" (Acts 7:2–53; Acts 4:8–12; 6:15–7:55 also discussed)

Remember, we noticed a situation like this earlier when Peter was pictured as not answering the charges against him before the sanhedrin. Instead he gave a kerygmatic sermon (Acts 4:8–12).

As we did then, we should remember that Luke is editing inherited material. The primary conversation is not between Stephen and the sanhedrin but between Luke and his audience. What is Luke teaching his audience through his narrative about Stephen?

One must admit that Stephen's speech seems to be obviously inserted into the story. At the end of chapter six we read, "And gazing at him, all who sat in the council saw that his face was like the face of an angel" (Acts 6:15).

Next comes the longest speech in Acts, followed by: "But he, full of the Holy Spirit, gazed into heaven and saw the glory of God, and Jesus standing at the right hand of God . . ." (Acts 7:55).

The speech seems to interrupt an independent account of Stephen's martyrdom.

This is not to say that Luke, as an editor, does a poor job of combining his material. On the contrary, by inserting this talk into the narrative of Stephen's martyrdom, Luke demonstrates Christ's central role in the course of salvation history. Through the speech Luke shows how events which preceded Christ foreshadowed him. In the person of Stephen, Luke shows how events which came after

Christ reflected an extension of Christ's presence in and through his disciples. Each of these statements needs further explanation.

The theme of Stephen's speech is that those who are rejecting him are following in the footsteps of the Jews who, through history, have rejected God, a rejection that culminated in their rejection of Jesus.

In the course of illustrating this theme, Luke pictures Stephen using what biblical scholars call "typology." A "type" exists when certain persons or events in the Old Testament are shown to foretell or prefigure a person or event in the New Testament.

In Stephen's speech, as he reviews Jewish history starting with Abraham, he demonstrates that Moses was a type for Jesus.

Stephen explicitly states that Moses is a type for Jesus when he says, "This is the Moses who said to the Israelites, 'God will raise up for you a prophet from your brethren as he raised me up' " (Acts 7:37). However, the explicit statement is simply emphasizing a comparison that is apparent throughout the narrative.

In Luke's description of Moses many details are included which remind one of Jesus. Moses grew in wisdom (Acts 7:23) as Luke had said Jesus did (Lk 2:52). Both became powerful in word and deed. Both "defended the oppressed man" (Acts 7:24). Both Moses and Jesus were chosen to give the people "deliverance" (Acts 7:25), but in both cases the people failed to understand (Acts 7:25). Both tried to "reconcile men" (Acts 7:26). Both withdrew and were visited by an angel (Acts 7:30). Both heard the voice of God (Acts 7:33). Finally, both were rejected by those whom they meant to deliver (Acts 7:39ff).

Stephen's point is that the Israelites, throughout their history as a chosen people, have turned against God and that they are still doing it. "You stiff-necked people, uncircumcised in heart and ears, you always resist the Holy Spirit. As your fathers did, so do you" (Acts 7:51).

In addition to emphasizing how Jewish salvation history has prefigured Jesus, Luke shows how Jesus' disciples reflect Jesus' presence in their own being. Just as Moses prefigured Jesus, so does Stephen reflect his Lord. Stephen is full of "grace and power" and does great wonders and signs among the people" (Acts 6:8). Both

EVENTS FORESHADOW CHRIST

MOSES IS A TYPE FOR JESUS

Both

- Grow in wisdom
- Are powerful in word and deed
- Defend the oppressed
- Deliver their people
- Suffer rejection
- Are reconcilers
- Are visited by an angel
- Hear God

CHRIST FORESHADOWS EVENTS

STEPHEN'S MINISTRY REFLECTS JESUS'

Both

- Are full of grace and power
- Perform signs and wonders
- Confound people by their wisdom
- Are accused of blasphemy
- Appear before the sanhedrin
- Are accused by false witnesses
- Have visions of the sky opening
- Pray that their persecutors will be forgiven

Stephen and Jesus confound people by speaking with the wisdom of the Spirit (Acts 6:12). Both are accused of blasphemy (Acts 6:11). Both are seized and brought before the sanhedrin (Acts 6:12). Both are accused by false witnesses (Acts 6:13). Both have a vision of the sky opening (Acts 7:55). Both pray that God will receive their spirits and that he will forgive their persecutors. "Lord, do not hold this sin against them" (Acts 7:60). Jesus still lives in his disciples.

The death of Stephen touched off a persecution in Jerusalem which caused the new Christians to disperse throughout the regions of Judea and Samaria. Persecution does not prevent the spread of the gospel; it causes it. Christianity starts to break with Judaism and spread to other peoples.

As Luke tells us the story of Stephen he does not get "off the subject" as the questioner suggests. Both in the content of Stephen's speech and in the narrative about Stephen, Luke shows that even though disobedience and persecution have always been present, God is still powerfully at work among his people.

Review Questions

1. What evidence is there that Luke inserted a speech into a narrative of Stephen's death?
2. What is a "type"?
3. How was Moses a type of Jesus?
4. What is Luke teaching through Stephen's speech?
5. How does Stephen resemble Jesus?
6. What is Luke teaching by the way he describes Stephen's death?
7. What effect does persecution have on the spread of the gospel?

Discussion Questions

1. "Typology" points out that Old Testament events foreshadow New Testament events. Do you think they do? Can you think of examples?
2. If Old Testament events foreshadow New Testament events, what significance is there to that fact?
3. What does it mean to say that the risen Christ lives on in his followers? Do you think this is true? Explain.

ARTICLE 12

The Church Reaches Out to the Unclean

Question: "Isn't the Holy Spirit received with baptism? Why does Luke say that the Samaritans 'had only been baptized in the name of the Lord Jesus' (Acts 8:16) and had not yet received the Holy Spirit?" (Acts 2:38; 8:1–24; 8:26–40; 10:44–48; 11:15–17 also discussed)

This question raises an issue which has been a problem for scripture scholars. The questioner is correct in thinking that the Holy Spirit is received at baptism. Earlier in Acts we read Peter saying, "Repent, and be baptized every one of you in the name of Jesus Christ for the forgiveness of your sins; and you shall receive the gift of the Holy Spirit" (Acts 2:38).

In the Acts of the Apostles, however, Luke pictures here the reception of the Spirit as coming after baptism, and as coming before baptism on another occasion which we will be discussing soon (see Acts 10:44–48; 11:15–17).

These passages, in which baptism and the reception of the Spirit are separate, are not teaching about the normal practice and effect of baptism. Rather, by departing from the norm, Luke is emphasizing another point. What is Luke's point?

This particular passage, in which the coming of the Spirit is after baptism, is part of Luke's narrative of the spread of the word to Samaria (Acts 8:9–24). Philip's missionary work in Samaria could have been seen as extremely controversial. Philip is reaching out to the likes of Simon the magician (Acts 8:9–24) and the eunuch (Acts 8:26–40), both of whom would have been considered outcasts by the Jews. Because of the controversial nature of Philip's activities, Luke is careful to make it clear that the outreach was approved by

God, by God's chosen apostles, and by the apostles' chosen "deacons." Once again we see that church authority and structure are important to Luke.

Jews were supposed to have nothing to do with Samaritans or eunuchs. Samaritans were unclean and eunuchs were excluded from the assembly, as was spelled out in Deuteronomy. "He whose testicles are crushed or whose male member is cut off shall not enter the assembly of the Lord" (Deut 23:1).

So for Philip to be out converting such people was astounding. Who gave Philip the authority to do it? Philip was one of the seven Hellenists chosen by the apostles to serve the church. Because the Hellenists were persecuted in Jerusalem after Stephen's murder, Philip went to Samaria and continued his missionary activity.

Luke seems to want to assure his audience that what Philip was doing was good. So Luke explains that Peter and John, the apostles from Jerusalem, came down and approved of Philip's work. Luke does this, as the questioner noted, by showing Philip baptizing the Samaritans but the apostles laying on hands for the reception of the Spirit. In this way Luke emphasizes that God is directing the course of events, but God is doing this through his chosen leaders.

Luke next makes it very clear, through the story of Simon the magician, that the authority and power which belong to the apostles are not God's gift to them but God's gift to the community through them. Simon greatly admires the power to lay on hands and give the gifts of the Holy Spirit. He wants this power himself and offers to buy it (the sin now called simony). Peter is outraged. This is not a power to buy and sell, or even to think of as a personal power. This is God's power being given to God's people.

This theme, that God's chosen leaders are the channel through which God's gifts are distributed, continues in the story of the conversion of the eunuch. The eunuch, despite his desire to understand the scripture, is unable to understand what he is already reading. The eunuch needs help. Philip finds the eunuch in the midst of the struggle and leads him to the truth. "Then Philip opened his mouth, and beginning with this scripture, he told him the good news of Jesus" (Acts 8:35).

In this account of the conversion of Samaria, then, Luke emphasizes that the movement away from the Jews and toward the Samaritans and the pagans (the eunuch was from Africa) was not simply the work of human beings. The apostles did not decide to move on. Rather, forced to move on by persecution, the apostles and deacons followed the lead of the Spirit and acted as God's instruments in bringing the good news to non-Jews.

Review Questions

1. Is the Holy Spirit received at baptism?
2. Why would Philip's missionary work in Samaria be controversial?
3. What is Luke emphasizing by picturing the apostles laying hands on the Samaritans some time after their baptism?
4. What is Luke teaching through the story of Simon the magician?
5. What is simony?
6. What is Luke teaching through the story of the eunuch?

Discussion Questions

1. Who are the outcasts of our society? Do churches reach out to these people and try to include them in the community? Explain.
2. Do you know of any examples of simony in our culture? Explain.
3. Do you think God is directing the church today? Have any bold new steps been taken in this century? Explain.
4. Is church structure important to you? Explain.

ARTICLE 13

Three Accounts of Paul's Conversion

Question: "Why would Ananias argue with the Lord in a vision (Acts 9:13–14)? You'd think if the Lord told him to help Saul he'd just go and do it." (Acts 9:1–22; Acts 8:3; 9:26–29; 22:1–16; 26:9–18 also discussed)

Once more we have a question that gets off the point by assuming that we are reading a journalistic account of events. Dialogues in Acts, as well as speeches, are composed and/or edited by Luke in order to teach the significance of historical events.

In this case the historical event is the conversion of Saul on the road to Damascus. We have already met Saul. He was present at the death of Stephen. "Then they cast him (Stephen) out of the city and stoned him; and the witnesses laid down their garments at the feet of a young man named Saul . . ." (Acts 7:58). "But Saul was ravaging the church, and entering house after house, he dragged off men and women and committed them to prison" (Acts 8:3).

As Luke picks up the story of Saul again he begins just where he had ended. "But Saul, still breathing threats and murder against the disciples of the Lord, went to the high priest and asked him for letters to the synagogues at Damascus so that if he found any belonging to the Way, men or women, he might bring them bound to Jerusalem" (Acts 9:1–2).

However, as Saul proceeds to Damascus he has an experience that profoundly changes not only his life but the life of the whole world. Luke emphasizes the importance of this event by telling us about it three times in Acts, here as well as in two speeches (see Acts 22:1–16 and 26:9–18).

Because we have three accounts of the same event we can compare the accounts and get a clearer idea of what are the core events and what are details included for emphasis. In comparing the accounts it becomes evident that Luke simply didn't care about minor inconsistencies. For us to care about them is to miss Luke's point because we have misunderstood the kind of writing we are reading.

In each account Saul is on the road to Damascus with the intent of persecuting Jesus' followers when he is surrounded by a great light, falls to the ground, and hears a voice say, " 'Saul, Saul why do you persecute me?' And he said, 'Who are you Lord?' And he said, 'I am Jesus whom you are persecuting' " (see Acts 9:4–5; 22:7–8; 26:14–15). Exactly what those who were traveling with Paul saw and heard is unclear as the accounts differ on these details.

Ananias appears in two accounts (chapters 9 and 22), but his arguing with the Lord about helping Saul appears only in chapter 9. Thus it is clear that to ask "Why would Ananias argue with the Lord?" is to focus on the wrong point. However, once again, it may be best to respond directly to this misfocused question in order to move on to the important question, "What is Luke teaching through his account of Saul's/Paul's conversion?"

Ananias' arguing with the Lord is a literary technique which enables Luke to put into the mouth of the Lord the significance of the conversion of Saul. In answer to Ananias' warning about Saul the Lord says, "Go, for he is a chosen instrument of mine to carry my name before the Gentiles and kings and the sons of Israel . . ." (Acts 9:15). With these words the readers understand the pivotal nature of the event about which they are reading. As we continue to read Acts we will see Paul do exactly this—preach to Gentiles, kings, and Jews. However, his missionary vocation will be primarily aimed toward the Gentiles.

In the second account of Paul's conversion this explanation of Paul's vocation is put in the mouth of Ananias, speaking to Paul (see Acts 22:14–15). In the third account, the explanation of Paul's vocation is again placed on the Lord's lips, but this time addressed directly to Paul (see Acts 26:16–18).

It is obviously important to Luke that, as he tells the story of Paul's conversion, his Gentile readers understand the pivotal nature of the event in their own lives.

THREE ACCOUNTS OF PAUL'S CONVERSION

(Acts 9:1–19; 22:1–16; 26:9–18)

Events in common

- Saul is on the road to Damascus with the intent of persecuting Jesus' followers.
- Saul is surrounded by a light.
- Saul falls to the ground.
- A voice says, "Saul, Saul why do you persecute me?"
- Paul responds, "Who are you, Lord?"
- The voice says, "I am Jesus whom you are persecuting."

Details which differ

- What do those traveling with Paul see and hear?
- What role does Ananias play?
- What does Ananias say?
- In whose mouth does the explanation of Paul's conversion appear?

In addition to highlighting the significance of Paul's conversion in the life of his audience, Luke re-emphasizes a point which he has been making all along. Jesus continues to be present in his disciples. We have seen this in the way in which the apostles' ministry mirrors Jesus'. We have seen it in the way Stephen's story reflected Jesus' story. Now we see it clearly stated in Jesus' own words: "I am Jesus, whom you are persecuting." In persecuting Jesus' disciples, Paul was persecuting Jesus himself.

After showing how Paul has been chosen directly by Jesus, Luke incorporates Paul into the early church. Paul is baptized (Acts 9:18) and later is introduced to and finally accepted by the apostles in Jerusalem (Acts 9:26–29).

The "acts of Paul," foreshadowed in the Lord's words to Ananias, will soon take center stage in the Acts of the Apostles. However, as we read Acts, it is becoming abundantly clear that the acts of the apostles and the acts of Paul are all the fruit of the acts of God, directing the early church to spread the good news to God's people.

Review Questions

1. What do the three accounts of Paul's conversion experience have in common?
2. How do the three accounts of Paul's conversion differ from one another?
3. What is Luke able to emphasize in his account by having Ananias argue with the Lord?
4. What is the significance of the words, "I am Jesus whom you are persecuting"?
5. How is Paul incorporated into the church?

Discussion Questions

1. Why do you think Luke told basically the same story three times?
2. Does it bother you that there are some inconsistencies in the three accounts? Why or why not?
3. Is it possible to persecute Jesus today? Explain.

ARTICLE 14

The Gentiles Are Included in the Covenant

Question: "It is obvious that Luke wants us to realize that something momentous is happening in Peter's dream on the rooftop (Acts 10:9–16), but I can't figure out what it is. It looks to me as if Peter was hungry and dreamed of food. What am I missing?" (Acts 10:23–48 also discussed)

You are missing the meaning of the dream, the effect it had on Peter's thinking, and so the effect it had on Peter's behavior.

By positioning the dream between an account of Cornelius' vision and the arrival of Cornelius' messengers at Peter's house, Luke shows us how Peter himself figured out the meaning of the dream and acted on it.

The whole significance of the dream and the interaction between Cornelius and Peter is missed if one forgets the background of each person. Peter is a Jew. He has lived according to Jewish law. Peter considers some food clean and unclean, even some people clean and unclean.

Cornelius is a Gentile, a good person who prays and gives alms—but, nevertheless, a Gentile. From Peter's point of view, it would be wrong to accept hospitality from such a person, who did not follow the law. Peter refers to this fact himself when he says to Cornelius and to Cornelius' guests, "You yourselves know how unlawful it is for a Jew to associate with or to visit anyone of another nation; but God has shown me that I should not call any man common or unclean" (Acts 10:28).

How did God show Peter that he should not call any man unclean? By the dream which Peter had had about food while he was hungry.

54

In the dream Peter saw something like a great sheet let down from heaven, and on it were all kinds of animals. A voice said, " 'Rise, Peter; kill and eat.' 'No, Lord: for I have never eaten anything that is common or unclean.' And the voice came to him a second time, 'What God has cleansed, you must not call common' " (Acts 10:13–15).

Peter himself does not know what the dream means. However, immediately after the dream he does something that he previously would have considered wrong. When Cornelius' messengers arrive and tell him about Cornelius' dream he invites these unclean men to be his guests. "So he called them in to be his guests" (Acts 10:23).

By juxtaposing the story of Peter's dream and the arrival of Cornelius' messengers Luke is making it clear that Peter did not decide on his own to act outside the Jewish law. Rather he did it because he believed that God had revealed to him that he should.

After going to Cornelius' house and hearing Cornelius' story, Peter preaches the kerygma as it was preached to Gentiles. The speech contains an account of Jesus' life, death, and resurrection, and ends with the words, "To him all the prophets bear witness that everyone who believes in him receives forgiveness of sins through his name" (Acts 10:43).

"Everyone" includes the Gentiles, people who don't even follow the law, but who have been "made clean" of sin.

The truth of this assertion is immediately made evident as "the Holy Spirit fell on all who heard the word. And the believers among the circumcised who came with Peter were amazed, because the gift of the Holy Spirit had been passed out even on the Gentiles" (Acts 10:44).

The "Pentecost" of the Gentiles did not come after baptism as we noticed in the "Pentecost of the Samaritans" (Acts 8:17). Rather, it came before. The presence of the gifts of the Spirit in the community persuaded Peter that it was God's will that these Gentiles be baptized. " 'Can anyone forbid water for baptizing these people who have received the Holy Spirit just as we have?' And he commanded them to be baptized in the name of Jesus Christ. Then they asked him to remain for some days" (Acts 10:47–48).

As Luke's Gentile audience reads this story it is completely evi-

---

BAPTISM AND THE SPIRIT

The Norm: The gifts of the Spirit are received at baptism (Acts 2:38).

The Exceptions:

1. The "Pentecost" of the Samaritans (Acts 8:16). The Samaritans received the Spirit after baptism when the apostles "laid on hands."

   Teaching: Luke shows that God affirms Philip's work among the Samaritans.

2. The "Pentecost" of the Gentiles (Acts 10:44). The Gentiles received the Spirit before baptism.

   Teaching: Luke shows that God wanted Peter to know that he should baptize even the Gentiles.

---

dent to them that they were included in the covenant by the direct intervention of God. However, God worked through his chosen apostles. It is also evident that there is no reason why Jewish Christians who obey the law and Gentile Christians who do not cannot be together in each other's homes. God has made the Gentiles clean, and what God has made clean no one should call unclean.

Peter's dream, when interpreted within the context of the events which surround it, is seen to be God's way of revealing God's will to his chosen apostle. It is God's will that Gentiles be included in the covenant.

Review Questions

1. What was Peter's dream?
2. What would Peter's attitude toward Cornelius have been before the dream?

3. Why does the dream change Peter's attitude toward Cornelius?
4. What is Luke emphasizing by describing the gifts of the Spirit as falling on the Gentiles before baptism?
5. What might Luke's audience learn about their own relationships with Jews from this account?

Discussion Questions

1. Do you believe God continues to guide his people through dreams? Explain.
2. Are there any rules in our society which arbitrarily divide people from each other? What are they?
3. Are the gifts of the Spirit manifest in our society? Explain.
4. Are there any changes in the course of events, which have occurred in the last five years, that you would attribute to the action of the Holy Spirit? Explain.

ARTICLE 15

The Council of Jerusalem

Question: "Why do Barnabas and Paul bother to go to Jerusalem to ask whether or not a person has to be circumcised to be saved (Acts 15:1–34)? They already know the answer." (Acts 11:22–25; 13:1–14:28 also discussed)

Paul and Barnabas certainly believe that a Gentile does not have to be circumcised to be saved. Luke tells us that Paul and Barnabas "had no small dissension and debate" with those who thought otherwise (Acts 15:2). Still, Paul and Barnabas go to Jerusalem to get a definitive decision on the matter.

Luke has been at great pains to show that the church at Antioch, which becomes the second great missionary church and which sends Barnabas and Paul on Paul's first missionary journey (Acts 13:1–14:28), is not a church independent of the Jerusalem church. Nor are Barnabas and Paul independent people acting separately from the community.

Barnabas had originally been sent to the church in Antioch from Jerusalem, after those in Jerusalem had heard that the Lord Jesus was being preached to the Greeks in Antioch. "News of this came to the ears of the church in Jerusalem, and they sent Barnabas to Antioch" (Acts 11:22). Barnabas then went to Tarsus to find Paul and brought him back to Antioch (Acts 11:25).

This Antiochan community, acting under the influence of the Spirit, commissioned Barnabas and Paul to go on the first missionary journey (see Acts 12:2–3). Far from being independent agents, the two are obviously accountable to the church, for on their return they report on all their experiences. ". . . and from there they sailed to Antioch, where they had been commended to the grace of God

58

PAUL AND CHURCH STRUCTURE

- Paul's conversion: A direct intervention by God in Paul's life.
- The Jerusalem church sends Barnabas to Antioch. Barnabas brings Paul to Antioch to work with him.
- Barnabas and Paul are commissioned by the church in Antioch to go on mission.
- Barnabas and Paul appoint local church leaders—elders.
- Barnabas and Paul go to Jerusalem for the Jerusalem council. They receive the commendation of the apostles for their work among the Gentiles.

---

for the work which they had fulfilled. And when they arrived they gathered the church together and declared all that God had done with them, and how he had opened a door of faith to the Gentiles" (Acts 14:26–27).

Just as Barnabas and Paul had been chosen for their roles, so did they choose leaders in the various churches which developed as a result of their preaching. "And when they (i.e. Barnabas and Paul) had appointed elders for them in every church, with prayer and fasting they committed them to the Lord in whom they believed" (Acts 14:23).

So it is certainly no surprise that when an extremely divisive argument developed in the church in Antioch the church appointed representatives, Barnabas and Paul among them, to go to Jerusalem so that a decision could be made in union with the apostles.

In Jerusalem the first church council is held. The apostles and elders gather together and all listen as Peter reminds the group of his experiences as the apostle to the Gentiles (Acts 15:6–11). Barnabas and Paul likewise tell of the "signs and wonders God had done through them among the Gentiles" (Acts 15:12). James, the head of the Jerusalem church, agrees. The council decides unanimously that the Gentile Christians need not become Jewish to become Christian. They need not be circumcised.

A letter is sent back to Antioch with Barnabas and Paul which states, "For it has seemed good to the Holy Spirit and to us to lay upon you no greater burden than these necessary things: that you abstain from what has been sacrificed to idols and from blood and from what is strangled and from unchastity. If you keep yourself from these you will do well. Farewell" (Acts 15:28–29).

The council of Jerusalem, with its official recognition of the missionary efforts to the Gentiles, is a turning point in the Acts of the Apostles. No longer will we hear of Peter or of the apostles as a group. The Gentile church, now less tied to its Jewish roots, will spread, through Paul's missionary activity, to the ends of the earth.

Review Questions

1. What church became the second great missionary church?
2. Why did the Jerusalem church send Barnabas to Antioch?
3. Who commissioned Paul and Barnabas to go on Paul's first missionary journey?
4. What question needed to be decided at the council of Jerusalem?
5. What decision was made at the council of Jerusalem?

Discussion Questions

1. Why is it important that the church be united as one body? Do you know of efforts to achieve this unity in our time? Explain. Do you feel any responsibility to work for unity? Explain.
2. How is authority handed on in the church today? How are definitive decisions made? Why is it necessary to have a formal and visible way to hand on authority and to come to decisions?
3. What church council was held most recently? Do you know what questions came before this council or what was decided? Explain.

ARTICLE 16

Paul's Personality in Acts

Question: "Did Paul and Barnabas go separate ways because they had a fight (Acts 15:36–40)? This seems out of sync with everything else." (Acts 8:1; 9:1; 16:37; 18:5–6; 20:22–24 also discussed)

Luke does tell us that Paul and Barnabas parted ways because they had an argument over whether or not Mark should accompany them. For Luke, disagreements as well as persecution result in the word being spread more and more. Because of the fight, two missionary teams set out: Barnabas and Mark to Cyprus, Paul and Silas to Syria.

Why does this detail seem "out of sync" to the questioner? Perhaps because the questioner would expect two people who are each acting under the influence of the Holy Spirit to agree with each other. Perhaps the questioner brings to Acts a presumption that there were no serious disagreements in the early church, that everyone agreed.

Such a presumption would blind one to the fact that the early Christians exhibit the same problems in achieving unity that we experience today. People's personalities do not always mesh. People have a variety of insights that sometimes blind them to the insights of others which are equally valid. Wherever people are involved with each other, personality conflicts are likely to arise.

As Luke describes Paul's activities, decisions, and reactions, we get a picture of Paul's personality as he appears in Acts. After examining this picture one is no longer surprised to hear that Paul had an argument with someone else and had the self-confidence to go the way he thought he should. Paul has a very strong personality. He seems to be a person who likes, rather than avoids, contention.

61

Remember how we first met Paul? He was taking the initiative to persecute Christians and drag them off to prison (Acts 9:1). Paul didn't seem to flinch at the murder of Stephen (Acts 8:1). Paul's conversion did not mean that he had a personality change, only that he had a new vision of the truth and so redirected his energies.

In Paul's new vocation he still exhibits the characteristics we saw in him before his conversion: He does not avoid contention but courageously charges forth doing what he believes to be right.

We see this when Paul is imprisoned in Philippi. When the magistrates decide to release Paul, he refuses to go. "But Paul said to them 'They have beaten us publicly, uncondemned men who are Roman citizens, and have thrown us into prison, and do they now cast us out secretly? No! Let them come themselves and take us out' " (Acts 16:37).

Paul retains not only his relish for confrontation but his deep anger at those who thwart him. Luke tells us Paul's reaction to the Jews in Macedonia who opposed him. "When Silas and Timothy arrived from Macedonia, Paul was occupied with preaching, testifying to the Jews that the Christ was Jesus. And when they opposed and reviled him, he shook out his garments and said to them, 'Your blood be upon your heads! I am innocent. From now on I will go to the Gentiles' " (Acts 18:5–6).

However, Luke does not picture Paul as a person incapable of compromise. In the beginning of Paul's second journey, Paul recruits Timothy in Lystra as a missionary. Timothy's mother was Jewish, his father Greek. Jews would have disapproved of their marriage. Jews would also have disapproved of Timothy's being uncircumcised since Jews considered children to be the same religion as their mothers. Timothy, uncircumcised, would be rejected by Jews. If Timothy were a missionary, not only would Timothy be rejected, but so too would be the truth which Timothy taught. So, even though Paul believed that circumcision was unnecessary, and even though the council of Jerusalem had declared it unnecessary, Paul had Timothy circumcised so that he could be a more effective missionary to the Jews.

In addition to picturing Paul as a person capable of compromise, Luke's Paul exhibits a lack of fear in the face of hostility and a courage to persevere even in the face of death. We will see this clearly when we read the farewell speech which Paul is pictured as giving to the elders of Ephesus. "And now, behold, I am going to Jerusalem bound in the Spirit, not knowing what will befall me there; except that the Holy Spirit testifies to me in every city that imprisonment and afflictions await me. But I do not account my life of any value nor as precious to myself, if only I may accomplish my course and the ministry which I received from the Lord Jesus, to testify to the gospel of the grace of God" (Acts 20:22–24).

Paul does have a fiery personality, but it is this very personality, channeled in the service of the gospel, which enables Paul to be the missionary to both the Jews who rejected him and the Gentiles who did not.

Review Questions

1. What was the result of the disagreement between Paul and Barnabas?
2. What was Paul doing when we first met him in Acts?
3. What evidence is there that Paul didn't try to avoid confrontation?
4. What evidence is there that Paul was capable of compromise?
5. What motivated Paul? Why was he able to persevere even in the face of death?

Discussion Questions

1. Do you know of instances where persecution or disagreement has resulted in people being stronger and more dedicated? Can you give examples? Why do you think this happens?
2. What does this statement mean: "Paul's conversion did not mean that he had a personality change, only that he had a new vision of the truth and so redirected his energies?" Do you agree with this statement? Why or why not?
3. What do you think of Paul's agreeing to have Timothy circumcised? Would you call this a moral compromise? Explain.

ARTICLE 17

Acts' Structure: Not Journeys
But "Other Christs"

Question: "I'm getting all mixed up here (Acts 15:36ff). Is Luke with Paul? All of a sudden he says, '*We* sought to go. . . .' Also, I can't keep track of the trips, they are moving around so much. And Paul's experiences seem so similar to Peter's. It's hard to keep it all straight. Help!" (Acts 12:25–14:20; 15:40; 16:10–17; 18:18–23; 20:5–15; 21:1–18; 27:1–28:16 also discussed)

It is hard to feel "in control of the plot" as you move into the accounts of Paul's second and third journeys for the very reasons which the questioner raises. Let us respond to each of these difficulties individually.

"Is Luke with Paul?" Scholars debate the significance of the fact that the narrator's voice suddenly switches from third person ("he") to first person plural ("we"). While Acts 16:10 is the first instance of this, it is not the only instance. The narrative voice slips into "we" in Acts 16:10–17, 20:5–15, 21:1–18, and 27:1–28:16. We know that Luke is editing inherited sources. Is one of his inherited sources a personal travel diary? Did Luke accompany Paul? Or is the "we" a convention used when narrators talk of sea journeys? If so, Luke does not use the convention consistently (see Acts 18:18–19). The traditional explanation is that Luke was a companion of Paul's and did accompany him on some journeys.

The reader's inability to keep track of Paul's itinerary is perfectly understandable and not a real impediment to understanding Acts. The first journey of Paul and Barnabas is clearly delineated (see Acts 12:25–14:28). As we noted, there was a formal "sending off"

PAUL'S MISSIONARY JOURNEYS

First Journey: Acts 13–14

Second Journey: Acts 15:40–18:22

Third Journey: Acts 18:23–21:17

---

for the journey (Acts 13:3) and a formal report on their return (Acts 14:27). The beginning of the second journey is also clearly mentioned (Acts 15:40). However, the end of the second journey (Acts 18:22) and the beginning of the third (Acts 18:23) is barely noticeable. "On landing at Caesarea, he went up and paid his respects to the congregation, and then went down to Antioch. After spending some time there he set out again, traveling systematically through the Galatian country and Phrygia to reassure his disciples" (Acts 18:22–23).

It seems evident that this traditional division into three journeys is arbitrary and not at all essential to understanding the points which Luke is teaching as he writes Acts. The best way to solve this difficulty is simply to keep a map handy so that the journey can be followed without the structure into three journeys taking on undue importance.

Much more essential to understanding Luke's point is the reader's comment that Paul's experiences sound so similar to Peter's that it is hard to remember which is which. This is true and points to a much more important structural pattern than the division into three journeys.

As we read of Paul's ministry, practically every event recalls Peter's ministry. At the source of each man's activities lies the inspiration of the Holy Spirit. Both heal the lame and raise the dead. Both suffer persecution and imprisonment, but are miraculously freed. Both have run-ins with magicians and are worshiped by Gentiles. Both are great preachers who, at the Spirit's direction,

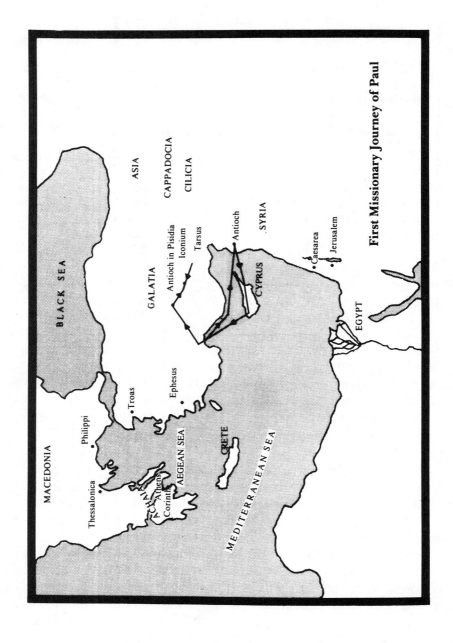

First Missionary Journey of Paul

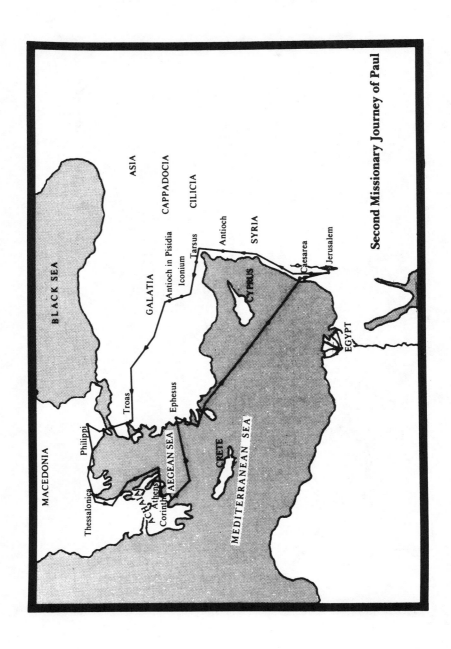

Second Missionary Journey of Paul

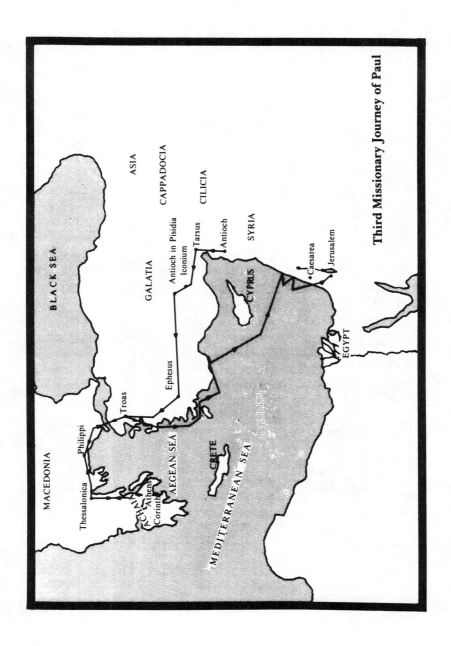

Third Missionary Journey of Paul

"WE SECTIONS" IN ACTS

16:10–17
20:5–15
21:1–18
27:1–28:16

---

preach to Jews and Gentiles, lay on hands, and appoint other leaders as both give their lives to spreading the gospel.

In modeling Paul's ministry after Peter's in this way, Luke is making the same point which we noted that he made in modeling Peter's and Stephen's ministries after Jesus'. All of Jesus' disciples represent an extension of Jesus' presence in time and space. Where Jesus' disciples are present, so is Jesus.

We noted that one way in which Luke teaches this truth is by emphasizing Jesus' words to Paul on the road to Damascus. "Why are you persecuting *me*?" A second way is by emphasizing the similarities between Jesus' ministry and those of his disciples. Peter's and Paul's ministries appear so very similar because each is

---

PETER'S MINISTRY AND PAUL'S MINISTRY

(Each reflects Christ's ministry)

- Each acts under the inspiration of the Holy Spirit.
- Each performs mighty signs.
- Each suffers persecution and imprisonment but is miraculously freed: Peter by an angel; Paul by an earthquake.
- Each encounters magicians.
- Each is worshiped by Gentiles.
- Each preaches to both Jews and Gentiles.
- Each appoints new leadership.

---

modeled after Jesus', whose ministry also started with the guidance of the Spirit, who also healed the lame and raised the dead, who also experienced persecution, who also appointed other leaders, and who also preached as he gave his life to spreading the good news.

Luke's point is not that his audience be able to name the towns on Paul's journeys, or recite exactly what happened to Peter or Paul. Rather, Luke wants his audience to understand that both Peter and Paul were "other Christs" who faithfully followed the direction of the Holy Spirit as they brought the good news of Christianity to the Gentiles.

Review Questions

1. What explanations are given for the "we sections" of Acts? Why are these sections called "we sections"?
2. Is the traditional division of Paul's travels into three journeys an important structural device in Acts? Explain.
3. What is a more important structural pattern?
4. What point is Luke making in modeling his account of Paul's experiences after Peter's?
5. What do Paul's, Peter's, and Jesus' ministries have in common?

Discussion Questions

1. Do you think being able to name Paul's routes is important to understanding Acts? Why or why not?
2. What does it mean to say that Peter and Paul were "other Christs"?
3. Do you think anyone in our society is another Christ? Do you think you are? Explain.

ARTICLE 18

Preaching to the Stoics
and the Epicureans

Question: "Doesn't Paul pretty much drop the ball in this talk in Athens (Acts 17:16–32)? He doesn't get around to talking about Christ until the very end. Instead he talks about God the creator. Why does Paul compromise his teaching so much?"

This questioner seems to have slipped back into the presumption that the speech on Paul's lips gives us an accurate historical picture of Paul's preaching in Athens. Remember that the speeches in Acts are Luke's compositions, aimed primarily at Luke's Gentile audience.

In this speech Luke has Paul argue against the thoughts of two Hellenistic philosophies with which Luke's Gentile audience would have been very familiar, the Stoics and the Epicureans. We know that these are the philosophies which are being challenged because Luke says so (see Acts 17:16–18). So in order to understand what Luke is teaching his audience through Paul's speech, it would be helpful to know what ideas were held by the Epicureans and Stoics.

Epicureans did not believe in life after death. Therefore, they saw no reason to fear what the gods might do to one after death. In fact, Epicureans did not think that the gods involved themselves with human beings, so not only was there no reason to fear, but there was no need to pray or to offer sacrifice.

For the Epicureans the goal of life was pleasure, which meant freedom from pain and anxiety. A wise person, according to the

Epicureans, would live a life of virtue because such a life would result in pleasure.

The Stoics' basic belief was that unity, order and purpose in life resulted from the fact that all was permeated by reason or "logos." This reason also exists in every person. One need only live a life in obedience to this inner reason in order to find purpose. To achieve happiness one must accept the order with which reason has permeated the universe with "apatheia" or lack of feeling.

Neither the Epicureans nor the Stoics denied the existence of gods. However, the Epicureans would have objected strongly to the idea of resurrection.

Notice, Paul mentions the resurrection, the point of contention, only at the end of his talk. No sooner does he mention it than he is interrupted. "Now when they heard of the resurrection of the dead, some mocked, but others said, 'We will hear you again on this' " (Acts 17:32).

The fact that Paul is interrupted as soon as he brings up a contentious point gives us a hint as to why this speech to the Gentiles differs from the basic kerygmatic speeches which we have already read. Paul is pictured as beginning in such a way as to avoid immediately antagonizing his audience.

In fact, Paul begins with flattery. "Men of Athens, I perceive that in every way you are very religious" (Acts 17:22). Next Paul discusses God in terms which might well be compatible with the beliefs of his audience. God the creator is responsible for the harmony and unity which exists in the universe. "And he made from one every nation of men to live on all the face of the earth, having determined allotted periods and the boundaries of their habitats . . ." (Acts 17:26).

Human beings are part of this created harmony. "In him we live, and move, and have our being, as some of your poets have said. 'For we are indeed his offspring' " (Acts 17:28).

So far Paul has not lost his audience. What he has said certainly has its roots in the Old Testament, but it is not incompatible with the ideas of order and purpose which the Greeks already held.

After laying this groundwork, Paul does move on to beliefs with which we are familiar from the kerygma. He tells his audience that God calls them to repentance because judgment is coming. "The times of ignorance God overlooked, but now he commands all men everywhere to repent, because he has fixed a day on which he will judge the world in righteousness by a man he has appointed, and of this he has given assurance to all men by raising him from the dead" (Acts 17:30–31).

Given the audience, one presumes that those who mocked Paul at this mention of the resurrection were the Epicureans and that those who were intrigued were the Stoics.

In the speech in Athens, Luke does not picture Paul "dropping the ball" by failing to immediately emphasize the kerygma. Rather, Luke gives his audience an example of how the kerygma can be reworked when used in missionary outreach to the Gentiles. A missionary talk to the Gentiles should begin with those points with which Greeks and Christians might agree and should then move on to the specific message of Christianity. The hope is that if Christianity were presented in a reasoned way, in a way initially compatible with Greek thought, the reaction might well be a show of interest. This is the reaction Paul is pictured as eliciting. "We will hear you again about this" (Acts 17:32).

In addition, some Gentiles, like those in Luke's audience, believed Paul's words and became disciples themselves. "But some men joined him, and believed . . ." (Acts 17:34).

Far from picturing Paul as dropping the ball, in this speech to the Gentiles Luke presents Paul as being both sensitive to the ideas which his audience already holds, and successful in his proclaiming the good news to the Gentiles.

Review Questions

1. What two schools of philosophy was Paul arguing against in Athens?
2. With what Christian beliefs would the Epicureans have disagreed?
3. Why does Paul begin his talk by speaking of God the creator who gives harmony and unity to creation?
4. What might Luke's audience learn from this speech of Paul's?

Discussion Questions

1. If you were going to explain Christianity to a Jew and then to an atheist, would you begin in the same place? How might you approach each group? Why would this be your approach?
2. Do you think it is a good idea or manipulative to flatter your audience and first speak of ideas you have in common? Explain.

ARTICLE 19

Paul's Farewell Discourse

Question: "Paul's speech before the elders from Ephesus sounds defensive. Why is it necessary for Paul to keep defending himself? He brags a lot too. This is a strange speech." (Acts 20:17–38; Acts 19:10 also discussed)

The defensive tone which the questioner has noted, and which appears several times in Paul's speech to the elders, is a characteristic of the kind of speech which Luke pictures Paul giving, a farewell discourse. This discourse plays an important role in Acts because it serves as the dividing point in Paul's life between his missionary activity and his "passion." Jesus' farewell discourse at the last supper played much the same role in Jesus' life (Lk 22:1–38).

Farewell speeches were common in the literature of the time. They were composed by authors and placed on the lips of significant characters who were about to die. (So Paul wasn't really bragging.)

The farewell speech traditionally shows the leader calling together his followers, speaking of the past as he holds up his own actions as an example, reflecting on the meaning of his work and that he did not fail in his duty, speaking of the future as he exhorts his followers to likewise serve well, warning his followers about trouble ahead, and, finally, blessing and praying for his followers as he passes authority on to them and says goodbye.

On close examination we can see that Luke has utilized these characteristics of a farewell discourse in Paul's speech, the only speech which we see Paul give to Christians.

First Paul, who is in Miletus, calls the elders from Ephesus to come to him. You will remember that we read about Paul's recent

---

COMPONENTS OF A FAREWELL DISCOURSE

- The leader calls together his followers.
- He reflects on the past and holds himself up as a good example; he did not fail in his duty.
- He envisions the future and encourages his followers to serve well too.
- He warns about trouble ahead.
- The leader blesses and prays for his followers as he passes on his authority and says goodbye.

---

stay in Ephesus in chapter 19. Paul had stayed in Ephesus for more than two years (see Acts 19:10). Paul begins by reminding the elders of his past work among them, which he holds up as an example. "You yourself know how I lived among you all the time from the first day I set foot in Asia, serving the Lord with all humility and with tears and trials which befell me through the plots of the Jews" (Acts 20:18–19).

As Paul refers to the fact that he knows imprisonment lies ahead, he reflects on the meaning of his work and the fact that he has not failed. "But I do not account my life of any value nor as precious to myself, if only I may accomplish my course and the ministry which I received from the Lord Jesus, to testify to the gospel of the grace of God . . ." (Acts 20:24). "Therefore I testify to you this day that I am innocent of the blood of all of you, for I did not shrink from declaring to you the whole counsel of God" (Acts 20:27).

This does sound unnecessarily defensive. However, the explanation lies not in the plot of the story but in the literary form, the genre of the speech. The defensive tone is a convention of a farewell discourse.

Next Paul looks to the future and exhorts the future leaders of the church to do a good job too. "Take heed to yourselves and to all the flock, in which the Holy Spirit has made you overseers, to care for the church of God which he obtained with the blood of his own Son" (Acts 20:28).

After warning of trouble ahead and again holding himself up as a model (remember, it is actually Luke and not Paul who is holding Paul up as a model), Paul commends the elders to God. "And now I commend you to God and to the word of his grace, which is able to build you up and to give you the inheritance among all those who are sanctified" (Acts 20:31).

Once more Paul's example is held up as a model. Paul never allowed economic profit to become his motivation. Instead he earned his own living. "You yourselves know that these hands ministered to my necessities, and to those who were with me" (Acts 20:34). As Paul did, so should his followers.

As Luke's audience read that Paul knelt, prayed with his followers, and then departed from them, Luke's audience would have realized from the form of this farewell discourse that they too would soon be reading no more about Paul. The farewell discourse would have made it clear to them that Paul's mission, indeed his life, was coming to an end.

Review Questions

1. What elements are traditionally present in a farewell discourse?
2. Why does Paul sound so defensive?
3. What does it mean to say that the defensive tone is a "convention" of a farewell discourse?
4. Was Paul bragging in this speech? Explain.
5. Why would Luke's audience have known from this speech that the account of Paul's life was coming to an end?

Discussion Questions

1. What does it mean to say that it is Luke and not Paul who is holding Paul up as a model in this farewell discourse?
2. Do you see any resemblances between this farewell discourse of Paul's and Jesus' farewell to the apostles at the last supper (Lk 22:1–38)? What are they?
3. Are there parts of this speech that strike you as exactly right for the kind of person you imagine Paul to have been? What are they? How would you balance this impression with the idea that Luke has used the form of a traditional farewell discourse?

ARTICLE 20

Paul's "Passion" and Time in Rome

Question: "I'm all mixed up reading these trial scenes, but at least I can see that details resemble Jesus' passion. Is this resemblance the point? If so, why don't we read of Paul's death? Why does Luke leave the story up in the air?" (Acts 21–26)

The resemblance between Paul's "passion" and Jesus' passion is certainly Luke's point in chapters 21 to 26, but it is not Luke's point in the Acts of the Apostles as a whole. First let's look at Paul's arrest and trials, and see how Luke, through the way in which he tells the story, pictures Paul as "another Christ." Then we will discuss why Acts ends as it does.

There is a great deal of similarity in Luke's account of the events of Paul's imprisonment and in Luke's account of Jesus' imprisonment in the gospel. Both Jesus and Paul try to defend themselves to the groups which are responsible for their arrests (Lk 22:47–53; Acts 22:1–21). Both have trials before the Sanhedrin (Lk 22:66–71; Acts 23:1–10). Both are tried before a Roman governor. Jesus is tried before Pilate twice (Lk 23:1–6; 23:13–25), Paul is tried before two Roman governors, Felix (Acts 24:1–22) and Festus (Acts 25:6–12). Both Jesus and Paul are tried before a Jewish Herodian king: Jesus before King Herod (Lk 23:6–11) and Paul before King Agrippa (Acts 26:1–29).

The similarities between Jesus' passion and Paul's extend even to details. Both are ridiculed, in both cases the crowds shout, "Kill him, kill him," and both are clearly found innocent by the Roman authorities. After each of Paul's trials Paul's innocence is clearly stated (see Acts 23:29; 26:31–32).

The questioner is right in concluding that Luke has purposefully

78

PAUL'S PASSION A SHARING IN CHRIST'S PASSION

- Both defend themselves to the group arresting them.
- Both are tried before the Sanhedrin.
- Both are tried before a Roman governor.
- Both are tried before a Jewish Herodian king.
- Both are found innocent by Roman authorities.
- Both are ridiculed by the crowds.

---

paralleled Jesus' and Paul's passions as a way of saying that Paul is an extension of Christ's presence on earth. Paul is another Christ who, under the guidance of the Holy Spirit, is continuing Christ's work on earth.

Why, then, do we not read of Paul's death? Why does the story end with Paul miraculously making it to Rome and unsuccessfully preaching to the Jews in Rome?

Remember, Acts as a whole is not about Peter, as we may have thought through the early chapters, nor about Paul, as we may have thought through the later chapters. You may remember that we noted that Luke tells us what Acts is about when he pictures the risen Christ saying to the disciples, "But you shall receive power when the Holy Spirit comes upon you; and you shall be my witnesses in Jerusalem, and in all Judea and Samaria, and to the end of the earth" (Acts 1:8).

Paul's arrival in Rome, however, is not the arrival of Christianity in Rome. You may have noted that Luke explicitly states that Christians already in Rome greeted Paul on his arrival. "And so we came to Rome. And the brethren there, when they heard of us, came as far as the Forum of Appius and Three Taverns to meet us. On seeing them, Paul thanked God and took courage" (Acts 28:14–16).

Paul's arrival in Rome was a proclamation of the gospel to the Jews in Rome. This too has been a pattern all through Acts. As Paul arrives in each town he preaches first to the Jews. Only when the Jews reject the gospel does he turn to the Gentiles. This pattern is not broken in Rome. Paul's last words in Acts, directed to the Jews, are, "The Holy Spirit was right in saying to your fathers through Isaiah the prophet, 'Go to the people and say, "You shall indeed hear but never understand, and you shall indeed see but never perceive. For this people's heart has grown dull, and their ears are heavy of hearing, and their eyes they have closed; lest they should perceive with their eyes, and hear with their ears, and understand with their heart, and turn for me to heal them." ' Let it be known to you then that this salvation of God has been sent to the Gentiles; they will listen" (Acts 28:25–29).

Luke concludes Acts, having made the birth and direction of the early church understandable to his Gentile audience. The "Way" has its roots in Judaism. Jesus was born a Jew and ministered to the Jews. Jesus chose his disciples. After Jesus' resurrection those disciples were empowered by the Holy Spirit. Under the Spirit's influence the word was offered first to the Jews, but they rejected it. It was the Holy Spirit who directed that the word be offered to the Gentiles. The Gentiles, including Luke's audience, listened. So Luke ends Acts with Paul asserting this fact. The Gentiles, who listen, continue to hear the good news about the kingdom of God and the teaching about the Lord Jesus Christ. In Acts, Luke has shown how the risen Christ has become light to the Gentiles.

Review Questions

1. Name some similarities between Jesus' imprisonment and Paul's.
2. What is Luke's point in stressing these similarities?
3. What is Acts about?
4. Is Paul's arrival in Rome the arrival of Christianity in Rome? How do you know?
5. What fact does Paul assert as Acts ends?
6. Why is this fact of particular importance to Luke's audience?

Discussion Questions

1. Why do you think it was so important to Luke to stress that Paul always tried to teach the Jews but was rejected by them?

2. If Paul were to come to teach in our country how do you think he would be received? Why?
3. Did you like Paul as he appears in Acts? Why or why not?
4. If you had been writing Acts would you have ended it the way Luke did? Why or why not?

Summation and Transition
from Acts to Paul's Letters

As you now know, the Acts of the Apostles is made up of a variety of kinds of writing, edited and arranged to meet the needs of Luke's audience. As we read the Acts of the Apostles we became well acquainted with Paul, with his missionary activities, and even with his personality. However, the picture that we got was not first-hand. The emphasis brought about by the selection and arrangement of incidents was Luke's emphasis. The speeches that were attributed to Paul were, to some extent, Luke's compositions.

Now, as we start to read Paul's letters, we will meet Paul first-hand. Through Paul's correspondence we will become acquainted with a number of first century churches, with the questions they had, with the problems they confronted, and with Paul's personal relationship with them.

In this next section you will find a number of articles written in response to questions which students have asked during a first reading of Paul's letters. Do not start with these articles. Start with Paul's first letter to the Thessalonians. Read the letter as you would read a letter from a friend. Jot down whatever questions come to mind. Do the same with each of Paul's letters: read the letter before you read the articles about the letter. Most likely, many of the questions which come to your mind will be addressed in the following articles.

■ PAUL'S LETTERS ■

ARTICLE 1

Letters: Insights into the Message
and the Messenger

1 THESSALONIANS

Question: "Why are we reading 1 Thessalonians first?" (1 Thes 2:1–3:7)

Scholars believe that 1 Thessalonians is the earliest writing we have in the New Testament. So, as we begin to read Paul's letters, we will start with 1 Thessalonians.

As with all biblical writing, in order to understand the revelation which this letter contains we must read it as a "contextualist." A contextualist asks, "What is the literary form of this writing?" "What is the social context in which the author is addressing the audience?" "How does this writing fit into the process of revelation which we find in the Bible?"

1 Thessalonians is an "epistle" or letter. Because we have letters in our culture too, the form will not be difficult for you to understand. Still it is important to describe the form because, even though you are familiar with letters and know how to understand them, you may not realize that you should apply this knowledge to letters in the Bible.

Just as in our culture a letter has a conventional form, beginning with a salutation such as "Dear," and concluding with a farewell such as "Sincerely," so did letters of Paul's time have an accepted form.

Both Graeco-Roman and Jewish letters began with an opening

FORM OF GRAECO-ROMAN AND JEWISH LETTERS

I. *Opening formula* Paul includes the sender, the receiver and a blessing.

II. *Thanksgiving* This section introduces the theme of the letter.

III. *Body* This is the message of the letter. Paul expands the body to include doctrinal and ethical matters.

IV. *Closing* This section includes personal greetings, doxologies, and benedictions.

---

formula, included a thanksgiving which introduced the theme of the letter, moved on to the body of the letter, and then closed with personal greetings, doxologies and benedictions. Paul adjusted this form as he wrote to various churches, addressing specific problems which he heard they were facing.

Among the letters in the New Testament, thirteen are attributed

---

**PROBABLE ORDER OF PAUL'S LETTERS
AND ACTS WITH APPROXIMATE DATES**

50 A.D.	1 Thessalonians
54 A.D.	Galatians
55 A.D.	Philippians (major portion)
54–56 A.D.	1 Corinthians
55–57 A.D.	2 Corinthians
57 A.D.	Philemon
58 A.D.	Romans
85 A.D.	Acts

to Paul. However, scholars believe that Paul is the author of only seven of these letters: 1 Thessalonians, Galatians, Philippians, 1 and 2 Corinthians, Philemon and Romans. It is these seven Pauline letters which we will now read, in the order in which they were most probably written.

1 Thessalonians is believed to be the earliest, probably dating to 50 A.D. That date means that 1 Thessalonians precedes all four gospels, written between 65 and 95 A.D., the Acts of the Apostles, written around 85 A.D., and the book of Revelation, written between 90 and 100 A.D.

Once more we see that the New Testament as we now have it is an edited arrangement. The gospels are placed first not because they were written first but because their content, their plot, speaks of the historical Jesus' life, ministry, death and resurrection. Editors placed the Acts of the Apostles next because its plot chronologically follows the plot of the gospels. The setting for the Acts of the Apostles is the time right after the ascension when the earliest preaching took place.

The editors arranged the letters next. However, the letters are not arranged in the order in which they were written. Rather they are arranged from the longest to the shortest. This order is a perfectly logical order; it is just not the order in which a contextualist would choose to read the letters. A contextualist would prefer to read the letters in the order in which they were written in order to understand any growth in understanding which took place over time. Only if one reads the letters in the order in which they were written can one address the question, "How do the insights contained in this letter fit into a process of revelation?"

Since you have already studied Acts you are aware that Acts pictures Paul on a number of missionary journeys and describes Paul's activities in several of the cities to which Paul later writes. Since Acts precedes Paul's letters in the New Testament you may be tempted to allow Acts to set the scene for Paul's letters. For instance, you may try to understand Paul's first letter to the Thessalonians by placing it in the context of Paul's visit to Thessalonica which we read about in Acts 17.

To allow Acts to dictate your understanding of Paul's letters is a

---

A CONTEXTUALIST

Reads scripture passages in context.

- What is the literary form?
- What is the social context within which the author is addressing the audience?
- How does this writing fit into the process of revelation which we find in the Bible?

---

mistake. As you recall, Acts was not written to teach history. The author of Acts is teaching theological insights. The literary form of Acts does not allow us to treat it as though the author were providing a completely accurate historical setting for Paul's letters. Rather, Paul's letters, which are, after all, first-hand accounts from one person's point of view, are more likely to contain realistic details of Paul's mission activities than is Acts.

So, as we read Paul's first letter to the Thessalonians, we should allow the letter itself to provide us with the setting. Paul tells us something about the setting for this letter when he describes his earlier preaching in Thessalonica, his longing to see the Thessalonians again, and Timothy's return with news of them (1 Thes 2:1–3:7). As with all the letters, Paul's first letter to the Thessalonians is our best guide to the social setting in which the letter was written.

As we read Paul's letter to the Thessalonians we should keep in mind the questions which a contextualist always asks. By noticing the literary form, the social setting, and the process of revelation, we will grow in our knowledge both of Paul's message and of Paul himself. Letters, we will see, reveal not only the message but the messenger.

Review Questions

1. What three questions should a contextualist ask?
2. Name six elements of the form of a Graeco-Roman or Jewish letter.

3. What seven letters do scholars believe Paul wrote?
4. According to what criteria was the order of the letters in the New Testament decided?
5. Where is the best place to look to understand the social setting for each of Paul's letters?

Discussion Questions

1. Do you agree with the editors of the Bible that writings need not be arranged in the order in which they were written? Why or why not? What are the advantages of the editors' order? What order might be better?
2. Given what you know about the kinds of writing in Acts, which would you expect to be more accurate in reporting realistic details: Acts or Paul's letters? Explain.
3. Why do letters reveal not only the message but the messenger? What might letters you write reveal about you?

ARTICLE 2

Preaching by Word and Deed

1 THESSALONIANS

Question: "Paul seems terribly concerned with his reputation in this letter. Why is this?" (1 Thes 1:5–7; 2:1–2; 2:7–8; 2:9; 2:11–12; 3:6–8; 4:11)

Paul does seem concerned with his reputation. There are at least two reasons for this. One is that Paul is sensitive to abuses which the Thessalonians might have experienced at the hands of other preachers. The second is that Paul is acutely aware that he preaches even more by who he is than by what he says.

Paul points out to the Thessalonians that he and his fellow preachers differ from manipulative, self-seeking preachers in a number of ways.

First, Paul, Silvanus, and Timothy persevered in the face of persecution. "For you yourselves know, brethren, that our visit to you was not in vain, but though we had already suffered and been shamefully treated at Philippi, as you know, we had courage in our God to declare to you the gospel of God in the face of great opposition" (1 Thes 2:1–2).

Paul then goes on to say that because God is the source of the truth of the appeal which had been made to the Thessalonians, that appeal was not made in error, not with guile, nor to please men, nor as a cloak for greed, nor to seek glory.

Paul wants the Thessalonians to know that he has grown to love them as a parent. He uses two beautiful images to describe this

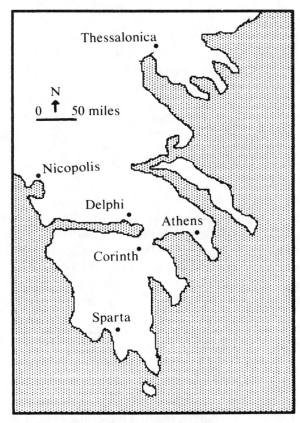

MAP OF GREECE

nurturing love. "But we were gentle among you, like a nurse taking care of her children. So, being affectionately desirous of you, we were ready to share with you not only the gospel of God but also our own selves, because you had become very dear to us. . . . For you know how, like a father with his children, we exhorted each one of you and encouraged you and charged you to lead a life worthy of God, who calls you into his own kingdom and glory" (1 Thes 2: 7–8; 11–12).

Paul urges the Thessalonians to live lives like his so that they too may be witnesses to the truth of the gospel. He wants them to live quietly, to mind their own business, and to work with their hands as Paul did, "so that you may command the respect of outsiders, and be dependent on nobody" (1 Thes 4:11).

As long as there is even a hint of personal gain, a preacher's words become less convincing and more suspect. That is why Paul and his fellow preachers earned their own living as they preached the gospel. "For you remember our labor and toil, brethren; we worked night and day, that we might not burden any of you, while we preached to you the gospel of God" (1 Thes 2:9).

The preaching of the gospel was, therefore, not only in words but in actions. Paul has modeled himself after Jesus. So, as the Thessalonians model themselves after Paul, they too model themselves after Jesus and become witnesses to others. "You know what kind of men we proved to be among you for your sake. And you became imitators of us and of the Lord, for you received the word in much affliction, with joy inspired by the Spirit, so that you became an example to all the believers in Macedonia and in Achaia" (1 Thes 1:5–7).

Not only have the Thessalonians become witnesses to those who have not yet heard the gospel, but they have become witnesses to Paul himself. "But now that Timothy has come to us from you, and has brought us the good news of your faith and love and reported that you always remember us kindly and long to see us, as we long to see you—for this reason, brethren, in all our distress and affliction we have been comforted about you through your faith; for now we live, if you stand fast in the Lord" (1 Thes 3:6–8).

Paul is concerned about his reputation and the reputation of the Thessalonians. He prays that each may be good witnesses of the gospel not only to others but to each other. Their mutual faith and love will help both of them persevere in the face of persecution.

Review Questions

1. For what two reasons was Paul so concerned about his reputation?
2. What two images does Paul use to describe his nurturing love?
3. Why did Paul earn his own living instead of using his ministry as a source of income?
4. What motivations does Paul give the Thessalonians to remain faithful in living the gospel?

Discussion Questions

1. How do preachers today sometimes exploit their listeners? Explain.
2. Do you think you say more by what you say or what you do? Explain.
3. Of all the people you know personally, who do you think lives a life that witnesses the gospel most faithfully? Why?

ARTICLE 3

Can the Lord Save the Dead?

1 Thessalonians

Question: "Considering the fact that this letter is our earliest written presentation of Christianity, it doesn't give us a very balanced picture. Why is there so much emphasis on what will happen at the second coming?" (1 Thes 4:15–17; 1 Thes 1:1; 1:3; 1:6; 2:2; 2:12; 4:1; 4:13; 5:1; 5:27 also discussed)

Behind this question lie two presumptions which are wrong and so will make understanding Paul's letters more difficult. One is that we are the primary audience. The other is that Paul was conscious of producing the first written presentation of Christianity.

Paul's letter is an "occasional" letter. Although Paul wanted the letter to be read to the whole church in Thessalonica (1 Thes 5:27) the letter is more similar to a personal letter than to a modern-day pastoral letter. Paul is not writing an ordered account of the Christian gospel. Rather, he is responding to recent news of beloved friends, news which included a misunderstanding or question on the part of the Thessalonians.

Thessalonica was a port city in Macedonia which Paul had visited during his second missionary journey, probably in 50 A.D. Acts tells us that Paul and Silvanus were expelled because their preaching caused a riot. The letter itself speaks of opposition to Paul's preaching (1 Thes 2:2). After leaving the Thessalonians Paul felt such a longing to see them that when he was unable to come himself he sent Timothy to bring him a first-hand report.

Perhaps it was Timothy's report that caused Paul to address the

94

subject of the second coming and to begin his comments with, "We would have you be clear about those who sleep in death, brothers" (1 Thes 4:13). Perhaps the Thessalonians had sent him a question in writing. Either way, Paul emphasizes the second coming because he knows that this topic is of particular concern to the Thessalonians.

Paul and the early Christians were expecting the second coming imminently. Paul refers to this expectation when he presumes that some of those who are presently alive will be alive when Jesus returns. "For this we declare to you by the word of the Lord, that we who are alive, who are left until the coming of the Lord, shall not precede those who have fallen asleep. For the Lord himself will descend from heaven with a cry of command, with the archangel's call, and with the sound of the trumpet of God. And the dead in Christ will rise first; then we who are alive, who are left, shall be caught up together with them in the clouds to meet the Lord in the air . . ." (1 Thes 4:15–17).

Paul is addressing a real concern of the Thessalonians. They have recently been converted to Christianity, perhaps earlier in the same year in which Paul is writing. Central to their new belief is that the Lord will come again. Now some of those converts who had anxiously awaited the second coming have died. Does this mean that they have missed out on salvation? Could the Lord still save them?

Paul assures the Thessalonians that the Lord can and will save those who have died as well as those who are still alive.

As Paul starts to talk about the second coming he slips into what is called "apocalyptic imagery." If something is "apocalyptic" it is about the end times. "Apocalyptic images" are those used to describe what is really beyond our comprehension and so indescribable. The description of Jesus coming on the "clouds of heaven" among "trumpet blasts" is an example of apocalyptic imagery. One understands apocalyptic passages much better if one realizes that the images are used to probe mysteries which are beyond our experience rather than to give realistic descriptions of future events.

Paul's teaching, and the revelation which the letter contains, is that the risen Lord will save both the living and those who have already died.

You may remember that the belief that the risen Lord would come again was one of the core Christian beliefs taught in the "kerygma," the early Christian preaching. Even though in his letter to the Thessalonians Paul doesn't attempt to give an ordered account of the core kerygma, he nevertheless does refer to other core teachings too.

The kerygma called people to repentance. Paul congratulates the Thessalonians on having turned their lives to God and refers to the fact that he had exhorted them "to lead a life worthy of God, who calls you into his kingdom and glory" (1 Thes 2:12).

The kerygma declared that Jesus is the messiah. Paul refers to this fact routinely as he calls Jesus "Lord" (1:1; 1:3; 1:6; 4:12; 5:1).

So although this "occasional" letter does not give equal emphasis to the core truths which were part of the earliest preaching, it nevertheless does reflect that preaching clearly. Paul's first letter to the Thessalonians, by addressing the Thessalonians' specific problems, gives us a clear picture not only of early issues, but of the life, love, and faith of an early Christian church and its preacher.

Review Questions

1. What two misperceptions lie behind the question?
2. What is the difference between an "occasional" letter and a modern-day pastoral letter?
3. About what specific problem were the Thessalonians worried?
4. What does "apocalyptic" mean?
5. Name some apocalyptic images.
6. What does Paul teach in response to the Thessalonians' main question?
7. Why does 1 Thessalonians not give an ordered account of the kerygma? Does it contradict the kerygma? Explain.

Discussion Questions

1. What does this sentence mean: "Apocalyptic images are used to probe mysteries which are beyond our experience rather than to

give realistic descriptions of future events"? Can you name such images in modern movies or songs? What are they?

2. What do you think this sentence from the creed means: "He (Christ) will come again to judge the living and the dead"?

3. Do you expect the world to last for eons more time, or do you expect it to end soon? Why?

Justification Not by Obedience to Law But by Faith in Christ

GALATIANS

Question: "Paul sounds so angry. Why would he curse and insult people?" (Gal 1:6–9; Gal 1:1; 1:9; 1:11–12; 1:16–17; 2:7–9; 2:14; 2:16; 4:14; 5:12 also discussed)

Paul does sound angry in his letter to the Galatians. Scripture scholars are not sure who these Galatians were, but we can tell from the letter why Paul was angry both with them and with certain "agitators."

Paul had been with the Galatians and had taught them the gospel, evidently arriving with some physical ailment. "You know it was because of a bodily ailment that I preached the gospel to you at first; and though my physical condition was a trial to you, you did not scorn or despise me, but received me as an angel of God, as Christ Jesus" (Gal 4:14).

After Paul left, some "agitators" arrived and challenged the Galatians both on Paul's authority to teach and on the content of Paul's teaching.

So part of Paul's anger is due to the fact that his authority has been questioned. This is why Paul interrupts the usual opening formula of his letter to start defending himself. "Paul, an apostle, not from men or through man, but through Jesus Christ and God the Father who raised him from the dead . . ." (Gal 1:1).

This defensive tone continues as Paul insists on his authority to

98

teach. "For I would have you know, brethren, that the gospel which was preached by me is not man's gospel. For I did not receive it from man, nor was I taught it, but it came through a revelation of Jesus Christ" (Gal 1:11–12).

Since Paul had received his mission directly from God he was supremely confident. "I did not confer with flesh and blood nor did I go up to Jerusalem to those who were apostles before me but I went away into Arabia" (Gal 1:16–17).

It was fourteen years after Paul's conversion (35 A.D.) that Paul went to the council in Jerusalem (49 A.D.) and was affirmed in the very teaching about which the Galatians have been challenged, the question of whether or not Gentiles must follow the Jewish law and be circumcised. The leaders in the Jerusalem church did not ask Paul to alter his teaching. "On the contrary, when they saw that I had been entrusted with the gospel to the uncircumcised, just as Peter had been entrusted with the gospel to the circumcised . . . and when they perceived the grace that was given to me, James and Cephas and John, who were reputed to be pillars, gave to me and Barnabas the right hand of fellowship, that we should go to the Gentiles and they to the circumcised . . ." (Gal 2:7–9).

So Paul had been teaching the Galatians that they need not follow the Jewish law, that they need not be circumcised. Now Paul is very angry because these agitators have been teaching the Galatians that they must be circumcised.

This disagreement cuts to the core for Paul because central to his understanding of the gospel is that "a man is not justified by works of the law (such as circumcision) but through faith in Jesus Christ" (Gal 2:16).

Not only is Paul upset because the agitators are contradicting a core belief and the Galatians are being persuaded away from the truth, but he is exasperated because he has been fighting many a battle on this question for years.

After the council of Jerusalem when all had agreed that Gentiles would not have to follow the Jewish law in order to be Christians, Paul had gotten into an argument about the same question in Antioch. Peter (Cephas) had agreed that Gentiles would not have to follow the Jewish law. But when some who did observe the law, "some circumcised," arrived, Peter all of a sudden stopped eating with the Gentiles and started obeying the Jewish dietary laws. For Paul, such behavior was tantamount to being unfaithful to the truth of the gospel. So Paul confronted Peter. "But when I saw that they were not straightforward about the truth of the gospel, I said to Cephas (Peter) before them all, 'If you, though a Jew, live like a Gentile and not like a Jew, how can you compel the Gentiles to live like Jews?' " (Gal 2:14).

Paul is certainly angry and disappointed with the Galatians. He sees their actions as deserting him "who called you in the grace of Christ and turning to a different gospel . . ." (Gal 1:16). As Paul says, their actions have him completely "perplexed" (Gal 4:20).

However, Paul's greatest anger is toward the agitators who have led the Galatians astray. It is they whom Paul curses. "If any one is preaching to you a gospel contrary to that which you received, let him be accursed" (Gal 1:9).

Paul is so angry with these agitators that he says, "I wish that those who unsettled you would mutilate (castrate) themselves" (Gal 5:12).

Paul's letter to the Galatians is an angry letter. It broke Paul's heart to see his converts turn away from the gospel which he had taught them.

Review Questions

1. On what two subjects did the "agitators" challenge the Galatians?
2. How did Paul defend his authority to teach?
3. What specific teaching of Paul's disturbed the agitators?
4. What core teaching is brought into question when people insist on the necessity of circumcision?
5. What had been decided at the council of Jerusalem?
6. Why did Paul find fault with Peter?
7. Whom does Paul curse? Why?

Discussion Questions

1. Have you ever questioned someone else's authority? What was that person's response? Have you ever had your authority questioned? How did you feel?
2. Do you think Paul was justified in being so angry? Why or why not?
3. Does it disturb you that so much anger would be present in a person who we claim is inspired? Why or why not?

ARTICLE 5

Galatians and Acts:
Are They Contradictory?

GALATIANS

Question: "Doesn't Galatians contradict Acts? How can they both be scripture if they contradict each other?" (Gal 1:18–22; 2:9–10; Acts 9:26–28; 15:19–20)

Galatians and Acts do not entirely agree. Whether or not this disagreement should cause us to doubt the value of one or the other depends entirely on the kind of writing we are reading. If both Galatians and Acts had been written in order to teach history, their lack of agreement would certainly cause us problems. However, neither was written as a history. Let us look at the disagreements and at the literary form of each in order to understand why each is included in the New Testament canon despite the lack of agreement.

In his letter to the Galatians Paul gives us a picture of his relationship to the leaders in the Jerusalem church as well as an account of the council of Jerusalem. In both of these areas, Paul's account in Galatians and Luke's account in Acts differ.

In Galatians Paul says that his first trip to Jerusalem was some three years after his conversion, three years which had been spent in Arabia. "Then after three years I went up to Jerusalem to visit Cephas, and remained with him fifteen days. But I saw none of the other apostles except James the Lord's brother. (In what I am writing to you, before God, I do not lie!) . . . And I was still not known by sight to the churches of Christ in Judea" (Gal 1:18–22).

102

GALATIANS AND ACTS: POINTS OF DIFFERENCE

- When Paul first went to Jerusalem did Paul meet all the disciples or only Peter and James?
- While in Jerusalem on this first visit did Paul preach and become well known or not?
- Was the Jerusalem council a public meeting or a private one?
- Were dietary laws discussed at the Jerusalem council or only the law regarding circumcision?

In Acts Luke describes Paul's first visit to Jerusalem quite differently. There is no mention of three years in Arabia. Acts says, "And when he had come to Jerusalem he attempted to join the disciples; and they were all afraid of him, for they did not believe that he was a disciple. But Barnabas took him, and brought him to the apostles, and declared to them how on the road he had seen the Lord, who spoke to him, and how at Damascus he had preached boldly in the name of Jesus. So he went in and out among them at Jerusalem, preaching boldly in the name of the Lord" (Acts 9:26–28).

Did Paul meet all of the apostles in Jerusalem or only Peter and James? Did Paul preach or was he not known by sight? The accounts simply differ.

In addition to this inconsistency, Paul's account of the council of Jerusalem differs from the one which we have already read in Acts.

Paul tells us that, prompted by a revelation, he took Titus with him to Jerusalem where he had a private meeting (Gal 2:2) and laid before those of repute the gospel which he preached to the Gentiles. James, Cephas (Peter) and John "gave me (Paul) and Barnabas the right hand of fellowship, that we should go to the Gentiles and they to the circumcised; only they would have us remember the poor, which very thing I was eager to do" (Gal 2:9–10).

Acts pictures the council at Jerusalem as a public meeting (Acts 15:6) at which a number of decisions were reached. "Therefore my (James') judgment is that we should not trouble those of the Gentiles who turn to God, but should write to them to abstain from the pollutions of idols and from unchastity and from what is strangled and from blood" (Acts 15:19–20).

What was decided at the council of Jerusalem? Would Paul have agreed to "abstain from what is strangled"? Wouldn't observing this dietary law have compromised his belief that man is saved by faith and not by observance to the law?

In order to understand how these differences could exist, without causing the believing community to reject one work or the other as scripture, we must review what has already been said about the literary form of Acts and letters.

Acts cannot accurately be described as historical writing. Luke is writing around 85 A.D., a generation after the events he is describing. Luke has edited and arranged various sources. As an editor looking at events in hindsight, he sometimes combined or "telescoped" events into a single account which had actually occurred over time. He also composed speeches for his characters which enabled Luke to teach, through the characters, what he wanted his audience to learn. None of these techniques were unique to Luke but were common among the authors of the time.

Just as Acts cannot accurately be described as historical writing, neither can a personal letter written in anger. In Galatians we do not find a cool Paul giving a carefully developed, logical presentation of his teaching. We find an angry Paul defending his authority and his teaching in the face of severe criticism.

So, in his letter to the Galatians, Paul emphasizes the fact that his authority is from God, not from the other apostles, because his authority has been questioned. Luke, on the other hand, wants to emphasize that the Spirit united and guided the church. So while he tells the story of Paul's direct revelation from God three times, he also emphasizes the fact that Paul was not a free agent, unattached to the Jerusalem church. Rather, Paul was accepted and affirmed by the Jerusalem leaders. The point which each is making is accurate, and while these points are in tension they are not incompatible with each other. This difference in emphasis, as well as the literary forms which Paul and Luke have employed, account for the inconsistencies in the picture of the relationship between Paul and the leaders of the Jerusalem church.

The difference in the accounts of the Jerusalem council are probably due to Luke's habit of telescoping several events into a single event. Scripture scholars believe that the question at the Jerusalem council was the question of circumcision, as Paul states. Also, as Paul states, later arguments developed about the eating laws. At a later date a compromise was reached on this question. Luke combines these two arguments about the Gentiles' relation to the Jewish law (i.e. circumcision and dietary questions) in his account of the Jerusalem council, and places the agreed-upon compromise regarding the eating laws in the mouth of James. Historically, the second controversy was probably settled after the council of Jerusalem, while the controversy over circumcision was settled at the Jerusalem council.

Neither Acts nor Paul's letters are written as modern-day history is written, nor is history the main interest of either author. However, if one asks historical questions it is best to look to Paul first and then see what Luke might have to add to our insights. Paul's letters, first-hand accounts, are more reliable as history than is Acts, written a generation later and employing techniques common at the time which a modern-day historian would not use.

Review Questions

1. Name some ways in which Acts and Galatians differ in their descriptions of Paul's first visit to Jerusalem and his relationship with the other apostles.
2. In what ways do Acts and Galatians differ in their description of the council of Jerusalem?
3. Name two things about Luke's method of writing in Acts which prevent Acts from accurately being described as historical writing.
4. What about Galatians prevents it from accurately being described as historical writing?
5. What does Paul want to emphasize in Galatians? Why?
6. What does Luke want to emphasize in Acts? Why?
7. What two things account for inconsistencies between Galatians and Acts as each pictures the relationship between Paul and the leaders of the Jerusalem church?

8. How can we explain the differences in the accounts of the Jerusalem council?
9. If one asks historical questions, would Luke or Paul be more likely to be an accurate source? Why?

Discussion Questions

1. What does it mean to say that Luke "telescoped" events in his account? Do you think this is honest? Why or why not?
2. Do you agree that a difference in emphasis results in differing accounts, but not necessarily contradictory accounts? Can you think of examples of this in your own life? Explain.
3. Do these kinds of apparent inconsistencies bother you? Should they? Why or why not?

ARTICLE 6

Gentile Circumcision:
A Falling Away from Grace?

GALATIANS

**Question: "How could Paul say that Christ could be of no use to a
person who has himself circumcised? Paul is circumcised and
Christ is certainly 'of use' to him" (Gal 5:2). (Gal 1:14; 2:15–16;
2:21; 3:4–5; 5:4; 5:6 also discussed)**

When Paul says that "if you have yourselves circumcised, Christ
will be of no use to you" (Gal 5:2), he is not speaking to an audience
of people like himself who were faithful Jews and circumcised before they ever heard of Christ. Rather, he is speaking to people who
are uncircumcised and thinking of becoming circumcised after
they have come to know Christ.

Paul is telling these Gentile Christians that if they become circumcised they will take on themselves an obligation to obey the rest
of the law. They will thus buy into a way to salvation which is not
Christ's way and which is in error. Paul is positive that this way is in
error because it is the way from which he has been converted.

Paul's original understanding as a Jew was that he could earn
salvation by obedience to the law. As Paul says, "I advanced in
Judaism beyond any of my own age among my people, so extremely zealous was I for the traditions of my fathers" (Gal 1:14).

However, after his conversion Paul realized that observance to
the law is not what justifies a person. "We ourselves, who are Jews
by birth and not Gentile sinners, yet who know that a man is not

justified by works of the law but through faith in Jesus Christ, even we have believed in Christ Jesus in order to be justified by faith in Christ, and not by works of the law, because by works of the law shall no one be justified" (Gal 2:15–16).

If Jews who have observed the whole law realize that they too must believe in Christ in order to be saved, why would a Gentile who already knows Christ consider being circumcised? Such an action is a clear expression of denial that salvation comes from faith in Christ. It is as much as to say that Christ accomplished nothing. "I do not nullify the grace of God; for if justification were through the law, then Christ died to no purpose" (Gal 2:21).

As Paul realizes from his own experience of grace that Christ, rather than obedience to the law, saves, so he thinks that the Galatians should realize this from their own experience. "Did you experience so many things in vain—if it really is in vain? Does he who supplies the Spirit to you and works miracles among you do so by works of the law, or by hearing with faith?" (Gal 3:4–5).

After having experienced grace and power through faith in Christ, why would one then turn around and act as though it is law and not faith that saves? Such an action not only is senseless but it has the effect of turning one away from Christ. "You are severed from Christ, you who would be justified by the law; you have fallen away from grace" (Gal 5:4).

It is because a choice to be circumcised after knowing Christ is tantamount to turning away from faith in Christ that Christ will be of no use to the Gentile Christians who choose to be circumcised. For a Jew who was already circumcised and later becomes a Christian, circumcision is not a block but simply irrelevant. "For in Christ Jesus neither circumcision nor uncircumcision is of any avail, but faith working through love" (Gal 5:6).

Paul's knowledge of Jesus Christ and freedom from the law is such a precious gift to him that he has devoted his entire life to spreading this good news to others. He sees his particular vocation as spreading this good news to the Gentiles who never were slaves to the law. Now, after converting these Gentiles, he finds that others are trying to undo his good work and enslave these newly baptized Christians with the very law which Paul knows to be ineffective. Paul is begging the Galatians not to turn away from the freedom which Christ has won for them, and not to turn away from faith in Christ by accepting circumcision.

Review Questions

1. Why does Paul not want the Galatians to submit to circumcision?
2. As a convert to Christianity, what did Paul come to believe about obedience to the law?
3. Why does Paul believe that a Christian Gentile who submits to circumcision has turned away from grace?

Discussion Questions

1. What do you think results in salvation—obeying all the rules or having faith in Christ?
2. What is the difference between Paul's having been circumcised and a Christian Gentile deciding to be circumcised? Explain.
3. Both Paul and the Galatians had had personal experiences that enabled them to know God as a powerful, saving God. Have you had any such experience? What was it?

ARTICLE 7

Paul and the Old Testament

GALATIANS

Question: "Does Paul believe in the Old Testament or not? He seems not to when he says you don't have to obey the law, but then he keeps holding up the Old Testament as an authority." (Gal 3:6–9; 3:10; 3:13; 3:19; 3:24; 4:21–31)

Paul believes that the Old Testament tells the story of God's action among God's people. The Old Testament helps one understand how God's people got to "where they are now." However, Paul understands "where they are now" to be quite a different place than where they were previously, due to the saving acts of Jesus Christ.

So Paul is not dismissing the truth contained in the first five books of the Old Testament, the torah, or the value of these books when he insists that God's people are no longer subject to the law. In fact, Paul uses the torah to explain this truth.

Modern readers often have trouble understanding the way in which Paul uses the Old Testament. We often bring to our reading of Paul a presumption that Paul is using scripture to prove that his conclusions are correct. In fact, Paul did not arrive at his conclusions from reading scripture but from personal experience. He uses scripture to explain his insights, not to prove them. You will have a much easier time understanding Paul's arguments from scripture if you understand them as explanations through analogy rather than as "proof texts."

Paul's first explanation by analogy from the Old Testament involves the story of Abraham. The Jewish patriarch, Abraham, lived around 1850 B.C., some 600 years (Paul says 450 years) before Moses and the law (1250 B.C.). That means that Abraham did not obey the law because he preceded the law. Yet Abraham was justified, not by obedience to the law, but by faith. "Thus Abraham believed God, and it was reckoned to him as righteousness. So you see that it is men of faith who are the sons of Abraham. And the scripture, foreseeing that God would justify the Gentiles by faith, preached the gospel beforehand to Abraham, saying, 'In you shall all nations be blessed.' So then, those who are men of faith are blessed with Abraham who had faith" (Gal 3:6–9).

Paul's audience, then, like Abraham, is justified by faith and is heir to the promise made to Abraham.

Paul's second argument from scripture attempts to support Paul's insight that Christ has delivered us from the law. To make this point Paul begins by quoting the law to show that those who depend on the law are under a curse unless they obey the whole law. "Cursed be every one who does not abide by all things written in the book of the law, and do them" (Gal 3:10).

Next Paul points out that the law put a curse on Jesus. The law says, "Cursed be every one who hangs on a tree" (Gal 3:13). Since Jesus was crucified (hung on a tree) and thus cursed by the law, he took the curse of the law upon himself, thereby redeeming us from the law (Gal 3:13).

Having used scripture to explain that God's people are now free from the law, Paul addresses the question, "Why then the law?" (Gal 3:19). Again Paul uses an analogy, this time from everyday life. Paul says that the law acted as a "custodian" (Gal 3:24) until Christ, Abraham's offspring, should come to inherit the promise of faith made to Abraham and free from the law those who are sons of God through faith in Christ.

Paul repeats his teaching that the Galatians are free from the law by drawing an analogy between them and Abraham's two sons (Gal 4:21–31). One son was born of the promise. This son compares to Paul's audience if they remain uncircumcised. The other son was born of the flesh. This son compares to those who want to live by the flesh and be circumcised. Paul points out that then, as now, those who were of the flesh (the agitators and those who accept

---

**PAUL'S ARGUMENT THAT OBEDIENCE
TO THE LAW DOES NOT SAVE**

	1850 B.C.	Abraham was justified by faith.
Paul's Jewish ancestors and finally Paul relied on obedience to the law to earn salvation.	1250 B.C.	Moses taught the law.
	7–6 B.C.	Jesus was born.
	35 A.D.	Jesus died and rose from the dead. Paul is converted: Paul realizes that salvation is through faith in Christ. Abraham has always been an example of this truth because he was saved even though he never even knew the law.

---

circumcision) persecuted those who were of the Spirit (the Galatians who refuse circumcision). By analogy Paul says that the son of the slave, born of the flesh (the agitators and those who want to live by the law and be circumcised), should be thrown out. They will not inherit with the son of the free woman (those who have faith in Christ and remain uncircumcised).

In many of his letters we will see Paul use the Old Testament to explain what he is trying to teach. While Paul does not consider the old law, the torah, as binding, he still sees it as a source of wisdom about the relationship between God and God's people.

ANALOGY OF ABRAHAM'S TWO SONS

Isaac: The son born of the promise

↓

Paul's audience, if they remain uncircumcised, are like Isaac. Salvation is a gift.

Ishmael: The son born of the flesh

↓

Paul's audience, if they accept circumcision, are like Ishmael. The agitators are like Ishmael. They rely on the flesh (circumcision) rather than the promise.

Review Questions

1. What does Paul think one can learn from the Old Testament?
2. How did Paul arrive at his conclusions?
3. In what way does Abraham serve as an example of a person saved by faith, not law?
4. In what way did the law put a curse on Jesus?
5. What analogy does Paul use to explain the function of the law?
6. What is Paul teaching through the analogy to Abraham's two sons?

Discussion Questions

1. What does this sentence mean: "Paul uses scripture to explain his insights, not to prove them"?
2. Can you follow Paul's explanations when he draws analogies from the Old Testament? Why or why not? What might help you?
3. Do you learn more from experience or from tradition? Explain. Has any personal experience of yours caused you to question something you have been taught? Explain.

ARTICLE 8

Philippians: One Letter or Three?

PHILIPPIANS

Question: "Twice I thought Paul was concluding this letter and both times he seems to take off on a new track. Why is this?" (Phil 3:1; 4:8; Phil 1:3–8; 2:25; 2:29; 3:2; 3:4; 3:18; 4:10–20 also discussed)

Paul does seem twice to conclude his letter and then start up a different subject. At 3:1 Paul writes, "Finally, my brethren, rejoice in the Lord . . ." (Phil 3:1). Then with a complete change of tone Paul writes, "Look out for the dogs, look out for the evil-workers, look out for those who mutilate the flesh . . ." (Phil 3:2).

Again Paul seems to conclude his letter when he says, "Finally, brethren, whatever is true, whatever is honorable, whatever is just, whatever is pure, whatever is lovely, whatever is gracious, if there is any excellence, if there is anything worthy of praise, think about these things. What you have learned and received and heard and seen in me, do; and the God of peace will be with you" (Phil 4:8–9). But instead of ending, Paul launches off on an extended thank-you to the Philippians for their help (Phil 4:10–20).

Why does Paul do this? Scripture scholars think the explanation lies in the possibility that in Philippians we have not one letter from Paul to the Philippians but three letters, written on separate occasions for separate reasons, and later combined by an editor.

The short thank-you note in Philippians 4:10–20 may well have been the first letter sent. Epaphroditus had been sent to Paul by the Philippians in order to express the Philippians' support and con-

114

THREE LETTERS COMBINED IN PHILIPPIANS

Written first: Phil 4:10–20: A short thank-you letter.

Written second: Phil 1:1–3:1a; 4:4–7; 4:21–23: This is the joyful letter written while Paul is in prison and delivered by Epaphroditus.

Written third: Phil 3:1b–4:3; 4:8–9: This is an angrier, more polemical letter. Paul is no longer in prison.

---

cern and to give Paul money. Paul was imprisoned at the time, scholars conjecture, in Ephesus between 54–57 A.D. In response, Paul wrote and thanked the Philippians.

The second letter is the longest letter. Scholars suggest that it consists of Phil 1:1–3:1a; 4:4–7 and 4:21–23. From internal evidence it seems that Epaphroditus got sick and almost died while with Paul. He has recovered and perhaps is carrying this second letter as he returns to the Philippians. "I have thought it necessary to send to you Epaphroditus my brother and fellow worker and fellow soldier, and your messenger and minister to my need . . ." (Phil 2:25). "So receive him in the Lord with all joy" (Phil 2:29).

The tone of this second letter is joyful even though the Philippians are suffering some opposition from outsiders and some dissension within their own ranks.

In contrast, the tone of the third letter is more polemical, more angry. In this letter Paul is warning the Philippians not to be influenced by those who think salvation rests in keeping the law rather than in having faith in Christ. Instead of seeming joyful, Paul is anxious and suffering. "For many, of whom I have often told you and now tell you even with tears, live as enemies of the cross of Christ" (Phil 3:18).

This third letter makes no reference to Paul's being in prison. Scholars conjecture that Paul's imprisonment had ended. He had heard disturbing news about these Judaizers, as well as disturbing news about the continued lack of unity within the Christian community itself, and so wrote this third letter, probably around 57–58 A.D.

It seems that an editor combined the three letters into one by inserting the thank-you and the polemical letter into the joyful letter at places where he thought they fit. In doing so he removed the introductions and thanksgivings from the two inserted letters but not the conclusions. The joyful conclusion to the long letter begins at 3:1 with, "Finally, my brethren, rejoice in the Lord . . ." (Phil 3:1), and continues after much of the polemical letter with, "Rejoice in the Lord always; again I say rejoice" (Phil 3:4).

Why were the letters combined? Again, scholars conjecture that the Philippians treasured Paul's letters and so sent the contents of them on to other communities. By combining the letters, and omitting the introductions and thanksgivings, which would have been redundant, the Philippians could hand on all of Paul's teaching in a shorter form.

Although the "seams" of this compiled letter are obvious, so are aspects of its final unity. Not least among these unifying characteristics is Paul's love for the Philippians which shines through all three letters. Paul had been to Philippi, a Roman city in Macedonia, on his second missionary journey (see Acts 16:11–40). His love for the men and women in this church which he had founded is clearly expressed. "I thank my God in all my remembrance of you always in every prayer of mine. . . . It is right for me to feel this way about you all, because I hold you in my heart. . . . For God is my witness, how I yearn for you all with the affection of Christ Jesus . . ." (Phil 1:3–8).

Paul's love for the Philippians and his pastoral tone when writing to them, which appear in all three of the original letters, are two of the distinguishing characteristics of our compiled letter of Paul to the Philippians.

Review Questions

1. How many letters do scholars think have been collected in our present form of Philippians?

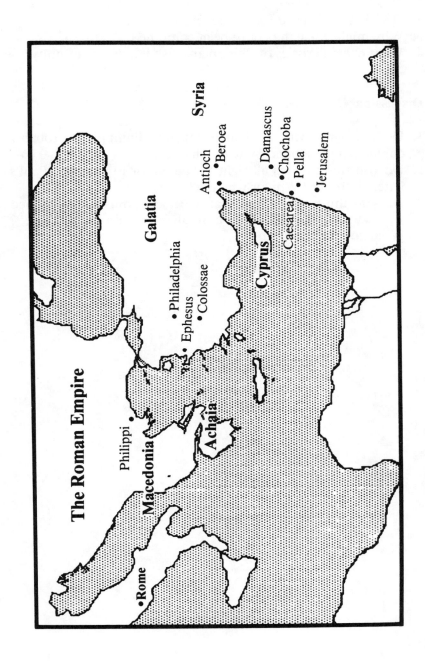

2. On what evidence does this conclusion rest?
3. Why might the letters have been combined?
4. What characteristics of Philippians give it a degree of unity?

Discussion Questions

1. Do you agree with the conclusion that Philippians probably contains three letters? Why or why not?
2. Do you think it was all right for an editor to combine Paul's letters into one? Why or why not?
3. Do you think it unusual that a person unjustly imprisoned would write, "Rejoice in the Lord always; again I say, rejoice"? What could Paul mean?

ARTICLE 9

Paul and Suffering

PHILIPPIANS

Question: "Why does Paul say that he is glad to suffer? (Phil 2:17). Is he a masochist?" (Phil 1:13; 1:16; 1:20; 2:8; 3:8–11)

Paul is not a masochist. He is a person who has grown to understand the place that suffering has in the Christian scheme of things.

Remember, Paul was raised in a community that believed suffering was punishment for sin. Also remember that at the time of his conversion, Paul was going about causing a great deal of suffering for those who followed Christ. At the time of his conversion, Paul heard the risen Christ say, "Why are you persecuting me?"

At the time Paul is writing the Philippians he is on the receiving end of the suffering meted out to those who follow Christ. ". . . it has become known throughout the whole praetorian guard and to all the rest that my imprisonment is for Christ" (Phil 1:13). "I am put here for the defense of the gospel . . ." (Phil 1:16).

Paul is in jail and he does not know if this imprisonment will end in life or death. ". . . it is my eager expectation and hope that I shall not be at all ashamed, but that with full courage now as always Christ will be honored in my body, whether by life or by death" (Phil 1:20).

Paul, of all people, could take courage and hope from his suffering because he saw clearly the connection between his suffering and Christ's suffering.

Paul explicitly states this union in suffering with Christ in the

119

inserted letter. "For his sake I have suffered the loss of all things, and count them as refuse, in order that I may gain Christ and be found in him . . . that I may know him and the power of his resurrection, and may share his sufferings, becoming like him in his death, that if possible I may attain the resurrection from the dead" (Phil 3:8–11).

For Paul, suffering is a sharing in the suffering of Christ and will lead to eternal life. It is for this reason that Paul can honestly say, "Even if I am to be poured as a libation upon the sacrificial offering of your faith, I am glad and rejoice with all of you" (Phil 2:17).

However, as Paul writes the Philippians, he is not the only one suffering for the sake of the gospel. The Philippians too are suffering persecution at the hands of their opponents. Paul urges them to ". . . stand firm in one spirit, with one mind striving side by side for the faith of the gospel, and not frightened in anything by your opponents. . . . For it has been granted to you that for the sake of Christ you should not only believe in him but also suffer for his sake, engaged in the same conflict which you saw and now hear to be mine" (Phil 1:27–29).

Paul considers suffering for the sake of the gospel a privilege, a privilege for him and for the Philippians. When one suffers one enters into an ever closer union with Christ who "became obedient unto death, even death on a cross" (Phil 2:8).

Scripture scholars think that Paul added the phrase "on a cross" to a pre-existent hymn. The hymn (Phil 2:6–11) celebrates the universal lordship of Christ. By adding "on a cross" Paul emphasizes the suffering which preceded this universal lordship.

Mention of the cross was omitted from many early hymns and creeds because it was associated with shame. Death on a cross was the most ignominious death a person could have. Only slaves or people who had committed crimes which deprived them of all rights died on a cross.

To say that Jesus died on a cross is to say that Jesus suffered the most degrading of deaths. Yet this death resulted in resurrection and redemption.

Jesus' suffering on the cross, Paul's suffering in the service of Christ and the gospel, and the Philippians' suffering for their faith in Christ were all one in Paul's mind. Suffering was a privilege and a joy because it joined one to Christ not only in his death but in his resurrection.

Review Questions

1. What did Paul's community think was the reason for suffering?
2. Why was Paul able to take courage and hope from his suffering?
3. What is Paul's hope?
4. What hope does Paul offer the Philippians?
5. How does Paul emphasize the role of suffering which preceded Christ's present universal lordship?
6. Why was mention of the cross omitted from many early hymns and creeds?

Discussion Questions

1. Have you ever suffered? Did you feel hopeless or hopeful? Did you learn anything about yourself? Did you think of Christ's suffering? If so, did this affect your ability to handle the suffering?
2. What does it mean to say that all suffering when united to Christ's suffering is redemptive?
3. Have you ever been unjustly punished? What did you feel? Did you use these feelings for good or ill? How might you use such feelings for good or for ill?

ARTICLE 10

Salvation: A Gift That
Demands a Response

PHILIPPIANS

Question: "Why does Paul tell the Philippians to 'work out your own salvation' (Phil 2:12)? I thought Paul taught that salvation was a gift." (Phil 1:6; 1:27; 2:3–4; 2:6–8; 3:8–11; 3:12–14 also discussed)

Paul does teach that salvation is a gift. We saw this clearly in Paul's letter to the Galatians. We will see it again in Paul's letter to the Romans. We even see it in this letter to the Philippians, in the inserted letter in which Paul is arguing against the Judaizers. Paul, after describing his own obedience to the law, claims that whatever gain he had from this obedience he now counts as a loss. "Indeed, I count everything as loss because of the surpassing worth of knowing Christ Jesus my Lord. For his sake I have suffered the loss of all things and count them as refuse, in order that I may gain Christ and be found in him, not having a righteousness of my own, based on law, but that which is through faith in Christ, the righteousness from God that depends on faith, that I may know him and the power of his resurrection, and I may share his sufferings, becoming like him in his death, that if possible I may attain the resurrection from the dead" (Phil 3:8–11).

Why, then, does Paul tell the Philippians to "work out your own salvation with fear and trembling" (Phil 2:12)? Is Paul contradicting himself here and suggesting that salvation is earned? To answer this question we need to look at the passage in the context in which

Paul says it. By looking at the passage in context we will be able to see what Paul is teaching the Philippians.

In this letter Paul is lovingly admonishing the Philippians to "let your manner of life be worthy of the gospel of Christ" (Phil 1:27). As an example of a life that is worthy of the gospel, Paul uses Christ Jesus. As he quotes the hymn celebrating Jesus' lordship Paul emphasizes the selflessness which characterized Christ's actions. Paul says that Christ, "though he was in the form of God, did not count equality with God a thing to be grasped, but emptied himself, taking the form of a servant, being born in the likeness of men. And being found in human form he humbled himself and became obedient unto death, even death on a cross . . ." (Phil 2:6–8).

Just as Christ lived for others, so should the Philippians. "Do nothing from selfishness or conceit, but in humility count others better than yourselves. Let each of you look not only to his own interests, but also to the interests of others" (Phil 2:3–4).

So Paul is teaching that the Philippians should "work out their salvation in fear and trembling" not because they are earning their salvation but because the gift of salvation demands a response on their part, a "life worthy of the gospel."

That the kind of life one lives matters even though salvation is a gift is later referred to, using the metaphor of a race. Again, this metaphor appears in the inserted letter in which Paul is arguing against the Judaizers who evidently believed that perfection was attainable by obedience to the law. Paul teaches the Philippians that perfection has not yet been reached. Using himself as an example he says, "Not that I have already obtained this (i.e. resurrection from the dead) or am already perfect; but I press on to make it my own, because Christ Jesus has made me his own. . . . I press on toward the goal for the prize of the upward call of God in Christ Jesus" (Phil 3:12–14).

The destiny of a Christian is to join Christ in his suffering, death and resurrection. Paul teaches that perfection comes only when the "race" is over, when one rises with Christ.

In the meantime, the Philippians must have faith in Christ's gift of salvation and work out that salvation in fear and trembling by living a life worthy of the gospel. A life worthy of the gospel is not a life of obedience to the law but a life spent in love of neighbor. It is because the Philippians persevere in love that Paul is "sure that he who began this good work in you will bring it to completion at the day of Jesus Christ" (Phil 1:6).

Review Questions

1. According to Paul, how is one saved?
2. Whom does Paul hold up as having lived a life worthy of the gospel?
3. What quality of this person's life does Paul particularly emphasize?
4. What response does the gift of salvation demand?
5. What is Paul teaching through his metaphor of a race?

Discussion Questions

1. What does this sentence mean: "Let your manner of life be worthy of the gospel of Christ"?
2. Who is the least selfish person you know? Why do you consider this person so selfless?
3. Reflect on these two statements: "Salvation is a gift." "I press on to make it (salvation) my own." Do you consider them contradictory or compatible? Explain.

ARTICLE 11

The Wisdom of Philo and
the Wisdom of Paul

1 CORINTHIANS

Question: "Isn't Paul insulting his audience when he says that God, in choosing them, didn't choose the wise?" (1 Cor 1:26–29; 1 Cor 1:11; 1:12; 1:26; 2:1–5; Acts 18:11; 19:1 also discussed)

When Paul tells his Corinthian audience that God, in choosing them, did not choose "the wise," Paul is using the word "wise" ironically. Paul is saying that God did not choose those who think they are wise because they have been particularly chosen to receive a wisdom reserved only for a few. Paul's use of the word "wisdom" is a reference to a kind of "wisdom" associated with Philo, a Jewish Hellenist philosopher, who may have been introduced to the Corinthians by Apollos, a contemporary of Paul's.

In order to understand this explanation of Paul's words to the Corinthians we should step back and ask ourselves, "Who are the Corinthians? What has occasioned Paul's letter to them? What is the intellectual climate?" When we put Paul's words in the context of the answers to these questions we will better understand the way in which Paul uses the word "wisdom."

Paul is writing his letter to the Corinthians from Ephesus (1 Cor 16:8) in the spring, probably in 54 A.D. The Corinthians live in what might have been called a boom town. Located on an isthmus, Corinth had access to the Aegean and Adriatic Seas and controlled the land route to the Greek mainland.

125

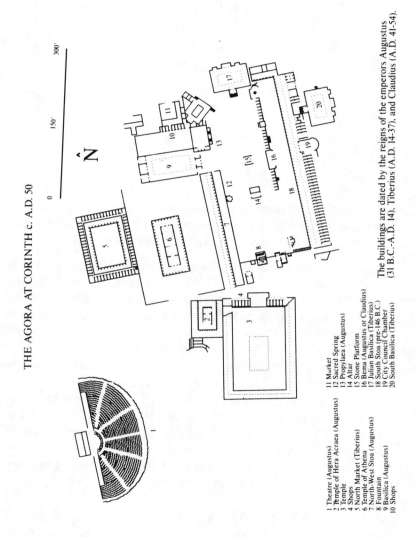

THE AGORA AT CORINTH c. A.D. 50

1 Theatre (Augustus)
2 Temple of Hera Acraea (Augustus)
3 Temple
4 Shops
5 North Market (Tiberius)
6 Temple of Athena
7 North-West Stoa (Augustus)
8 Fountain
9 Basilica (Augustus)
10 Shops

11 Market
12 Sacred Spring
13 Propylaea (Augustus)
14 Altar
15 Stone Platform
16 Bema (Augustus or Claudius)
17 Julian Basilica (Tiberius)
18 South Stoa (pre-146 B.C.)
19 City Council Chamber
20 South Basilica (Tiberius)

The buildings are dated by the reigns of the emperors Augustus (31 B.C.-A.D. 14), Tiberius (A.D. 14-37), and Claudius (A.D. 41-54).

Corinth had been destroyed in 146 B.C. and restored by Julius Caesar in 44 B.C., so the population did not have deep roots in Corinth. There was no long-standing upper class, as most of the first settlers were freedmen. Paul refers to this fact when he says, "For consider your call, brethren; not many of you were wise according to worldly standards, not many were powerful, not many were of noble birth" (1 Cor 1:26).

Corinth was a city where wealth was a possibility and competition was intense. At the time Paul was writing, Corinth was probably the most important Greek city.

People of many cultural backgrounds were attracted to the commercial possibilities in Corinth. A thriving Jewish community existed, especially after Claudius expelled Jews from Rome. Temples dedicated to Greek, Egyptian, and Oriental gods give evidence of a large and varied pagan population.

Acts tells us that Paul stayed in Corinth for eighteen months (Acts 18:11) during his second missionary journey. After Paul left, Apollos also preached in Corinth (Acts 19:1). Apollos was a native of Alexandria and was known for his eloquence. It seems that some of the Corinthians found Apollos more to their liking than Paul (1 Cor 1:12).

Part of Apollos' charm may have resulted from his introducing the Corinthians to the speculations of another Alexandrian Jew, Philo.

Philo, born around 20 B.C. to a Hellenized Jewish family, attempted to turn the Pentateuch into Greek categories of thought. The Jewish concept of heavenly wisdom became associated with the Greek idea of logos. The result of Philo's philosophical efforts included the subordination of the visible to the invisible, of matter to reason, and of the body to the soul.

Perhaps Apollos, influenced by Philo, preached in a way that enabled some in his Greek pagan audience to equate Apollos' preaching of Christianity with Greek categories of thought which they already had and resulted in their misunderstanding the content of Apollos' preaching.

At any rate, Paul is upset to hear from Chloe's people (1 Cor 1:11) that divisions exist among those who claim to be his followers and those who claim to "belong to Apollos." In addressing those who make this claim, Paul couches his argument in words that seem to be addressing the misconceptions which resulted from the thinking of Philo.

Christians who had been affected by Philo's thought considered themselves superior to others because they had been granted "wisdom." This "wisdom" made them more spiritual than those who were concerned with the body.

So when Paul says that "God didn't choose the wise," he is arguing against those who think themselves superior in their own wisdom. The same ironic meaning of the word "wisdom" is present when Paul says, "When I came to you, brethren, I did not come proclaiming to you the testimony of God in lofty words or wisdom. For I decided to know nothing among you except Jesus Christ and him crucified. And I was with you in weakness and in much fear and trembling; and my speech and my message were not in plausible words of wisdom, but in demonstrations of the Spirit and of power, that your faith might not rest in the wisdom of men but in the power of God" (1 Cor 2:1–5).

So when Paul writes to the Corinthians he writes to people whom he knows well. He writes, based on information he has received from Chloe's people, to correct problems which the Corinthians themselves have not recognized as problems (1 Cor 1:10–6:20) and also to answer questions which the Corinthians have sent him by letter (1 Cor 7:1–11:1).

Only when we put Paul's words in the context of a conversation between Paul and his specific audience, living in a particular intellectual climate, will we begin to understand what misunderstandings Paul hopes to correct when he says such things as, "God did not choose the wise."

Review Questions

1. What does Paul mean by the word "wise"?
2. Who was Philo?
3. Why did Corinth have no long-standing upper class?
4. Who was Apollos?
5. What did Philo attempt to do?

6. What were some of the results of Philo's philosophical efforts?
7. How did Christians who had been influenced by Philo's thought regard themselves?
8. Based on 1 Cor 2:1–5, what does Paul consider more persuasive than "plausible words of wisdom"?

Discussion Questions

1. Do you see any danger in someone's believing that he or she is superior to others because that person has been granted superior wisdom? Explain.
2. Do you see any danger in being suspicious of the goodness of the body? Explain. Is this suspicion present in our culture? Explain.
3. Which do you think would be more persuasive, "plausible words of wisdom" or "demonstrations of the Spirit and power"? Have you experienced the latter? How?

ARTICLE 12

Paul's Metaphors for Church

1 CORINTHIANS

Question: "What does Paul mean when he says the people are God's building, God's temple?" (1 Cor 3:9–17; 1 Cor 3:5–9; 3:9–13; 3:16–17; 12:12–16; 13:4–5; 13:27 also discussed)

Paul uses a number of metaphors in his letter to the Corinthians to help them understand their identity as church. Among these metaphors are a field, a building, a temple, and a body. Each metaphor is used to teach a slightly different truth.

Paul uses the metaphor of a field when he is trying to help the Corinthians understand their unity. "What then is Apollos? What is Paul? Servants through whom you believed, as the Lord assigned to each. I planted, Apollos watered, but God gave the growth. So neither he who plants nor he who waters is anything, but only God who gives the growth. He who plants and he who waters are equal, and each shall receive his wages according to his labor. For we are God's fellow workers: you are God's field" (1 Cor 3:5–9).

That the people should be divided as to whether they were Paul's or Apollos' made no sense at all. They are all one field in whom the Lord is causing growth. The name of the "planter" or the "waterer" is irrelevant to their unity as God's chosen people.

Next Paul compares the growing church to a building under construction. "You are . . . God's building. According to the grace of God given to me, like a skilled master builder, I laid a foundation, and another man is building upon it" (1 Cor 3:9–10).

With this metaphor Paul stresses that the building is not yet

130

PAUL'S METAPHORS FOR CHURCH

A field
A building
A loaf
A temple
A body

---

complete. The one and only possible foundation is laid—Christ. Yet there are a variety of materials with which people could continue to build—some suitable and strong, others unsuitable and weak. One must build carefully on the foundation and realize that each will be held accountable for the quality of his or her work.

That the church is in the process of being built rather than being a finished product is a very important concept. We often use the metaphor "pilgrim church" or "the church on a journey" to teach the same truth today.

Next Paul moves from the metaphor of a building to a very specific building, a temple. "Do you not know that you are God's temple and that God's spirit dwells in you? If any one destroys God's temple, God will destroy him. For God's temple is holy, and that temple you are" (1 Cor 3:16–17).

With this metaphor Paul is teaching the imminence, the "dwelling within" of God. The fact that God is holy and transcendent does not mean that God is distant, that he dwells far away from his people. Rather God dwells in the midst of his people. By dwelling in their midst God makes his people holy too.

This close identity between God and his people is emphasized again as Paul uses the metaphor of a body to explain the diversity of gifts which exists in this one holy church. "For just as the body is one and has many members, and all the members of the body, though many, are one body, so it is with Christ. . . . For the body does not consist of one member but of many. If the foot should say, 'Because I am not a hand, I do not belong to the body' would that make it any less a part of the body? . . . Now you are the body of Christ and individually members of it" (1 Cor 12:12, 14, 15, 27).

OUTLINE OF 1 CORINTHIANS

I. Introduction (1:1–9)

II. Responding to news of factions in the community (1:10–4:21)

III. Emphasizing the importance of the body to the "Spirit people" (5:1–6:20)

IV. Answering specific questions (7:1–14:40)

V. Defending the resurrection of the body (15:1–58)

VI. Conclusion (16:1–24)

With this metaphor Paul is teaching the Corinthians that each of them is a precious and necessary member of the church. Some should not feel superior to others because of their "wisdom" or their "spiritual gifts." No member is expendable. Each member needs to lovingly serve the body, the church, with whatever gifts and talents that person has been given by God. The variety of gifts in the church should not result in competition or feelings of superiority or jealousy. Rather, this variety should result in a loving interdependence. Only when each member of the body uses his or her gifts in the service of the body is the church whole.

Evidently the Corinthians were allowing their competitiveness to cause them to bicker even over spiritual gifts. Paul wants to put an end to such bickering by reminding the Corinthians that the supreme gift is the ability to love one another. "Love is patient and kind, love is not jealous or boastful, it is not arrogant or rude. Love does not insist on its own way; it is not irritable or resentful . . ." (1 Cor 13:4–5).

Love is the gift of the Spirit which binds the one, holy, growing body of the church into unity with Christ and with each other. As the church grows in love, the church will grow in its own understanding of itself as God's field, God's building, God's temple, and as the body of Christ.

Review Questions

1. Name four metaphors which Paul uses to help the Corinthians understand their identity as church.
2. What is Paul teaching through the metaphor of a field?
3. What is Paul teaching through the metaphor of a building under construction?
4. What is Paul teaching through the metaphor of the temple?
5. What is Paul teaching through the metaphor of the body?
6. Which is the most important spiritual gift?

Discussion Questions

1. Do you understand the church as "a finished product" or as "under construction"? What are the advantages of understanding the church as "under construction"?
2. Do you believe that it is important to maintain unity in the church? Do you regard the disunity among Christian denominations as a scandal? Why or why not?
3. Paul says, "Love does not take offense." What is the difference between "offense taken" and "offense given"? Which do you think causes more hurt?

ARTICLE 13

Love as the Basis
for All Moral Judgments

1 CORINTHIANS

Question: "Why would Paul say that the Corinthians should deliver anyone to Satan (1 Cor 5:5)? Doesn't this contradict Paul's teaching on the importance of love and the necessity for unity?" (1 Cor 5:2; 5:6–7; 6:7; 8:1; 8:9; 8:11–13; 11:20; 11:22; 11:24; 11:29; 14:26–28 also discussed)

When Paul advises the Corinthians to expel from their midst a man who is living with his father's wife, Paul is not condemning the man to hell but advising the Corinthians to act in a way that might bring the man to his senses and result in his conversion. Paul's intention is clear when he says, ". . . you are to deliver this man to Satan for the destruction of the flesh, that his spirit may be saved in the day of the Lord Jesus" (1 Cor 5:5).

Paul is very upset with the Corinthians for not recognizing that the man's actions are wrong. Evidently their understanding of the superiority of the spiritual over the material has resulted in their failing to see that what one does with one's body affects one spiritually. The Corinthians, in their spiritual pride and false "wisdom," were evidently proud of their ability to accept such behavior as part of their newfound freedom in Christ. Paul is horrified with this misunderstanding. "And you are arrogant! Ought you rather to mourn?" (1 Cor 5:2).

Paul's teaching in this regard contradicts neither Paul's core

134

teaching on love nor his teaching on the importance of the unity and wholeness of the body.

Since the church is one, a diseased member affects the health of the whole community. "Your boasting is not good. Do you not know that a little leaven leavens the whole lump? Cleanse out the old leaven that you may be a new lump, as you really are un-leavened" (1 Cor 5:6–7).

Paul's hope is that if the community expels this sinful member the community's spiritual health will be maintained and the excommunicated member will, in the end, also be saved. So to expel the person is the most loving thing to do both for his good and for the good of the community.

In fact, no matter what the surface problem with which Paul is grappling, his solution is always the result of trying to figure out what the loving thing to do is in various circumstances.

For instance, what should Christians do if they feel wronged by each other? Paul is horrified at the thought that they might bring charges against each other in pagan courts. Surely someone is wise enough to settle such disputes. And if not, wouldn't it be more loving to suffer injustice than to accuse each other? "To have law-suits at all with one another is defeat for you. Why not suffer wrong? Why not be defrauded?" (1 Cor 6:7).

Should Christians eat food sacrificed to idols? Once again the decision should be made based on love, not on knowledge. "Knowl-edge puffs up, but love builds up" (1 Cor 8:1). The knowledgeable person knows that, since no other gods exist, food apparently of-fered to idols is not actually offered to idols. If such food is for sale in the market or served at a meal, it would not be wrong to eat it. But what if someone who doesn't know this sees you eat it and is scandalized? Love demands that you show concern for the effect of your actions on others. "Therefore, if food is a cause of my brother's falling, I will never eat meat, lest I cause my brother to fall" (1 Cor 8:13).

Love as the measuring rod for behavior should be particularly evident when the church gathers for eucharist. Paul corrects the Corinthians for their lack of consideration for each other's welfare. "When you meet together, it is not the Lord's supper that you eat.

PAUL'S TEACHING ON MORAL DILEMMAS

- For his sake, and yours too, expel the man living in incest. Maybe he will see the light and convert.
- Settle your own differences. Don't go to pagan courts.
- You may eat food sacrificed to idols except when it leads the weak astray.
- You must treat each other with consideration at eucharist. (OF ALL PLACES!)
- Use spiritual gifts only in service to each other.

For in eating, each one goes ahead with his own meal, and one is hungry and another is drunk. . . . Do you despise the church of God and humiliate those who have nothing?" (1 Cor 11:12; 11:22).

Paul reminds the Corinthians how Jesus had instituted this eucharistic celebration on the night before he died, saying, "This is my body" (1 Cor 11:24). Paul teaches the Corinthians that "any one who eats and drinks without discerning the body eats and drinks judgment upon himself" (1 Cor 11:29). To "discern the body" is to recognize Christ in the eucharist. It is also to recognize Christ in the church, the individual members of Christ's body. When one fails to love his or her fellow Christian one fails to recognize the body and fails to love Christ.

Not only in celebrating eucharist but in exercising all spiritual gifts, the law of love should prevail. To use a spiritual gift in a way that fails to help anyone is to waste it. Paul warns the Corinthians not to exercise their spiritual gifts to no purpose. "Let all things be done for edification. If any speak in a tongue, let there be only two or at most three, and each in turn; and let one interpret. But if there is no one to interpret, let each of them keep silence in church and speak to himself and to God" (1 Cor 14:26–28).

The church in Corinth faced many problems. Some problems they recognized, some they did not. No matter what the problem, Paul seeks a solution in the same way. What is the loving thing to do? If the Corinthians live in Christ's love, they will grow in unity and in holiness.

Review Questions

1. What misunderstanding has resulted from the Corinthians' understanding of the superiority of the spiritual over the material?
2. Does Paul's advice to expel the man from their midst contradict Paul's teaching on the importance of unity?
3. Does Paul's advice to expel the man contradict Paul's teaching on love? Explain.
4. What question is at the core of every moral decision? Give some examples found in 1 Corinthians.
5. What two meanings can be seen in the words "discern the body" at eucharist?

Discussion Questions

1. Do you think our society has come to accept some behaviors which are actually sinful?
2. Are there situations today in which we need to give up a freedom in order to act lovingly toward someone else? What are some examples?
3. Do you believe it is ever the loving thing to do to isolate someone from the group? Explain.
4. Do you believe that Christ is present in the members of the church? Do you believe Christ is present in you? Explain.

ARTICLE 14

Paul's Views on Marriage and Women

1 CORINTHIANS

Question: "Doesn't Paul have a warped view of marriage (1 Cor 7:1ff)? Why would he teach that it is 'well for a man not to touch a woman?' " (1 Cor 7:31; 11:3; 11:4–5; 11:14; 14:34–35)

Paul does not teach that "it is well for a man not to touch a woman." Rather, some Corinthians taught this, and Paul is stating their position before he argues against it.

In this section of Paul's letter he is responding to questions and problems raised by the Corinthians. Some of the Corinthians, in their exaltation of the spiritual over the material, have become so suspicious of the body that they are teaching that even married people should refrain from sexual relations. In a culture where women were owned by their husbands, such a decision could be unilateral on the part of the husband.

Paul does not agree that the spiritual life of married people would be improved by permanently abstaining from sexual relations. Paul teaches that married people have a mutual obligation to each other and that neither should deny the other.

However, this teaching of Paul's is in a larger context. Paul thinks that whatever state one is presently in—married or unmarried, slave or free—he or she should remain in that state. "For the form of this world is passing away" (1 Cor 7:31). Why make a change now when the end is so near?

Some scholars think a second example of Paul's stating a position with which he disagrees appears in chapter 14:34–35.

PAUL ARGUES AGAINST THESE IDEAS OF THE CORINTHIANS WHO HAVE BEEN INFLUENCED BY PHILO

1. Those of us who are "Spirit people" have a wisdom not available to others.

2. Spirit is much more important than matter. Therefore:

   ■ Perhaps married people should refrain from sexual relations.
   ■ The body has so little importance that "dress codes" at liturgical gatherings can be ignored.
   ■ We tolerate "sexual sin" because the body isn't all that important.
   ■ The resurrection of the body makes no sense.

"Women should keep silent in such gatherings (i.e. liturgical gatherings). They may not speak. Rather, as the law states, submissiveness is indicated for them. If they want to learn anything, they should ask their husbands at home" (1 Cor 14:34–35).

The reason these words demand an explanation is that they contradict an earlier section of 1 Corinthians in which Paul assumes that women will play prominent roles in liturgical gatherings. The question being addressed in this earlier passage is not *whether* women should have these functions. Rather Paul is discussing the appearance of both men and women when they fulfill important functions at liturgical gatherings. "Any man who prays or prophesies with his head covered brings shame upon his head. Similarly, any woman who prays or prophesies with her head uncovered brings shame upon her head" (1 Cor 11:4–5).

It seems the Corinthians were having disagreements over the proper appearance of both men and women. Each could give an unintended message by ignoring the cultural mores of the time. For example, for a man to have long hair was a statement that he was a homosexual. That is why Paul says, "Does not nature itself teach you that for a man to wear long hair is degrading to him . . ." (1 Cor

11:14)? For a woman not to wear a veil was to suggest that she was sexually available. Although "proper dress" is a cultural rather than a spiritual issue, it has spiritual dimensions because to ignore custom upsets people and causes division in the community. Again, loving consideration of others is all-important.

Since Paul assumes that women will pray and prophesy at liturgical gatherings in this passage, how can one explain his apparently forbidding women to do so in chapter 14? Is Paul once again stating an opinion with which he disagrees in order to argue against it?

A second, and preferable explanation is that 1 Cor 14:34–35 is a later interpolation addressing a problem that arose later in the century. Not only does this passage contradict Paul's earlier assumption that women would pray and prophesy, but it uses an argument appealing to the law, an argument which Paul would not have used. A passage similar to 1 Cor 14:34–35 appears in 1 Tim 2:11–14. Scholars surmise that the interpolation, like 1 Tim, is not Pauline but dates to the end of the first century.

Paul's view of marriage is not warped. It is just that Paul's teaching is within the context of a culture different from our own. Paul is addressing questions different from the questions our generation is asking. In addressing those questions both Paul and his audience share presumptions which we don't share. The result is that modern-day audiences sometimes attribute to Paul ideas which Paul did not hold.

For instance, in addressing the proper attire for men and women at liturgical gatherings Paul says, "I want you to know that the head of every man is Christ; the head of a woman is her husband, and the head of Christ is the Father" (1 Cor 11:3).

Many modern readers read this and take the word "head" to be an image used to teach the subordination of women in marriage. In fact, Paul is not addressing the role of women in marriage in this passage at all, nor is the word "head" used to teach a lesson about authority or superiority. In this passage "head" means "source" as in the "head" of a river. Paul is laying the foundation for his teaching that men and women should dress according to the customs for each by saying that men and women have been different since creation, since their "source." This difference should be reflected in their appearance. In arguing for this difference Paul alludes to the story in Genesis that woman was created from man's rib. Therefore the husband is woman's "source."

Paul's views on marriage will need explanation, but it is unfair to accuse Paul of being warped. Compared to his own society, Paul was a progressive. Paul did not think that baptism gave someone the right to back out of a marriage commitment, nor did Paul fail, as others did, to recognize the mutuality that should exist in marriage.

Review Questions

1. Does Paul teach that it is "well for a man not to touch a woman"? Explain.
2. Why does Paul advise people to stay in the state in which they are presently?
3. In Paul's culture, why did it matter whether or not a man had long hair or a woman left her head uncovered?
4. What two explanations are offered for the passage which says women may not speak at liturgical gatherings (1 Cor 14:34–35)?
5. What does Paul mean by the word "head"? What point is Paul making when he says "The head of every man is Christ; the head of a woman is her husband"?
6. In what ways was Paul more progressive than his contemporaries in his view of marriage?

Discussion Questions

1. Does Paul sound sexist to you? Why or why not?
2. Do you think you should take into account other people's reactions when you dress for church? Why or why not?
3. Do you agree with scripture scholars who say that Paul does not teach the subordination of women, only that men and women have been different since creation and that the difference should be apparent in their dress? Explain.
4. Based on what you have read so far, do you think you would like Paul if you met him? Why or why not?

ARTICLE 15

The Centrality of the Resurrection

1 CORINTHIANS

Question: "When Paul talks about the resurrection he distinguishes between a physical and a spiritual body (1 Cor 15:35–44). What does he mean?" (1 Cor 15:3–5; 15:12; 15:17; 15:35; 15:37–38; 15:42; 15:44 also discussed)

Once again Paul is couching his arguments in terminology that would appeal to his audience, influenced by the thinking of Philo, the Hellenized Jew who explained the Pentateuch in Greek categories of thought.

Paul is trying to make the resurrection more understandable and more acceptable to a group of people who have emphasized the spiritual so much that they attach no importance to the body. We have seen Paul struggle with the ramifications of this mistaken premise as he argued against abstinence from sexual relationships in marriage, and as he argued against neglecting proper attire in liturgical gatherings. Since Paul's audience considers the body merely a material thing of no account, the doctrine of the resurrection of the body has no meaning for them.

For Paul a belief in the resurrection is the absolute core to all that he has taught. Paul does not start his argument with philosophical theory but with core historical events and with experience. Paul quotes an early creed when he says, ". . . Christ died for our sins in accordance with the scripture, that he was buried, that he was raised on the third day in accordance with the scripture, and then he appeared to Cephas, and to the twelve . . ." (1 Cor 15:3–5).

Paul then goes on to challenge the belief held by some of the Corinthians that there is no resurrection from the dead. "Now if Christ is preached as raised from the dead, how can some of you say that there is no resurrection from the dead?" (1 Cor 15:12).

The ramifications of such a belief are that Christ did not rise, that faith in Christ is in vain, and that Paul's audience, who consider themselves "Spirit people," are still in their sins. "If Christ has not been raised, your faith is futile and you are still in your sins" (1 Cor 15:17).

Paul continues his dialogical argument by posing a question. "But some one will ask, 'How are the dead raised? With what kind of body do they come?' " (1 Cor 15:35).

At this point Paul is able to use language that will be more appealing to his "Spirit people." It is obvious from observing nature that seeds which are sown die and come to life with a body completely different than the seed itself. "And what you saw is not the body which is to be, but a bare kernel, perhaps of wheat or of some other grain. But God gives it a body as he has chosen and to each kind of seed its own body" (1 Cor 15:37–38). "So it is with the resurrection of the dead. What is sown is perishable, what is raised is imperishable. . . . It is sown a physical body, it is raised a spiritual body" (1 Cor 15:42; 15:44).

Paul is making it clear to the Corinthians that we do not know exactly what the resurrected body will be like. To equate the resurrected body with the body we now know is a mistake. Even more serious a mistake is to consider the body we now know of so little importance to the spiritual life that we deny the fact of Christ's resurrection and of the resurrection of those who, by faith in Christ, will join him not only in death but in resurrection.

What does Paul mean when he distinguishes the spiritual body from the physical body? A precise answer is impossible because Paul uses the words "spiritual body" to name something which is beyond his comprehension.

Paul knows that Christ has risen. Paul knows that after his resurrection Christ appeared. His presence was not an hallucination on the part of his followers. Neither was Christ's resurrected body identical to the body of the historical Jesus. By using the word "spiritual body" to describe this resurrected body, Paul picks a word that makes the idea of a resurrected body more acceptable to his audience.

Paul does not want to let the Corinthians' disdain for the physical body result in their denying the core of Christian belief. When these "Spirit people" deny the resurrection of the body, they deny not only the Christian faith but they deny their own claim to be "Spirit people," to have reason to expect eternal life. Paul warns the Corinthians that neither faith in Christ nor their own belief in eternal life makes any sense if they continue to deny the resurrection of the body.

Review Questions

1. What mistaken presumption caused the Corinthians to discount the resurrection of the body?
2. What are the ramifications of not believing in the resurrection?
3. How does Paul demonstrate from nature that the resurrected body need not be equated to the body we know now?
4. Why did Paul pick the expression "spiritual body" to name the resurrected body?
5. What exactly does "spiritual body" mean?

Discussion Questions

1. How do you understand the words "resurrection of the body"?
2. What might a "body" be other than flesh and blood?
3. Why is everything Christians believe dependent on Christ's having risen from the dead?

ARTICLE 16

A Deteriorating Relationship

2 CORINTHIANS

Question: "Paul's relationship with the Corinthians seems to have deteriorated. What has happened?" (2 Cor 2:1–4; 2 Cor 2:5–9; 9:1; 12:14; 13:2 also discussed)

We do not know exactly what happened between Paul and the Corinthians, but it does seem that things got worse rather than better.

Paul evidently visited the Corinthians after 1 Corinthians and before 2 Corinthians. In 2 Corinthians Paul mentions an approaching visit as a third visit (2 Cor 12:14) and refers to the fact that the second visit had involved some acrimony. "I warned those who sinned before and all the others, and I warn them now while absent, as I did when present on my second visit, that if I come again I will not spare them" (2 Cor 13:2).

In addition, it seems that a particular individual did something very offensive to Paul. Paul had asked that this individual be punished, but now asks that he be forgiven. "For such a one this punishment by the majority is enough, so you should rather turn to forgive and comfort him, or he may be overwhelmed by excessive sorrow" (2 Cor 2:6–7).

Paul refers to the letter he wrote previously as a tearful letter. "For I wrote you out of much affliction and anguish of heart and with many tears, not to cause you pain but to let you know the abundant love that I have for you" (2 Cor 2:4). This tearful letter is not 1 Corinthians.

So 2 Corinthians seems to be a letter attempting to further a

---

**POSSIBLE ORDER OF EVENTS BETWEEN PAUL
AND CORINTHIANS**

51–52 A.D.	■ Paul stops in Corinth on first missionary journey.
	■ Apollos preaches in Corinth.
	■ Paul hears from Chloe's people that divisions exist.
Sometime between	■ Paul writes 1 Corinthians.
54–56 A.D.	■ Paul visits the Corinthians. There is acrimony.
	■ Paul writes a tearful letter (now lost).
Sometime between	■ Paul writes 2 Corinthians (chapters
55–57 A.D.	1–9).
	■ Paul writes 2 Corinthians (chapters 10–13).

---

reconciliation between Paul and the Corinthians which was partially accomplished by the tearful letter.

However, scripture scholars believe that 2 Corinthians is not just one letter, but at least two. Chapters 10–13 are an abrupt change of tone. As you read the letter you will see that Paul's tone of reconciliation in the first chapters is replaced by anger and sarcasm in the last chapters. Paul probably wrote 2 Corinthians 1–9 in 55 A.D. and 2 Corinthians 10–13 later when his relationship with the Corinthians had once again taken a turn for the worse.

Other questionable sections of 2 Corinthians are 2 Cor 6:14–7:1 and 2 Cor 9:1–15. The first of these passages interrupts an appeal to the Corinthians to lay aside their differences with a warning against pagan contacts. Is this passage a digression of Paul's or a later, non-Pauline interpolation? The question is debated.

2 Cor 9:1–15, a second appeal for money for the Jerusalem collection, seems redundant. If this passage were originally part of 2 Corinthians, why does it begin, "Now it is superfluous for me to write to you about the offering for the saints, for I know your

---

MAKEUP OF 2 CORINTHIANS

2 Cor 1–9   One letter; however 6:14–7:1 may be a digression or may be a later interpolation.

9:1–15 may be a separate collection appeal.

2 Cor 10–13   An additional, later letter, more sarcastic in tone.

---

readiness . . ." (2 Cor 9:1). After all, Paul has already dwelt on this subject in chapter 8. Perhaps this section was originally a separate appeal and was inserted into 2 Corinthians at a later date.

All of these questions aside, one is still left with a curiosity about the nature of the trouble between Paul and the Corinthians. Who exactly were Paul's antagonists? Why was there so much tension between them? While no precise answer can be given, it is obvious that one problem between them is that the antagonists question Paul's authority as an apostle. Because the attack on Paul is personal, the defense or "apologia" is also personal. Paul reveals a great deal about his own character and personality as he seeks reconciliation, defends himself, and continues to accuse the Corinthians.

Review Questions

1. What two events occurred between Paul's first and second letters to the Corinthians?
2. What leads scripture scholars to suspect that 2 Corinthians contains more than one letter?
3. What three sections do scholars suggest might not be part of the original letter?
4. What is an "apologia"?

Discussion Questions

1. If you are in a relationship that is painful, would you prefer to try to straighten things out in person or in writing? Why?
2. Do you think an abrupt change of tone is reason to suspect that a particular section was not an original part of the letter? Why or why not?
3. Do you think Paul had a right to speak to the Corinthians as he did? Why or why not?

ARTICLE 17

The Ministry of Reconciliation

2 CORINTHIANS

Question: "What is the 'ministry of reconciliation' to which Paul refers?" (2 Cor 5:18; 2 Cor 2:8; 2:10–11; 5:9–10; 5:11; 5:12; 5:18–21 also discussed)

Paul understands his role as a minister and the role of other Christians who are also ministers to be to extend Christ's mission on earth. Central to Christ's mission is reconciliation. So, grounded in Christ, both Paul and the Corinthians should be ministers of reconciliation rather than people who stir up division.

As we saw in Paul's first letter to the Corinthians, Paul addresses particular problems by connecting them to core issues of Christianity. Here the particular problem is that the Corinthians are using false standards to judge their ministers, standards by which Paul has apparently come out on the short end. Those who have criticized Paul "pride themselves on a man's position and not on his heart" (2 Cor 5:12).

In his heart Paul knows that he has tried to be a faithful minister of the gospel and to do God's will. "So whether we are at home or away, we make it our aim to please him (the Lord). For we must all appear before the judgment seat of Christ, so that each one may receive good or evil, according to what he has done in the body" (2 Cor 5:9–10).

Paul is confident that the Lord knows his heart. He just wishes that his heart were known also to the Corinthians. "Therefore, knowing the fear of the Lord, we persuade men; but what we are is known to God, and I hope it is known also to your conscience" (2 Cor 5:11).

149

Paul wants the Corinthians to believe in him and to be proud of him not just for personal motives but because they could then defend not only him but his ministry to those who judge him falsely.

So Paul is trying to reconcile himself with the Corinthians. He is also trying to get the Corinthians to speak well of him to his accusers so as to bring about further reconciliation. All of this is proper to their role as Christians because Christ himself was the great reconciler. "All this is from God, who through Christ reconciled us to himself and gave us the ministry of reconciliation, that is, in Christ God was reconciling the world to himself, not counting their trespasses against them, and entrusting to us the message of reconciliation. So we are ambassadors for Christ, God making his appeal through us. We beseech you on behalf of Christ, be reconciled to God" (2 Cor 5:18–21).

Christ was God's instrument to reconcile the world to himself. This is the core of the gospel. Because of Christ, human beings' sins have been forgiven and the opportunity and the power to be reconciled to God and to each other are present. Paul then draws two conclusions from this core. First, "we are ambassadors for Christ, God making his appeal through us," and, second, "Be reconciled to God."

What does it mean to be an ambassador for Christ? What was an ambassador in the minds of the Corinthians? At the time Paul is writing, Corinth is the capital city of the Roman province Achaia. The ancient city of Corinth had been razed during the Roman conquest and had been rebuilt by Julius Caesar in 44 B.C.

In order to make a vanquished city a province, the Roman senate would send ambassadors to the soon-to-be province to arrange a settlement and to draw up terms. So the ambassadors were the ones who spoke for those in authority (the senate) and who arranged for others to be reconciled to Rome and to be made part of the Roman empire.

If Paul and the Corinthians are ambassadors for Christ, they are speaking for Christ and making it possible for others to be united to Christ.

However, God is not like the Romans, one who conquers and vanquishes. Rather, God is one who "makes an appeal" through his ambassador. God respects the freedom of those with whom God wishes to be reconciled.

So Paul beseeches the Corinthians, "Be reconciled to God." The opportunity and the power to be reconciled to God, to Paul and to each other can be accepted or rejected. Paul begs the Corinthians to open their hearts and be reconciled.

Because Paul understands the core gospel message of reconciliation he has earlier asked the Corinthians to forgive the person who had so offended Paul. The demand to be reconcilers, to be "forgivers," rests on every Christian. "So I beg you to reaffirm your love for him. . . . Any one whom you forgive, I also forgive. What I have forgiven, if I have forgiven anything, has been for your sake in the presence of Christ, to keep Satan from gaining the advantage over us; for we are not ignorant of his designs" (2 Cor 2:8, 10–11).

To fail to be reconcilers, to fail to forgive, is to give Satan rather than Christ power in your life.

So the "ministry of reconciliation" is core to being Christian. If one lives in Christ, one participates in Christ's ministry of reconciliation, living in peace and love with God and others.

Review Questions

1. How does Paul understand his role as a minister?
2. What false standard have the Corinthians used to judge their ministers?
3. In what way is Christ a reconciler?
4. What does it mean to be an "ambassador for Christ"?
5. Why does Paul ask that the man who offended him be forgiven?
6. What will happen if one fails to forgive?

Discussion Questions

1. Do you believe that your sins have been forgiven (as opposed to "will be forgiven")? Why or why not?
2. Do you believe you are an ambassador for Christ? Why or why not?
3. Do you believe it is essential for Christians to forgive? Why or why not?

ARTICLE 18

The Jerusalem Collection

2 CORINTHIANS

Question: "Isn't Paul terribly manipulative in his arguments about giving? How could he say that giving money is a measure of love?" (2 Cor 8:8; 2 Cor 8:5; 8:10–11; 8:20–21; 9:8; 9:13; 1 Cor 16:1–4; Gal 2:10 also discussed)

Paul is walking on thin ice when he writes to the Corinthians about the collection for Jerusalem. His relationship with them is already somewhat strained and he doesn't want to add fuel to the fire by doing anything that would appear to be self-seeking. On the other hand, the collection is extremely important to Paul, for reasons which we will explore. That Paul would broach the subject in these circumstances is testimony to its importance in his mind. When we understand the collection's importance we will better be able to respond to the question, "Is Paul being manipulative?"

You may remember from reading Galatians that the decision to have the Jerusalem collection was made at the Jerusalem council. Paul, Barnabas and Titus had gone to Jerusalem to check things out with the apostles in Jerusalem. Paul says that at the conclusion of the meeting, "when they perceived the grace that was given to me, James and Cephas and John, who were reputed to be pillars, gave to me and Barnabas the right hand of fellowship, that we should go to the Gentiles and they to the circumcised; only that they would have us remember the poor, which very thing I was eager to do" (Gal 2:10). For Paul this collection was an important sign of unity between the Jewish and Gentile churches.

You may also remember that the subject of the collection came up in 1 Corinthians. Paul writes, evidently in response to a question raised by the Corinthians, "Now concerning the contribution for the saints: as I directed the churches of Galatia, so you also are to do. On the first day of every week, each of you is to put something aside and store it up, as he may prosper, so that contributions need not be made when I come. And when I arrive, I will send those whom you accredit by letter to carry your gift to Jerusalem. If it seems advisable that I should go also, they will accompany me" (1 Cor 16:1–4).

Paul had evidently already told the Corinthians about the collection before this letter since his comments here deal only with the method of the collection and not with the theological or scriptural basis for participating.

The Corinthians must have responded positively to the idea but failed to actually come up with the money. ". . . it is best for you now to complete what a year ago you began not only to do but to desire, so that your readiness in desiring it may be matched by your completing it out of what you have" (2 Cor 8:10–11).

So Paul must broach the subject, despite the fact that he has already been accused of acting out of self-interest and wants to avoid any such accusation in the future. "We intend that no one should blame us about this liberal gift which we are administering, for we aim at what is honorable not only in the Lord's sight but also in the sight of men" (2 Cor 8:20–21).

Why is the collection so important to Paul? Paul considers giving to the collection a measure of one's acceptance of the gospel. "Under the test of this service, you will glorify God by your obedience in acknowledging the gospel of Christ, and by the generosity of your contribution for them and for all others" (2 Cor 9:13).

Paul does not want the Corinthians to give because he commands it but as an expression of love to a God who has showered them with gifts.

To persuade the Corinthians Paul holds up the Macedonians as a good example. The Macedonians gave out of their poverty. ". . . but first they gave themselves to the Lord and to us by the will of God" (2 Cor 8:5). Giving has its roots in the gift of self to God. Giving flows naturally out of a life lived in the light of the gospel.

So for Paul, to give is a proof of love. "I say this not as a command, but to prove by the earnestness of others that your love is also genuine" (2 Cor 8:8).

In chapter 9, which may or may not be a separate appeal to all of the province of Achaia, Paul claims to have held up the Corinthians as a generous example to the Macedonians, just as he had previously held up the Macedonians to the Corinthians. He reminds the Corinthians that they need not be afraid to give for fear they may be in need themselves someday. "And God is able to provide you with every blessing in abundance, so that you may always have enough of everything and may provide in abundance for every good work" (2 Cor 9:18).

Perhaps the tone of Paul's argument, a balance between the force of his personality and his desire not to further offend, could strike a resistant person as manipulative. But Paul is not manipulative in the sense that he is insincere or self-seeking. Rather Paul is promoting gospel living and the unity of the church when he teaches the Corinthians that they should give generously to the Jerusalem collection.

Review Questions

1. When was the decision made to have the Jerusalem collection?
2. Why is Paul walking on thin ice when he brings up the collection?
3. Why was the collection so important to Paul?
4. Why does Paul not want to command the Corinthians to give?
5. Is Paul manipulative?

Discussion Questions

1. Do you think giving to others is part of what is demanded of one who lives according to the gospel? Why or why not?

2. What do you consider acceptable ways to solicit funds? What are unacceptable ways?
3. Do you think many people neglect to give to the needy because they are saving for their own future? What would Paul have to say about this?

ARTICLE 19

Paul Boasts in His Weakness

2 CORINTHIANS

Question: "What does Paul mean when he says that he 'boasts in his weakness'? (2 Cor 12:9). No one wants to be weak." (2 Cor 3:1; 3:4–6; 4:7–10; 12:8–9 also discussed)

You may remember that in Paul's letter to the Philippians Paul said that he was "glad to suffer" (Phil 2:17). In exploring why Paul would say such a thing we found that Paul believed that suffering united him all the more closely to Christ, and that if Paul were united with Christ in his suffering and death he would also be united with Christ in his resurrection.

Paul's boasting of his weakness is in a similar vein. Paul boasts of his weakness because, in his weakness, Paul better reflects the "power of Christ."

As Paul says, to keep him from becoming proud because of the extraordinary graces which he had received, the Lord gave Paul a "thorn in the flesh." "Three times I besought the Lord about this, that it should leave me; but he said to me, 'My grace is sufficient for you, for my power is made perfect in weakness.' I will all the more gladly boast of my weakness, that the power of Christ may rest upon me" (2 Cor 12:8–9).

Paul makes somewhat the same point about weakness earlier in 2 Corinthians, using the image of treasure in an "earthen vessel." Paul is defending himself to the Corinthians, upset that they are questioning the authenticity of his ministry. ". . . do we need, as some do, letters of recommendation to you or from you?" (2 Cor 3:1).

Paul's letter of recommendation should be the Corinthians themselves since they know first-hand the power of the Spirit which has resulted from Paul's ministry to them. The Spirit has written Paul's letter of recommendation on the Corinthians' hearts. This makes Paul confident. "Such is the confidence that we have through Christ toward God. Not that we are competent of ourselves to claim anything as coming from us; our competence is from God who has made us competent to be ministers of a new covenant, not in a written code but in the Spirit, for the written code kills, but the Spirit gives life" (2 Cor 3:4–6).

Both Paul and the Corinthians are "ministers of a new covenant." How much greater is this covenant than was the old covenant ministered by Moses! The old covenant, deficient as it was, was accompanied with such splendor that Moses had to cover his face with a veil to shield the Israelites from God's splendor (see Ex 34:29–35). Just think what splendor accompanies the ministers of the new covenant!

But, cautions Paul, "we have this treasure in earthen vessels, to show that the transcendent power belongs to God and not to us" (2 Cor 4:7).

With this statement Paul makes it clear that he considers the experience of suffering and of weakness, always accompanied by an experience of God's healing, as a necessary qualification for a minister of the new covenant. Far from wanting to hide his weakness, Paul boasts about it because it is the very recommendation for which the Corinthians are looking.

Paul then expands on this suffering/healing experience which marks the ministers of the new covenant. "We are afflicted in every way but not crushed, perplexed but not driven to despair; persecuted but not forsaken; struck down but not destroyed; always carrying in the body the death of Jesus, so that the life of Jesus may also be manifested in our bodies" (2 Cor 4:8–10).

Why does Paul boast in his weakness? Paul believes that he is a minister of the new covenant, bringing others to a knowledge of and union with Christ. Paul also believes that Christ and the power of the Spirit are more visible in him when he is weak and suffering than when he is strong. Since weakness and suffering are necessary qualifications for ministers of the new covenant, Paul boasts in his weakness. Perhaps if the Corinthians understand the importance of weakness they will be more willing to accept Paul and the gospel which he preaches.

Review Questions

1. Why does Paul boast in his weakness?
2. What does "my grace is sufficient for you" mean?
3. What does Paul mean by "a treasure in earthen vessels"?
4. What does Paul consider a necessary qualification for a minister of the new covenant?

Discussion Questions

1. Do you believe that God's grace is always sufficient? Do you have a personal experience on which to base your answer? Explain.
2. What does Paul mean by "a thorn in the flesh"? Have you ever found that what initially appeared to be a cross in hindsight appeared to be a blessing?
3. Think of someone you know who has suffered. Has this person grown more loving through suffering or more self-pitying? Why do you think suffering can move a person in either direction?

ARTICLE 20

Paul, Goaded by His Critics, Defends Himself

2 CORINTHIANS

Question: "Why is Paul so sarcastic?" (2 Cor 11:20ff; 12:13; 2 Cor 10:12; 11:4; 11:17–18; 12:11; 12:14–16; 13:1–2 also discussed)

Paul is sarcastic in chapters 10–13 of 2 Corinthians. He is sarcastic when he refers to others as "super-apostles" (2 Cor 11:5 and 12:11) as well as when he asks the Corinthians to forgive him for the "injustice" (2 Cor 12:13) of not being a financial burden to them. Why is Paul sarcastic? The answer lies in Paul's personality and in the situation which Paul is addressing. Let us first explore the situation.

Scholars believe that chapters 10–13 of 2 Corinthians represent another letter entirely, probably written four to five months after the earlier chapters. It seems that problems have grown rather than diminished.

Two problems are easily identified. Some intruders, whom Paul never names, are disturbing the Corinthians with their preaching, in the process claiming to be true apostles and accusing Paul of not being a true apostle. In addition, some Corinthians are still living sinful lives.

Paul is terribly upset by the actions of the intruders and by the fact that the Corinthians accept them and criticize Paul. "For if some one comes and preaches another Jesus than the one we preached, or if you receive a different spirit from the one you re-

159

ceived, or if you accept a different gospel from the one you accepted, you submit to it readily enough" (2 Cor 11:4).

In addition to teaching a "different gospel" the intruders claim that they are true apostles and that Paul is not. We can deduce what claims they make on their own behalf and what charges they make against Paul by seeing how Paul defends himself. Evidently the intruders offered as their own credentials the facts that they were Jewish, that they worked mighty signs, and that they had received visions and revelations. Paul is terribly frustrated by this list of criteria for two reasons.

One reason is that Paul considers their approach wrong. True apostles should not be puffing themselves up, comparing themselves to others, and judging each other in a negative way. In addition, a true apostle would consider meekness, suffering, and service credentials rather than self-proclaimed power.

The second reason Paul finds the criteria so terribly maddening is that if he used it himself he would come out with high scores. He fulfills all the criteria, theirs and his too.

In chapter 10 Paul is resisting the temptation to compare himself to their criteria since he does not want to dignify their unseemly behavior by acting the same way himself. "Not that we venture to class or compare ourselves with some of those who commend themselves. But when they measure themselves by one another, and compare themselves to one another, they are without understanding" (2 Cor 10:12).

But later he succumbs to the temptation, acts like a fool, and points out that he fulfills the checklist of the intruders. We can hear Paul's ambivalence, for he begins by saying, "What I am saying I say not with the Lord's authority but as a fool, in this boastful confidence; since many boast of worldly things, I too will boast" (2 Cor 11:17–18), and ends with, "I have been a fool! You forced me to it, for I ought to have been commended by you. For I was not at all inferior to these superlative apostles, even though I am nothing" (2 Cor 12:11).

Why did Paul succumb to the temptation to dignify his critics and their false list of criteria for a true apostle by responding to the list and behaving in the same way he said an apostle should not behave? The answer lies in Paul's personality.

We already looked at Paul's personality as it appears in Acts (see Acts, Article 16). We noted that Luke pictures Paul as one who perseveres and as one who, far from backing away from confrontation, seems to relish it. We also noticed in the letter to the Galatians that Paul is capable of deep anger, and in the letter to the Philippians that he is capable of deep love. All of these characteristics seem to be operative in these last four chapters of 2 Corinthians.

Paul's deep love for the Corinthians makes him all the more vulnerable to deep hurt and anger when he is falsely accused by them. Evidently the intruders have suggested that there is some deceit in the way Paul handles money. Why is it that he won't accept financial payment for his personal services yet keeps asking for money for the collection? Paul accepted money from the Macedonians. To accept money is to accept support and love. To refuse money is to insult the benefactor. Does Paul think more highly of the Macedonians than he does of the Corinthians? Is Paul deceitful when it comes to money?

Based on Paul's defense of himself, these seem to be the kinds of accusations leveled against him. The Corinthians should know that Paul loves them, for he has spent himself on their behalf. "Here for the third time I am ready to come to you. And I will not be a burden, for I seek not what is yours, but you. . . . I will most gladly spend and be spent for your souls. . . . But granting that I myself did not burden you, I was crafty, you say, and got the better of you by guile" (2 Cor 12:14–16).

When Paul comes he hopes they will accept him in love. But this visit too will end up being painful unless those who are living in sin reform their lives. "I warned those who sinned before and all the others, and I warn them now while absent, as I did when present on my second visit, that if I come again I will not spare them" (2 Cor 13:1–2).

Since this is the last letter of Paul's to the Corinthians that we have, we do not know how this story ends. Was Paul accepted as a true apostle? Was the gospel Paul preached accepted so that those who were sinning reformed their lives? Did the intruders continue to be influential? Did the thinking of Philo continue to skew Christianity for the Spirit people? We do not know the answers to these questions. But we do know, judging from Paul's personality, that Paul continued to love, to challenge, to correct and to preach Christ crucified to the Corinthians.

Review Questions

1. What two problems can be identified between Paul and the Corinthians?
2. What credentials did the "intruders" offer on their own behalf?
3. Name two reasons why Paul is so frustrated by this list of credentials.
4. On what basis did the "intruders" call into question Paul's behavior in relation to money?
5. Why is Paul so vulnerable to the Corinthians' criticism?

Discussion Questions

1. Have you ever been falsely accused? Did you defend yourself? In hindsight do you think this was the best response? Explain.
2. Who can hurt you more, people you love or people who are only acquaintances? Why do you think this is so?
3. Have you ever realized, as you were doing something, that you were making a fool of yourself? What is the best way to handle such a situation? How did Paul handle it?

ARTICLE 21

Slavery and the Demands of Love

PHILEMON

Question: "Is Paul asking Philemon to free the slave Onesimus? I thought Paul taught in 1 Corinthians that each person should stay as he or she is." (Phlm 13–21; Phlm 5–6; 8; 16; 21 also discussed)

Paul does not directly ask Philemon to free Onesimus. Paul recognizes Philemon's rights as a slave owner. However, Paul definitely asks Philemon to view the relationship between himself and his runaway slave in a new light, a light that would demand he forgive the slave without punishing him. In addition, Paul hints that Philemon might consider freeing Onesimus so that Onesimus could become a partner with Paul in Paul's work.

Paul's request is bold, and as befits a bold request, his methods of persuasion are masterful.

Philemon is evidently a young slave owner whom Paul considers to be in his debt. "I would have been glad to keep him (Onesimus) with me, in order that he might serve me on your behalf during my imprisonment for the gospel; but I preferred to do nothing without your consent in order that your goodness might not be by compulsion but of your own free will" (Phlm 13–14).

We do not know why Paul thinks that someone should serve him on Philemon's behalf. Neither do we know to which imprisonment Paul refers, although the majority opinion holds that Paul refers to his imprisonment in Ephesus around 56–57 A.D.

Nevertheless, we do know that Paul uses his friendship, his influence, and his spiritual authority over Philemon to persuade him to forgive his runaway slave, and possibly to do even more.

163

Although Paul explicitly states that he wants Philemon to be free to choose his response in love, Paul puts a great deal of pressure on Philemon.

First he does not address his letter just to Philemon but to the church which meets in Philemon's house (see Phlm 2). This means that Philemon cannot privately refuse but must choose his response in view of everyone.

Next Paul flatters Philemon for living up to the demands of the gospel. "I hear of your love and of the faith which you have toward the Lord Jesus and all the saints, and I pray that the sharing of your faith may promote the knowledge of all the good that is ours in Christ" (Phlm 5–6). Such flattery would motivate Philemon to live up to his reputation for goodness when confronted with Paul's request.

As though this were not enough, Paul reminds Philemon that he could command rather than request that Philemon do as Paul desires. "Accordingly, though I am bold enough in Christ to command you to do what is required, yet for love's sake I prefer to appeal to you" (Phlm 8).

Then, before Paul makes his request, he plants in Philemon's mind a desire of Paul's that is more than Paul will end up requesting. He mentions that he would very much like to keep Onesimus with him but decided against this since he recognizes Philemon's rights as Onesimus' owner.

However, Philemon's rights take second place to another truth, and that is that baptism has turned slave owner and slave into brothers united in Christ. Paul does not claim that this spiritual relationship wipes out the previous relationship, but only that this spiritual relationship makes demands of its own. "Perhaps this is why he was parted from you for a while, that you might have him back for ever, no longer as a slave but more than a slave, as a beloved brother, especially to me, but how much more to you, both in the flesh and in the Lord" (Phlm 16).

Only at this point does Paul make his request, that Onesimus be received back without punishment. If debts are owed, Paul will pay them.

Next Paul says, "Confident of your obedience, I write to you, knowing that you will do even more than I say" (Phlm 21). What does "even more" mean? Perhaps it means only that Philemon will not ask Paul to pay the damages caused by Onesimus' flight from slavery. Or perhaps it means that Philemon will act on the suggestion which Paul so carefully planted in his mind and free Onesimus to be a fellow worker with Paul.

However Philemon took the "even more," he undoubtedly understood the core teaching in Paul's letter. Baptism changes the order of everything and makes all things new, especially relationships. For a person who has been baptized, every relationship becomes one in which Christ's love should be manifest.

The ramifications of this principle did not cause Paul to teach against slavery. But it did cause Paul to plant a seed which resulted in Christians questioning the validity of any relationship that is not based on freedom and love. The ramifications of this insight did, after nearly two thousand years, result in the abolishment of slavery.

Review Questions

1. At the very least, what is Paul asking Philemon?
2. How does Paul pressure Philemon?
3. What desire of Paul's does he mention to Philemon?
4. What difference does Onesimus' baptism make in his relationship with Philemon?
5. Name two things which "even more" might mean.

Discussion Questions

1. Do you think it was right or wrong for Paul to address his letter to the whole church? Explain.
2. What does it mean to say that baptism didn't wipe out the old relationship of slave and master but did radically change it?
3. What relationships in our society fail to meet the criteria of being based on freedom and love?

ARTICLE 22

Paul's Audience: Jews or Gentiles?

ROMANS

Question: "Is Paul writing primarily to Jews or Gentiles? The first few verses don't make this clear." (Rom 1:1–6; Rom 1:2; 1:5–6; 11:13; 15:15; 15:31; 15:24–25 also discussed)

The person who made this point has asked a very important question because, as we have constantly seen, to understand any of Paul's letters we need to think of them as addressed to their original audiences and understand them in that context before we try to apply Paul's teaching to our own lives.

The questioner is also right on the mark when she comments that the evidence is confusing. In his opening greeting Paul speaks of the gospel as "promised beforehand through his prophets in the holy scriptures" (Rom 1:2) and points out that Jesus was descended from David—comments that would be important for a Jewish audience rather than a Gentile audience. But then Paul says that his own vocation has been to the Gentiles. ". . . we have received grace and apostleship to bring about the obedience of faith for the sake of his name among all the nations ('Gentiles' in some translations) including yourselves who are called to belong to Jesus Christ" (Rom 1:5–6).

The evidence continues to be unclear throughout Romans. Many Old Testament quotations are used, including arguments derived from analogies to Adam and Abraham, the latter of which we read in Galatians. Would Paul have chosen this basis for his argument if his audience were not Jewish? However, Paul contin-

166

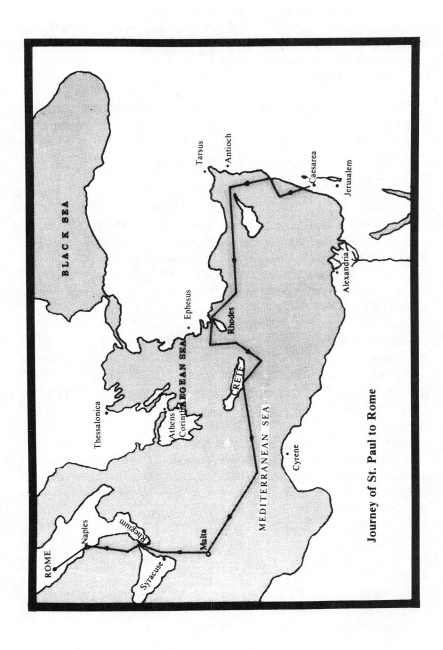

Journey of St. Paul to Rome

ues to refer to his readers as Gentiles throughout the letter. "Now I am speaking to you Gentiles" (Rom 11:13). "But on some points, I have written to you very boldly by way of reminder, because of the grace given me by God to be a minister of Christ Jesus to the Gentiles . . ." (Rom 15:15).

Since the evidence in the text does not solve our problem we can address two other questions which might cast some light on the subject: "What does history tell us about the Roman Christian church?" and "What was the context for Paul personally when he wrote this letter?"

Paul did not found the Christian church in Rome, nor does he say who did. Scholars surmise that Christianity had been introduced early on in Rome by Christian immigrants from Palestine. Once present, Christianity had attracted many pagan converts. In 49–50 A.D. Emperor Claudius had expelled Jews, including Jewish Christians, from Rome. However, Gentile Christians remained in Rome. After Claudius died, Jewish Christians were able to return to Rome in 54 A.D.

So, by the time Paul is writing, 57–58 A.D., there is a flourishing Christian church in Rome, including both Jews and Gentiles, but the Gentiles may have been in the majority and more entrenched.

However, even though Gentiles were the primary object of Paul's missionary activity and even though his audience was primarily Gentile, Jews rather than Gentiles may well have been on Paul's mind.

Paul writes this letter to the Romans, possibly from Corinth, as he prepares for a trip to Jerusalem to deliver the collection. We already know how important the collection was to Paul as a sign of unity between the Gentile converts and the Jewish Christian church in Jerusalem. Paul is worried about the reception he will receive in Jerusalem. He asks the Romans for "prayers to God on my behalf, that I may be delivered from the unbelievers in Judea, and that my service for Jerusalem may be acceptable to the saints . . ." (Rom 15:31).

Paul realized that he was still regarded with suspicion by many of the Jews in Jerusalem. In their eyes Paul was a dangerous enigma, an ex-Pharisee who taught people that they did not have to obey the law.

Perhaps, then, as Paul was composing Romans he was partially thinking of his Roman audience and partially thinking about how his teaching would fall on Jewish ears.

In many respects Romans seems less like a personal letter than other letters we have read because it is a clear and unimpassioned presentation of Paul's understanding of salvation through faith in Christ. Unlike previous letters, it was not written in response to questions, not written to correct abuses, and not written to warn against false teachers.

By writing to an audience to whom he was not personally known, Paul had an opportunity to treat at length themes which were merely touched upon in other, more personal letters.

As Paul tells the Romans, it was his hope that after visiting Jerusalem he would head for Spain and visit Rome on the way. "I hope to see you in passing as I go to Spain. . . . At present, however, I am going to Jerusalem with aid for the saints" (Rom 15:24–25).

However, Paul's fears about his reception in Jerusalem were fulfilled rather than his hopes that he would go to Spain. Paul did make it to Rome, but as a prisoner. Paul was arrested in Jerusalem, and after a two year imprisonment in Caesarea he went to Rome.

Was Paul's audience primarily Jew or Gentile? In numbers, his audience was primarily Gentile. However, the Jewish minority in Rome and the Jews in Jerusalem were probably very much on Paul's mind as he wrote his letter to the Romans.

Review Questions

1. Why is Paul's audience unclear in the greeting?
2. Why were Gentiles more entrenched than Jews in the Roman Christian church?
3. As Paul writes the letter to the Romans, what is he preparing to do? About what is he worried?
4. Why is the letter to the Romans less personal?
5. Was Paul's hope to visit Rome on his way to Spain fulfilled? Explain.

Discussion Questions

1. Why does it matter whether the audience was primarily Jew or Gentile?
2. Why is it an advantage to us to read Paul's ideas addressed to an audience he hadn't met?
3. Have you ever rehearsed your arguments to an antagonistic audience in front of a third party? Explain. Why do we do this? What does this question have to do with Paul's letter to the Romans?

ARTICLE 23

God's Justice: God's Saving Power

ROMANS

Question: "What does Paul mean by 'justice'? He doesn't seem to mean that people get what they deserve." (Rom 1:16–17; Rom 3:5–6; 3:21–26 also discussed)

In his letter to the Romans, Paul uses the word "justice" to describe an attribute of God. This attribute has nothing to do with God's judging people in such a way that they are punished for misdeeds, thus getting what they deserve. In fact, almost the opposite is true. God's "justice" is the attribute whereby God acquits his people, using his power to save.

Before exploring this idea further we must point out that English translations use a variety of words to translate the original Greek. While the New American Bible uses the word "justice," the RSV uses "righteousness." Other translations use "uprightness."

The original Greek had been translated by Jerome in the Latin Vulgate as *justitia Dei.* English translations often used "the justice of God." But because this translation was so often misunderstood (in exactly the way reflected by our question) as God doling out well-deserved punishments, some English translations have preferred "righteousness" or "uprightness."

No matter what word is used, it is extremely important to understand the concept behind the word when reading Paul's letter to the Romans.

Paul announces the theme of his letter immediately after the customary greetings and thanksgiving. "For I am not ashamed of

171

OUTLINE OF ROMANS

I. Introduction: 1:1–15.

II. Paul teaches his core doctrines: 1:16–11:36.

    A. God's justice is God's saving all who have faith in Christ.

    B. God has not been unfaithful to his promises to the Jews.

III. Paul gives advice on how to live in Christ's love: 12:1–15:13.

IV. Conclusion: 15:14–33.

---

the gospel: it is the power of God for salvation, to every one who has faith, to the Jews first and also the Greeks. For in it the righteousness (justice) of God is revealed through faith for faith; as it is written, 'He who through faith is righteous (just) shall live' " (Rom 1:16–17).

In other words, God's justice is God's power to save.

Perhaps it would be easier to let this meaning of the word "justice" sink in if we think a moment about the ways in which we use the word "just" in English. We might say, "The punishment was just because the accused was guilty." But we also use the word "just" to describe something that is appropriate, fitting, suitable, well balanced, or harmonious. So the proportions of a painting could be just or the closing measures of a song. This meaning of the word is perfectly evident in our phrase "just right" or "just as it should be."

So when God is described as "just" in the letter to the Romans you might think of God as acting just as God should act considering who God is. God is love, so God is acting just like God when God is revealing his saving power. A just God is a powerful, saving God.

The just God whom Paul is proclaiming is the God who acquits his people of sin. The just person is the person who has faith that God has acquitted human beings through the saving actions of Jesus Christ.

After proclaiming his theme so succinctly Paul goes on to elaborate on his teaching that justification is through faith and not through observance of the law. Some of the arguments Paul uses are very similar to the arguments which we have already read in Galatians, such as the analogy made with Abraham. In some of his arguments Paul continues to use the word "justice" as an attribute of God's in the way in which we have already described.

In chapter 3 Paul responds to certain objections to his teaching. He says, "But if our wickedness serves to show the justice of God, what shall we say? That God is unjust to inflict wrath on us? (I speak in a human way.) By no means! For then, how could God judge the world?" (Rom 3:5–6).

In this statement the first use of the word "justice" is the one we have been describing. The question is: If God's justice (his saving power) is made manifest by his saving reaction to our wrongdoing, then is God acting unjustly when he punishes? Paul say no. If this were true, then God would not be the judge of the world. For Paul's audience this was evidently explanation enough as they accepted the idea that God is the judge of the world.

Paul then goes on to teach that God's justice is operative in people's lives only if they have faith. "But now the righteousness (justice) of God has been manifested apart from the law, although the law and the prophets bear witness to it, the righteousness (justice) of God through faith in Jesus Christ for all who believe. For there is no distinction; since all have sinned and fall short of the glory of God, they are justified by his grace as a gift, through the redemption which is in Christ Jesus, whom God put forward as expiation by his blood, to be received by faith. This was to show God's righteousness (justice) because in his divine forbearance he had passed over former sins; it was to prove at the present time that he himself is righteous (just) and that he justifies him who has faith in Jesus" (Rom 3:21–26).

Here Paul is saying that obedience to the law has nothing to do with becoming just. Rather faith in Jesus Christ is what saves. All have sinned, Greek and Jew alike. All are saved by a free gift of grace. This gift of justification is made manifest in Christ Jesus and is received by faith. All of this shows God's justice, God's saving power for everyone who has faith.

One cannot understand Paul's teaching about justification by faith unless one understands what Paul means by the word "justice." God's justice is not God's punishing us or receiving satisfaction for our sins. Rather, God's justice is God's acquitting us of our sin as a free gift. God's justice is made manifest in Jesus Christ. All who have faith in Jesus Christ are justified, are acquitted of sin.

Review Questions

1. In Paul's letter to the Romans what does he mean by God's "justice"?
2. What words besides "justice" are used in some English translations? What misperception do some English-speaking readers bring to the word "justice"?
3. In addition to "just" as in "just punishment," what does the word "just" mean?
4. In Paul's sense of the word "just," what is a just God? A just person?
5. How does Paul respond to this question: "If God's justice is his saving power, does that mean that God is unjust when he punishes?"
6. How is the gift of justification received?

Discussion Questions

1. Do you believe that God wants to save everyone? Explain.
2. If God wants to save everyone, what do you think stands in the way of everyone living in God's love?
3. Have you ever loved anyone who wouldn't respond? Explain. Have you ever refused to respond yourself?

Paul's Moral Teaching

ROMANS

Question: "Why do Christians still argue over whether or not homo-sexuality is a sin? Doesn't Paul say clearly that it is?" (Rom 1:27; Rom 1:24–27; 1:28–29; 1:29–31; 1 Cor 11:13–16 also discussed)

This is the kind of question that many people would like to avoid. However, I think we should tackle it. By confronting the question directly we can learn not only about Paul's moral teaching but also about the correct way to interpret Paul's letters.

The passage which has been the catalyst for the question is this: "Therefore, God gave them up in the lusts of their hearts to impurity, to the dishonoring of their bodies among themselves, because they exchanged the truth about God for a lie and worshiped and served the creature rather than the creator, who is blessed for ever! Amen. For this reason God gave them up to dishonorable passions. Their women exchanged natural relations for unnatural, and the men likewise gave up natural relations with women and were consumed with passion for one another, men committing shameless acts with men and receiving in their own persons the due penalty for their error" (Rom 1:24–27).

Does Paul say clearly that homosexuality is a sin? Not quite. Paul says clearly that failing to recognize God in his sovereign power and so serving the creature rather than the creator is sin. That the Gentiles have committed this sin is evident in their behavior. "And since they did not see fit to acknowledge God, God gave them up to a base mind and to improper conduct. They were filled with all

175

manner of wickedness, evil, covetousness, malice . . ." (Rom 1:28–29).

So Paul says that the Gentiles have sinned as evidenced by the lack of love in their relationships. Paul goes on to say that the Jews have also sinned by thinking that salvation came through their own obedience to the law. All have sinned and all need to be reconciled to God.

More specifically in answer to the question—Paul does not say that homosexuality is a sin but that homosexual behavior is evidence that the persons engaged in this act have refused to recognize, acknowledge, and have faith in God.

The reason Christians still argue over the morality of homosexual actions is that they see some presumptions in Paul's description of homosexual actions which are brought into question by psychology. Paul assumes that homosexual behavior is freely chosen. Men "gave up" natural relations. The modern understanding of "sexual orientation" and the mysterious causes for it are completely unknown to Paul.

Paul assumes that homosexual behavior is the result of insatiable lust, that these men are "consumed with passion" for one another. Finally, Paul assumes that homosexual actions are unnatural. Men gave up "natural" relations.

Those Christians who debate the morality of homosexual actions do so not because they dismiss the Bible but because they separate Paul's teaching from Paul's presumptions. Paul's teaching is that idolatry is a sin. Paul's presumption is that homosexual behavior, which Paul believes is unnatural, freely chosen, and rooted in lust, is evidence that the sin of idolatry has already been committed.

Any behavior not based on love, including "gossips, slanderers, haters of God, insolent, haughty, boastful, inventor of evil, disobedience to parent, foolish, faithless, heartless, ruthless" (Rom 1:29–32), is seen by Paul as evidence that the Gentiles have not had faith in God's saving power through Jesus Christ.

So if a psychologist asks "Is homosexual behavior freely chosen, unnatural, and rooted in lust?" that psychologist is not questioning Paul's teaching but Paul's presumptions.

On less controversial issues we have no trouble realizing that we

---

PAUL'S MORAL TEACHING

Faith in God manifests itself in love.

Gentiles have failed to put their faith in God. Evidence is:
- homosexual acts
- gossip
- slander
- disobedience to parents
- faithless actions
- heartless actions
- ruthless actions

Jews have failed to put their faith in God. Evidence is:
- They still believe salvation is earned through obedience to the law.

Conclusion: All need to be saved. All need to put their faith in God and live in love with one another.

---

must put Paul's words in their cultural context to understand them. For instance, how many of us regard our hair length as natural or unnatural because Paul tells the Corinthians: "Judge for yourselves; is it proper for a woman to pray to God with the head uncovered? Does not nature itself teach you that for a man to wear long hair is degrading to him, but if a woman has long hair it is her pride? For her hair is given to her for a covering" (1 Cor 11:13–16).

To ask "Are Paul's presumptions correct?" is a fair question no matter whether the answer turns out to be "yes" or "no." To ask if Paul's presumptions are correct is not to attack Paul's teaching.

The core of Paul's moral teaching is that faith in God manifests itself in love. The question to ask in every moral dilemma is, "What is the loving response?" When it comes to sexuality, no behavior which is merely an expression of lust, which is exploitive, or which fails to recognize God's sovereignty in the created order would be considered loving, be it homosexual or heterosexual behavior.

Only that which is done in love is worthy of a person whose faith in God's power to save through Jesus Christ has made God's love operative in that person's life.

Review Questions

1. For Paul, what is a core sin?
2. What is the evidence that people have committed this core sin?
3. What are three presumptions which Paul has about homosexual behavior?
4. What are other behaviors besides homosexual activity which Paul considers evidence of sin?

Discussion Questions

1. What is the difference between saying something is a sin and saying something is evidence of sin?
2. Do you consider it wrong to ask if Paul's presumptions are accurate? Why or why not?
3. Among Paul's list of behaviors which evidence sin he names gossip and disobedience to parents. Do you consider these actions wrong? Explain.

ARTICLE 25

Has God Rejected the Jews?

ROMANS

Question: "Paul makes it sound as if God wants some people to reject him (Rom 9:18–23). Does Paul believe this?" (Rom 11:26; 11:29; chapters 9–11 also discussed)

Once again, in order to understand Paul's words, we must read them in the context in which they are written.

The passage which has triggered this question is, "So then he (God) has mercy on whomever he wills, and he hardens the heart of whomever he wills" (Rom 9:18). The passage appears as a comment on a biblical example (Moses and Pharaoh) which Paul has used to illustrate God's sovereignty. The illustration of God's sovereignty is itself just one step in a lengthy response to the question: "What is the relationship of unconverted Jews to Paul's teaching that one is saved through faith in God's saving power as manifested in Jesus Christ? How can one explain the Jews' apparent rejection in God's plan of salvation, given the fact that the original promises were made to them?"

As he responds to this question Paul uses scripture, as he did in the letter to the Galatians, to draw analogies and make more understandable the points he is trying to explain. Let us follow the argument from the beginning so that we can understand Paul's comment that God "hardens the heart of whomever he wills."

First Paul expresses his great love for his fellow Jews and enumerates seven gifts which God had given the Israelites, among them the sonship, the covenant and the promises. The Israelites were to be God's people in covenant love. Has God now broken that promise?

Paul uses Abraham and his two wives as an analogy. Not all of Abraham's children in the flesh were children of the promise. It is not just a physical relationship which makes a person an heir of God's promise but a spiritual relationship. The spiritual relationship rests on faith. All who have faith are heirs of the promise.

Obviously those who receive the inheritance are simply chosen. Look at Jacob and Esau. Jacob was chosen over Esau in the womb, so the choice obviously didn't rest on good works.

Is God then unjust? Of course not, Paul argues. God is the creator and he can choose just as he wills. That is God's prerogative. Paul then launches into the example that resulted in our original question. God, in his sovereignty, can bring good out of every situation. He can use a cooperative person or an uncooperative person to accomplish his will. Look at Moses and Pharaoh. God used both of them to accomplish his purposes. When Paul then says, "he hardens the hearts of whomever he wills," Paul is using a form of expression which is also used in Exodus. Pharaoh was hard-hearted. Sometimes this fact is attributed to Pharaoh (Ex 7:14; 8:15) and sometimes to God (Ex 4:21; 7:3). When Pharaoh's hard heart is attributed to God, the author is not saying that God wanted or caused the hard heart but that God recognized, accepted, and worked with the hard heart to accomplish his own will. Paul uses the phrase in the same way in which the tradition from which he is drawing used it. God does not cause hard-heartedness nor want it, but the fact of hard-heartedness does not thwart God in his saving actions on behalf of his people.

Paul then goes on to pose the question, "Why would God blame anyone for anything if part of the problem is that not all are chosen and God can use even resistance to accomplish his will?" Paul can't answer this question. He points out, though, that a creature shouldn't expect to be able to completely understand the creator.

Paul continues the discussion by reminding his audience that God has been very patient, and that God has, at present, saved a remnant. So hope is not lost. Paul begs the Romans to pray for the Israelites that they may be saved (Rom 10:1). The Israelites have not been rejected and will yet be saved. "Brothers, I do not want you to be ignorant of this mystery lest you be conceited; blindness has come upon part of Israel until the full number of Gentiles enter in, and then all Israel will be saved" (Rom 11:26). "God's gifts and his call are irrevocable" (Rom 11:29).

As Paul teaches his basic truths he constantly confronts mysteries. If God's justice is manifest in his saving power, then is God acting unjustly to judge? If God chooses some and not others, how can he find fault with anyone? If salvation is through faith rather than obedience to the law, what difference does it make how we act? Paul grapples with all of these problems. He insists that salvation is through faith in Jesus Christ, in whom God's saving power has become manifest. Faith itself is manifested in loving behavior. These are the core truths, and all other truths must somehow be compatible with these.

It is all right to ask the questions. It is necessary to admit that some answers are beyond our comprehension. But no matter what our background, Jew or Gentile, salvation comes through faith, and faith manifests itself in love.

Review Questions

1. What is it that makes a person heir to God's promise to the Jews?
2. How does Paul respond to this question: "Is God unjust to choose some and not others?"
3. Does God actually harden hearts?
4. What question is Paul unable to answer?
5. Does Paul have hope for his fellow Jews? Why?
6. Name two truths which are core for Paul so that all other truths need to be compatible with these.

Discussion Questions

1. Does it surprise you that Paul asks a question he can't answer? Why would Paul do this? Does it cause you to wonder if Paul is inspired? Why or why not?
2. Do you think it is necessary to admit that some things are beyond our comprehension? Are you willing to believe some things which you can't understand?
3. What belief do you find most mysterious? Why?

ARTICLE 26

Freedom and Conscience

Question: "Does Paul believe in freedom of conscience or not? First he says you should always obey authority (Rom 13:1ff). Then he says, 'Whatever does not accord with one's belief is sinful' (Rom 14:23). Aren't these contradictory teachings?" (Rom 13:2–3; 14:22–25 also discussed)

As always, each statement must be put in the context in which Paul said it. In addition, the questioner seems to be operating from a presumption that the word "conscience" means exactly the same thing for him as it did for Paul. We will see if this is true.

Let us look first at what Paul says about the Christian's conduct in relation to the state since that is the context of the first statement. "Let every person be subject to the governing authorities" (Rom 13:1).

At the time Paul was writing there had been no Roman persecution of Christians. As you already know, Paul was for remaining with the status quo in terms of social order. There is a presumption behind Paul's words that the government authority in question is acting for the good of the people governed. In such a situation, the government is contributing to the justice and peace of people's lives. That government should act for the good of the governed is emphasized by Paul's stating three times that the authority of governors comes from God. "For there is no authority except from God, and those that exist have been instituted by God. Therefore, he who resists the authorities resists what God has appointed . . ." (Rom

13:2–3; see also Rom 13:4; 13:6). These statements presuppose just authority.

Paul offers Christians two motivations for obeying just authority. "Therefore, one must be subject, not only to avoid God's wrath but also for the sake of conscience" (Rom 13:6). What does Paul mean by "conscience"?

Those in Paul's audience who were Jewish would not have had a modern-day sense of conscience as the subjective internal voice which judges, condemns, or praises a person's moral choices. For Jews, the law was the absolute norm of moral conduct. There was no encouragement to evaluate the law and decide independently whether or not one agreed with it.

For Paul's contemporaries, conscience was not formed by listening to an internal subjective voice but rather by internalizing an external objective voice. A person of conscience would ask, "Have I conformed my behavior to what others expect, given our shared knowledge of right and wrong?"

So Paul is telling his audience that they should obey just authority not only because they will be punished if they don't but because it is the right thing to do.

It may be that Paul thought it necessary to teach the Roman Christians to obey civil authority because they were interpreting their Christian freedom as a freedom from obedience to civil authority. Paul would not approve of this attitude because such a lack of cooperation and order would hinder rather than promote justice and peaceful living.

The word "conscience" also appears in the second quotation which was brought up in the original question. Paul says, "Happy is the man whose conscience does not condemn what he has chosen to do! But if a man eats when his conscience has misgivings about eating, he is already condemned, because he is not acting in accordance with what he believes. Whatever does not accord with one's belief is sinful" (Rom 14:22–25, New American translation).

Is this teaching in contradiction to Paul's teaching on obedience to just civil authority? No, it is not. At the core of each teaching is Paul's belief that Christians should choose to act in such a way that they promote peace and harmony.

The question behind this second teaching is one we saw in 1 Corinthians. Can Christians eat food that some other Christians consider unclean? However, the reason behind the question is a little different in Rome than it was in Corinth. The question is no longer, "Can one eat food which has been sacrificed to idols?" Now the question is, "Can one eat food which Jewish Christians consider unclean?" It is likely that Gentile Christians who had remained in Rome when Jewish Christians had been exiled grew less and less sensitive to the feelings of their fellow Jewish Christians when it came to obeying the laws about clean and unclean food. After Claudius died and the Jews returned, this insensitivity probably caused division. Certainly Gentiles are free from dietary laws, but they are not free from an obligation to act lovingly and with sensitivity for the feelings of others. So a Gentile Christian might in conscience (i.e. out of consideration for what is expected by the weak) have to give up the freedom to eat anything in order to promote unity in the community.

Paul does tell his fellow Christians that whether to eat or not eat in this setting is a personal decision and that one should not act contrary to one's conscience. But he encourages people to form their consciences based on what others think. Conscience would thus be an internalization not of the Christian's personal belief but of the reactions and opinions of others. As always in Paul, the deciding factor is the demand of love rather than the exercise of freedom.

Does Paul believe in freedom of conscience? For Paul freedom and conscience are not so easily linked. Christians are free from the law because salvation rests in faith and not in obedience to the law. However, that freedom cannot be exercised if it causes a weaker person distress and divides the community. The shared value system of the group should be assessed and internalized. Then actions which are compatible with one's conscience, one's internal sense of others' expectations, are right actions.

Such actions are motivated by love and promote unity and peace, as does obedience to just civil authority.

Review Questions

1. What presumption is behind Paul's teaching on obedience to governing authorities?
2. What two motivations does Paul suggest for obeying just authority?
3. For Paul's contemporaries what was the pertinent question in examining one's conscience?
4. What does Paul mean by "conscience"?
5. Does Paul believe in freedom of conscience?

Discussion Questions

1. What do you mean by the word "conscience"?
2. How do you form your conscience?
3. What role do the opinions and beliefs of others play in the formation of your conscience?
4. What do you mean by freedom of conscience?
5. Can you name any nationally known person who has exercised freedom of conscience in a way you admire? Who? Why?

■ SELECTED LETTERS ■

A Transition Note
from Paul to Other New Testament Letters

We have now read all of the letters which scholars agree were written by Paul. Other letters have been attributed to Paul but are thought to have been written by later authors. Since we do not have time to read all the remaining letters we will simply list them in traditional groupings and select one letter (*) from each group to read.

Deutero-Pauline Letters

These letters are often attributed to Paul but are believed to have been written by a disciple of Paul.
Colossians
* Ephesians
2 Thessalonians

Pastoral Letters

These letters are addressed to the pastors of Christian communities and deal with church life and practice.
* 1 Timothy
2 Timothy
Titus

Hebrews and Catholic Epistles

These epistles resemble sermons more than letters. All but Hebrews are named after the supposed writer rather than the receiver.

189

Hebrews
James
1 Peter
* 2 Peter
1 John
2 John
3 John
Jude

ARTICLE 27

Pseudonymity: A Convention of the Time

EPHESIANS

Question: "How can you say that this letter wasn't written by Paul? The author says he is Paul (Eph 1:1; 3:1). Is the author lying?" (Eph 2:14–16; 2:19–20 also discussed)

The author is not lying. However, the fact that the author claims to be Paul does not mean that the author is Paul.

The person who asked this question is bringing presumptions formed in our culture with her and is applying these presumptions to another culture in which they are inappropriate. The idea that an author owns a work, gets a copyright on it, is a modern idea. Such ownership was unheard of in Paul's day.

Instead "pseudonymity" was customary. "Pseudonymity" means that a writer ascribes his work to some other person. The purposes from the writer's point of view were several. The most obvious is anonymity. A writer may not want to attach his name to a writing for several reasons. Perhaps the writer is passing on oral tradition, or perhaps he attributes his insights to the Holy Spirit and does not want to take personal credit.

However, to remain anonymous is not identical to attributing the work to someone else. Pseudonymity was a literary convention, a way of writing about spiritual topics. One attributed one's writing to a venerable figure of the past. This is no more dishonest in a culture that accepts the convention than is beginning a letter "Dear Mr. Brown" when Mr. Brown is not dear to one at all. "Dear" is simply a convention of the form "letter" and no one is misled by it.

191

So letters are not included in Paul's corpus simply because the letter says Paul is doing the writing. Letters which do not belong to Paul's corpus are distinguished from those which do by their content, vocabulary, and style.

In particular, the letter to the Ephesians is recognized as being dependent on Paul's corpus but not part of it because the ideas contained in it are more highly developed, the sentence structure is not Pauline, and Ephesians appears to have been written from a perspective later in time.

For instance, the author of the letter to the Ephesians speaks of the church as being built on the foundation of the apostles and prophets. "So then you are no longer strangers and sojourners, but you are fellow citizens with the saints and members of the household of God, built upon the foundation of the apostles and prophets" (Eph 2:19–20).

Paul claimed to be one of the apostles. The view of the church in Ephesians is from a generation that looks back on the apostles as the foundation of the church.

The letter to the Ephesians reflects a greater unity between Jewish and Gentile Christians than we saw in Paul's letters. "For he (Christ) is our peace, who has made us both (Jew and Gentile) one, and has broken down the dividing wall of hostility, by abolishing in his flesh the law of commandments and ordinances, that he might create in himself one new man in place of two, so making peace, and might reconcile us both to God in one body through the cross, thereby bringing the hostility to an end" (Eph 2:14–16).

Notice, as you read this quotation, that it is all one sentence. This kind of complex sentence with long dependent clauses is nowhere near as prevalent in Paul's letters as it is in the letter to the Ephesians.

Ephesians is also much less personal in tone than Paul's letters. In fact, if you took away those parts of the letter which are conforming to the conventions of letter writing (i.e. greeting, thanksgiving, etc.) the remaining sections could have been addressed to anyone. Scholars think it very likely that Ephesians, while it observes the conventions of letter writing, was written as a "circular letter," a letter that was meant to be passed from community to

---

WHY EPHESIANS NOT ATTRIBUTED TO PAUL

- Ideas more highly developed

  —Cosmic view of Christ
  —Later understanding of church
  —Views on marriage

- Sentence structure not Pauline

- Perspective is later in time
  —Looks back at apostles
  —Greater unity between Jews and Gentiles

---

community. This would explain its impersonal tone and the fact that, in some of the earliest Greek manuscripts, "Ephesus" is not mentioned.

This anonymous writer also distinguishes himself from Paul by his cosmic view of Christ, his understanding of the church as universal, his expanded image of the church as the body of Christ, placing Christ as its head, and his more exalted view of marriage. (Some of these ideas will be explained in our next article.) Because of the highly developed concepts in Ephesus, scholars place it late in the century, between 80 and 100 A.D.

Such a late date would be another factor in our answer to the question, "Was the author lying when he claimed to be Paul?" Paul had probably been dead at least ten years and possibly twenty-five to thirty years by the time this letter was circulated. No one would have mistaken the intent of the author in attributing the letter to Paul. The author was not lying but was honoring an esteemed apostle of the church, acknowledging his debt to Paul's thinking and writing, and keeping Paul's memory and authority alive and present for another generation of Christians.

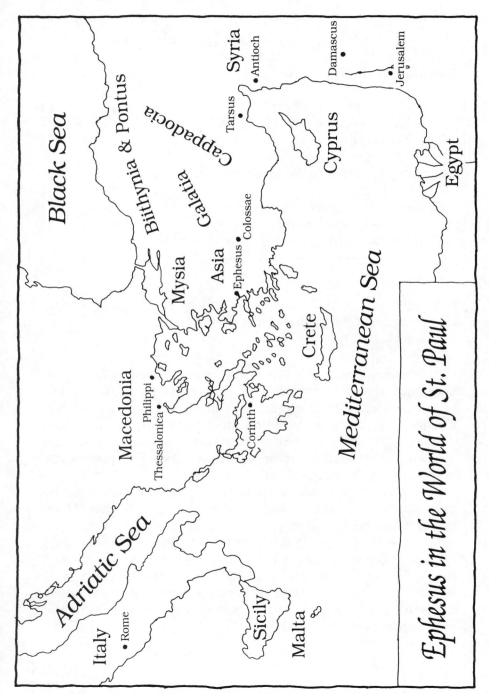

Ephesus in the World of St. Paul

Review Questions

1. What does "pseudonymity" mean?
2. Why might a writer attribute a work to someone else?
3. What is a literary convention? Give an example.
4. How are letters which do not belong to Paul's corpus distinguished from those which do?
5. Why is the letter to the Ephesians not considered part of Paul's corpus?
6. What conclusions have scholars drawn from the impersonal tone of Ephesians?
7. Why do scholars date this letter later than Paul's letters?
8. Was the author lying when he "claimed" to be Paul?

Discussion Questions

1. Did you already know that not all letters attributed to Paul are Paul's? Does this fact lessen their authority for you? Why or why not?
2. Do you agree with the arguments of scholars which cause them to date the letter later than Paul's letters? Why or why not?
3. Do you think authors should "own" stories? Musical compositions? Why or why not?

ARTICLE 28

The Church: United, Holy, Universal, Apostolic

EPHESIANS

Question: "What does Paul mean when he says that Christ is the head of the body, and the church is the body? This separates Christ and the church. I thought the church was Christ's whole body, not a separate part of the body from Christ." (Eph 1:22; Eph 1:19–23; 2:4–5; 2:5–7; 3:4–5; 4:46; Col 1:15–20 also discussed)

The person who asked this question is both very insightful and very literal.

She is insightful because she realizes that the image presented in Ephesians is a different image than the one we read in Paul. Remember, however, that this second image is not Paul's since Paul did not write Ephesians. Paul's image of the church as the body of Christ stressed the unity of the church with its variety of gifts. Ephesians is using an expanded image to teach that Christ is a cosmic Christ, and the church is a universal body. We will explore each of these ideas shortly.

First, however, we must notice how literally the questioner has understood the image. She has taken "head" to mean "the part of the body above the neck" rather than "the exalted one." That is why the image separated Christ from the church for her rather than identified Christ with the church.

The author uses the word "head" to mean "the exalted one who has dominion over all." This is clear from the context. ". . . and

196

what is the immeasurable greatness of his (the Father's) power in us who believe, according to the working of his great might which he accomplished in Christ, when he raised him from the dead and made him sit at his right hand in the heavenly places, far above all rule and authority and power and dominion, and above every name that is named, not only in this age but also in that which is to come; and he has put all things under his feet and has made him the head over all things for the church, which is his body, the fullness of him who fills all in all" (Eph 1:19–23).

The author is referring to a concept thoroughly developed in an earlier letter which we did not read (Colossians) in which Christ is proclaimed as a cosmic Christ who has dominion over the whole created world, even angels. Colossians includes this teaching in a beautiful hymn. "He is the image of the invisible God, the first-born of all creation; for in him all things were created, in heaven and on earth, visible and invisible, whether thrones or dominions or principalities or authorities—all things were created through him and for him. He is before all things, and in him all things hold together. He is the head of the body, the church; he is the beginning, the first-born from the dead, that in everything he might be preeminent. For in him all the fullness of God was pleased to dwell and through him to reconcile to himself all things, whether on earth or in heaven, making peace by the blood of his cross" (Col 1:15–20).

While the main focus and contribution of the letter to the Colossians is the highly developed christology of a cosmic Christ who preceded creation and reigns over all, the main focus and contribution of the letter to the Ephesians is its highly developed ecclesiology, its vision of the church as united, holy, universal and apostolic.

We have already mentioned in the previous article how the author of Ephesians stresses the unity of the church. Jew and Gentile have been made one in the one body of Christ.

The author pleads with his audience to preserve this unity, reminding them that "there is one body and one Spirit . . . one Lord, one faith, one baptism, one God and Father of all, who is above all, and through all, and is in all" (Eph 4:4–6).

The author insists that the church is already holy, having been saved through Christ. "But God who is rich in mercy, out of the great love with which he loved us, even when we were dead through

---

THE CHURCH IS

ONE: All who are baptized belong to the one
                body of Christ.

HOLY: The church has been redeemed by
                Christ.

CATHOLIC: The church is universal.

APOSTOLIC: The church is built on the foundation
                of the apostles.

---

our trespasses, made us alive together with Christ (by grace you have been saved), and raised us up with him . . ." (Eph 2:4–5).

The word "church" in Ephesians is used differently than it was in Paul's letters. Paul used the word to refer to an individual community of people gathered in Christ's name. In Paul, the plural, "churches," made sense. In Ephesians there is just one church. All are united in one body with Christ as the head. The fact that there is one church, one baptism and one Lord means not only that the church is "one," united, but also that it is "catholic," universal.

The author of Ephesians also stresses the apostolic roots of the church. It may be that by the time he is writing new ideas incompatible with the traditions taught by the apostles were being suggested. Not only does the writer attribute his work to the apostle Paul and say that the church is built on the foundation of the apostles and prophets, but he mentions that the apostles and prophets were specially gifted with revelation. "When you read this you can perceive my insight into the mystery of Christ, which was not made known to the sons of men in other generations as it has now been revealed to his holy apostles and prophets by the Spirit . . ." (Eph 3:4–5).

Perhaps one of the reasons that the concept of the church as Christ's body with Christ as the head is so highly developed in

Ephesians is that the church as an entity in itself became more important as the hope of an imminent return of Jesus faded. Ephesians never mentions the expectation that we saw in Paul that the world would soon end. Instead the emphasis is on the fact that those baptized into Christ already share in the resurrection. The Father "made us alive together with Christ . . . and raised us up with him, and made us sit with him in the heavenly places in Christ Jesus" (Eph 2:5–7).

Evidently the author is expecting not an imminent end but a long future for Christ's body, the united, holy, universal and apostolic church.

Review Questions

1. What is the author of Ephesians teaching through the image of Christ as the head of the body, the church?
2. What is the main focus and contribution of the letter to the Colossians?
3. What is the main focus and contribution of the letter to the Ephesians?
4. What does the author of Ephesians teach about the church?
5. How does the meaning of the word "church" differ in Ephesians as compared to Paul's letters?
6. What does the word "catholic" in the phrase "Catholic Church" mean?
7. What does the word "apostolic" in the phrase "apostolic church" mean?

Discussion Questions

1. What does this sentence mean to you: "Christ is the head over all things and the church is his body"?
2. What ramifications for the ecumenical movement are there to the teaching that Christ's body is one and there is one baptism?
3. Why is it so important that the church be apostolic?
4. When you say, "I believe in the one, holy, catholic, and apostolic church," what do you mean?

ARTICLE 29

Passing on the Leadership

1 TIMOTHY

Question: "When the author of 1 Timothy says, 'If any one aspires to the office of bishop, he desires a noble task' (1 Tim 3:11), is he saying that someone who wants the job should apply for it? Isn't this a big change?" (1 Tim 1:3–4; 1:18–19; 2:4–7; 3:11; 4:13; 4:14; 4:16; 5:17–18; 6:20 also discussed)

1 Timothy does represent "a big change" in the church if by "big change" we mean a different stage of growth. All the pastoral epistles (i.e. Titus, 1 Timothy, 2 Timothy) probably date to 95–100 A.D. and reflect a church which is a generation older than the church with which we became acquainted in Paul's genuine letters.

These pseudonymous letters, aimed at the churches in Asia Minor, are meant to extend Paul's legacy and make his core teaching applicable in a new setting. All these letters stress church order and morality.

One of the "changes" in church order revolves around the way in which leadership is chosen. The first apostles were appointed by Jesus. You will remember from Acts that lots were drawn to pick Judas' replacement. This was an expression of faith that the Spirit was selecting the leadership. In 1 Timothy it seems that people who feel called to leadership volunteer and are validated by the community.

1 Timothy talks about the call to be a bishop as well as to be a deacon. Rather than describing the duties of each, 1 Timothy de-

200

CHANGES IN CHURCH REFLECTED IN 1 TIMOTHY

- How leadership is chosen
- Concern for doctrinal purity
- Assumption that people will lead long lives on earth
- Less prominent role for women

---

scribes the kind of character and behavior which one would look for in people who feel called to these roles.

However, since the "Timothy" addressed in the letter functions as the type for a bishop or overseer, we can get a good idea of the duties of a bishop from looking at the instructions which he receives. Timothy is told to "attend to the public reading of scripture, to preaching, to teaching. . . . Take heed to yourself and to your teaching; hold to that, for by so doing you will save both yourself and your hearers" (1 Tim 4:13, 16).

The bishop's job is not primarily that of an evangelizer but includes ongoing care for those who are already converted. He is to read the scripture, give a good homily, faithfully teach, and live a life that is itself a witness to his beliefs.

The author of 1 Timothy is concerned that new church leaders be formally recognized. The letter itself, affirming Timothy's authority, is one way of expressing this concern. Another is the mention of the ritual which, by the time the letter is written, must remind the audience of an ordination rite known to them. "Do not neglect the gift you have, which was given you by prophetic utterance when the council of elders laid their hands upon you" (1 Tim 4:14).

In addition to pointing out the qualities for a bishop, the author describes what one should look for in a deacon. The list of qualifications is similar to that for a bishop. One cannot determine exactly what the duties are. Despite what is said about women in this letter (to be discussed in a separate article) it seems that women could be deacons. "The women likewise must be serious, not slanderers, but temperate, faithful in all things" (1 Tim 3:11).

In addition to bishops and deacons, the church is served by "elders." Again a clear understanding of their role is not possible. As we saw, their laying on of hands validated the ministry of bishops (1 Tim 4:14). Like a bishop, they teach and preach. The author is concerned that elders who perform such duties be fairly paid. "Let the elders who rule well be considered worthy of double honor, especially those who labor in preaching and teaching; for the scripture says, 'You shall not muzzle an ox when it is treading out the grain,' and 'the laborer deserves his wages'" (1 Tim 5:17–18).

One reason for being so concerned about handing on leadership in the church is so that legitimate designated leaders can help preserve the truth which has been received. The author makes this interest perfectly clear when he begins, "Remain at Ephesus that you may charge certain persons not to teach any different doctrine nor to occupy themselves with myths and endless genealogies, which promote speculations rather than the divine training that is in faith" (1 Tim 1:3–4).

The author solemnly charges Timothy to be faithful to the teachings which he has received. As he begins his letter he says, "This charge I commit to you, Timothy, my son, in accordance with the prophetic utterances which pointed to you, that inspired by them you may wage the good warfare, holding faith and a good conscience" (1 Tim 1:18–19). As he closes, the author once again begs Timothy to be faithful to teaching the truth. "O Timothy, guard what has been entrusted to you. Avoid the godless chatter and contradictions of what is falsely called knowledge, for by professing it some have missed the mark as regards the faith" (1 Tim 6:20).

The pastoral epistles clearly reflect the problems and concerns of a second generation church in which believers are instructed to live long, faith-filled lives rather than instructed to expect an imminent change of the world order.

The motivation of the writer is to preserve the truth. As he says, ". . . God our Savior . . . desires all men to be saved and to come to a knowledge of the truth. For there is one God, and there is one mediator between God and men, the man Christ Jesus, who gave himself as a ransom for all, the testimony to which was borne at the proper time. For this reason I was appointed a preacher and apostle . . . a teacher of the Gentiles in faith and truth" (1 Tim 2:4–7).

And for this reason others called to serve in the church have been appointed to preach and teach in faith and truth in each succeeding generation.

Review Questions

1. When were the pastoral letters written?
2. What do all three stress?
3. How are leaders chosen by the end of the century?
4. What were the duties of bishops?
5. How does the author of 1 Timothy show his concern that new church leaders be formally recognized?
6. Were women deacons? How do you know?
7. In addition to passing on leadership, what concerns the author of 1 Timothy?

Discussion Questions

1. Why is it important to have a formal way to hand on leadership in the church?
2. The author of 1 Timothy is concerned that elders be fairly paid. Do you think those who work for the church should be paid? Why or why not? Do you think they are? Why or why not?
3. Do you agree that 1 Timothy seems to give advice to women deacons? Why or why not?

ARTICLE 30

1 Timothy and Women

1 TIMOTHY

Question: "How did this letter ever get in the canon? Paul didn't even write it and the teaching on women is awful." (1 Tim 2:11–14; 1 Tim 3:11; 1 Cor 11:5; Acts 18:26; Rom 5:12–21 also discussed)

This is really two questions in one. To respond to the questioner we need to address the presumption that a pseudonymous letter shouldn't be in the canon. Next we need to look at the words on women in 1 Timothy which the questioner finds so offensive.

Since Paul didn't really write 1 Timothy, should it be excluded from the canon? How important is apostolic authorship? Apostolic authorship was extremely important to the early church fathers. It is still important today if, by apostolic authorship, one includes those works which were not physically written by an apostle but were written by a disciple of that apostle who was guided by the apostle's words and spirit. This understanding of apostolic authorship lies behind works included in both the Old and New Testaments.

Extremely important to canonicity is the conformity of the teaching in a given work to the rule of faith. The author of 1 Timothy is himself very concerned about faithfully preserving and handing on the truths which have been received.

In later years, by the time of the Council of Trent (sixteenth century), a criterion for inclusion was the long use of a particular book by the church. 1 Timothy fulfills that criterion too.

So let us look at the teaching on women and see how one is to interpret it, given the fact that 1 Timothy has been accepted as canonical.

The offending passage is this: "Let a woman learn in silence with all submissiveness. I permit no woman to teach or to have authority over men; she is to keep silent. For Adam was formed first, then Eve; and Adam was not deceived, but the woman was deceived and became a transgressor" (1 Tim 2:11–14).

As we mentioned in our last article, the pastorals reflect a change from earlier days, a change in the way leadership is chosen, a change in the emphasis on doctrinal purity, a change in their expectations of a long life on earth, and, we now see, a change in the way they regard women.

Jesus included women in his ministry and entrusted them to evangelize others (i.e. Mary Magdalene, the woman at the well). Women served in prominent roles in the Pauline churches, including preaching (1 Cor 1:5) and teaching (Acts 18:26). What we see here is a pulling back from the original freedom and equality which had existed in the early church. Even in the church to whom these words are addressed, women seem to have served as deacons (1 Tim 3:11).

The author seems to be choosing cultural norms and a desire for order over the counter-cultural freedom of the early church.

Remember, in Paul's letters Paul sometimes advised giving up the exercise of a freedom, such as eating unclean meat, in order to avoid scandalizing others and causing dissension in the community. These things are judgment calls. The core question is, "What is the loving action?" In various cultural settings one might come to opposite conclusions. This author thinks women should not teach or have any authority.

The author bolsters his conclusion by drawing an analogy between his conclusion and the story of Adam and Eve in the book of Genesis. A modern reader who mistakes the analogy for a core teaching, or who, perhaps like the author, draws historical arguments from a story (i.e. Genesis 2–3) which is not history is making a mistake. To say that Adam was formed first, not Eve, is to describe the plot elements of a story, not the actual order of creation. To claim that Eve was deceived, not Adam, is to misrepresent even

---

CRITERIA FOR INCLUSION IN CANON

- **Apostolic Authorship:** Is this work guided by the apostolic words and spirit?

- **Conformity to Truth:** Is the teaching in this work in conformity with the truth inherited from the apostles?

- **Spiritual Nourishment:** Has the church over the centuries been nourished by the work, thereby recognizing it as inspired?

---

the plot. Paul, of course, used the same story as an analogy and put the blame on Adam (Rom 5:12–21).

Why do we still value this letter if it contains a conclusion such as this? The letter is very valuable because it illustrates the difficulty and the necessity of taking the revealed core truth and applying it within a culture and for a generation different from the original setting.

First century communities developed the structures needed in their church. They struggled over how to live the gospel. They did not all come to the same decisions regarding structures and concrete ramifications of the core truth.

We are in the same situation. We have the same core truth but a different social setting. We too have to struggle to develop appropriate structures and to face the ramifications of gospel living within the context of our lives. We can look to 1 Timothy as an example of a community involved in the struggle.

While we too want to remain faithful to the core truths, we are under no obligation to accept the applications of that truth which 1 Timothy contains. We, like the first century churches, need to make our own applications. It is good that an example of the necessity and freedom to adapt the core truth to a new social setting appears in the canon.

Review Questions

1. What is today's understanding of the phrase "apostolic authorship"?
2. Besides apostolic authorship, what is important about a work for it to be included in the canon?
3. What criterion was important by the time of the Council of Trent?
4. How is the attitude expressed toward women in 1 Timothy a change from Jesus' attitude and Paul's attitude?
5. In what way does the author choose cultural norms over the freedom of the early church?
6. Does the argument from Genesis, with which even Paul would disagree, mean the letter should not be in the canon? Why or why not?
7. Why is the letter valuable?

Discussion Questions

1. What do you think of 1 Timothy's words on women?
2. Do you agree that 1 Timothy moves away from Jesus' and Paul's attitudes? Why or why not?
3. Do you see any value in 1 Timothy? Explain.

ARTICLE 31

A Last Will and Testament:
A Convention

2 PETER

Question: "Did Peter have a revelation that he was going to die (2 Pet 1:13–14)? Is that why he is writing this letter?" (2 Pet 1:13–15; 3:1–2; 3:15–16 also discussed)

Scripture scholars do not think that 2 Peter was written by Peter. Therefore, in order to respond to our questioner, we will first give the evidence within the letter which has resulted in scripture scholars concluding that 2 Peter is a pseudonymous letter written as late as 100 A.D. or even a little later. Then we will explain why the author of the letter says, "I think it right, as long as I am in this body, to arouse you by way of reminder, since I know that the putting off of my body will be soon, as our Lord Jesus Christ showed me. And I will see to it that after my departure you may be able at any time to recall these things" (2 Pet 1:13–15).

Since we have not read the other "Catholic epistles" you had no way to notice that 2 Peter includes a great deal of Jude. Jude dates to late in the first century. 2 Peter is thought to have been written after Jude.

In addition, 2 Peter ends with a reference to "all" Paul's letters. "So also our beloved brother Paul wrote to you according to the wisdom given him, speaking of this as he does in all his letters" (2 Pet 3:15–16). Such a reference reflects knowledge of a collection of Paul's letters, letters which were not collected until late in the first century.

208

REASONS FOR DATING 2 PETER LATE

- The author incorporates Jude—a later letter itself.

- The author refers to Paul's letters as a collected group. Paul's letters were collected late in the century.

Once more an author is presenting his ideas to his contemporaries in a conventional way which is not at all misleading to them. By the time 2 Peter is being written the apostle Peter was recognized as a foundational figure. The author wants his audience to know that he is teaching within the traditions of Peter.

Pseudonymity is not the only literary convention which the author of 2 Peter employs. In addition he uses a "testament" genre. As an occasion for the writing of this letter, he chooses the setting of Peter at the end of his life, passing on the truth to the church. Both Jews and Greeks had such a "testament" genre, a last will and testament of a dying leader. Using this setting, the author pictures Peter giving a definitive teaching which the whole church needs to understand for all time.

Perhaps it is because this letter is not addressed to any particular church but is appropriate for all churches that it has for many

---

LITERARY CONVENTIONS USED IN 2 PETER

- *Pseudonymity:* The author attributes his work to a venerable figure of the past and adopts that persona as the narrative voice.

- *A Last Will and Testament:* The author selects as the fictive occasion for his letter the imminent death of that purported author. That person thus writes his "last will and testament," his definitive teaching.

---

centuries been referred to as a "Catholic epistle." The descriptive title "Catholic epistle" is applied not only to 2 Peter but to James, 1 Peter, 1, 2 and 3 John, and Jude. All of these letters are named after the supposed sender rather than the receiver. The reason for the word "Catholic" may be, as we said, because the letters are addressed to all churches. (If so, 1 Peter and 2 and 3 John are exceptions.) Or the word "Catholic" may have been applied to these letters after they had been accepted in all the churches, after they had become canonical.

Instead of addressing his letter to a specific recipient, as is customary, the author sends it "to those who have obtained a faith of equal standing with ours in the righteousness of our God and Savior Jesus Christ" (2 Pet 1:1). It does seem that the author intends to include all the churches in his audience.

The real occasion for writing the letter is not the apostle Peter's imminent death but the presence of some "scoffers" in the community who are challenging some of the truth which the church has inherited from Peter and the other apostles. "This is now the second letter that I have written to you, beloved, and in both of them I have aroused your sincere mind by way of reminder, that you should remember the predictions of the holy prophets and the commandment of the Lord and Savior through your apostles" (2 Pet 3:1–2).

This reference to "your apostles" does not pretend to include the author as one of the apostles. Of course, the author is not one of the apostles. Nor is the author dying. Both the attribution to Peter and the setting of Peter's writing his last will and testament are accepted literary conventions which an end of the century author uses as he reaffirms the apostles' teaching for his contemporaries.

Review Questions

1. What evidence leads scholars to think that 2 Peter dates at least to the end of the first century?
2. What is a "testament" genre?
3. What might be the reasons for the "Catholic epistles" to be so named?
4. What is the real occasion for this letter?

Discussion Questions

1. If both the attribution to Peter and the setting of Peter's last will and testament are literary conventions, could the content of the letter possibly be true? Explain.
2. Do you think the author is misleading his audience? Why or why not?

ARTICLE 32

Explaining God's Ways to God's People

2 PETER

Question: "This letter seems to stress God's punishments rather than God's saving love (2 Pet 2:4–22). Why is this?" (2 Pet 1:21; 2:1; 2:9; 2:22; 3:4; 3:8–9; 3:14–15; 3:17–18 also discussed)

The emphasis in this epistle is much easier to understand when one places it in context. The author of 2 Peter is writing in response to "scoffers" and false teachers. He writes, "But false prophets also arose among the people, just as there will be false teachers among you, who will secretly bring in destructive heresies, even denying the Master who bought them, bringing upon themselves swift destruction" (2 Pet 2:1). Once we understand why the scoffers are scoffing and what the false teachers are teaching, we will be better able to understand the letter's apparent emphasis on punishment.

By the end of the century it was perfectly apparent to everyone that the second coming had not occurred as expected. Why not? The scoffers are saying, "Where is the promise of his coming? For ever since the fathers fell asleep, all things have continued as they were from the beginning of creation" (2 Pet 3:4).

These scoffers have evidently begun to deny God's presence and interest in the lives of his people. Since they do not think of God as paying any attention they have no motivation to live lives compatible with the gospel. What difference does it make? God is not coming to reward or punish, so we might as well do whatever we want.

The author of 2 Peter is arguing against these ideas. First he defends the expectation of the parousia. He holds up the transfiguration, at which Peter was present, as an event which foreshadowed the parousia. He regards this event as a prophecy of the parousia. Prophesies are not human concoctions but inspired by God. "No prophecy ever came by the impulse of man, but men moved by the Holy Spirit spoke from God" (2 Pet 1:21). The expectation of the parousia is still a valid expectation.

The author then warns that one need only look to scripture to see that God does punish evil-doers. Look at the angels who sinned! Look at those who lived at the time of Noah! Look at Sodom and Gomorrah! It is this section of 2 Peter (2 Pet 2:4–22) which caused our questioner to ask why the letter stresses God's punishment rather than God's love. However, this impression is slightly off balance, for the author is arguing not only that God punishes evil-doers but also that God saves those who do good. ". . . the Lord knows how to rescue the godly from trial, and to keep the unrighteous under punishment until the day of judgment" (2 Pet 2:9).

The author categorizes the scoffers as the worst kind of people who live evil lives and who will bring terrible destruction on themselves and on all who follow them. These people have heard the truth and have rejected it. "It has happened to them according to the true proverb, 'The dog turns back to his own vomit, and the sow is washed only to wallow in the mire' " (2 Pet 2:22).

The author then goes on to try to explain God's ways to his audience. If the expectation of the parousia rests on a valid prophecy, then why has it not happened? The author responds, "With the Lord one day is as a thousand years and a thousand years as one day. The Lord is not slow about his promise as some count slowness, but is forbearing toward you, not wishing that any should perish, but that all should reach repentance" (2 Pet 3:8–9).

In other words, the author suggests that it is God's mercy which accounts for his delay. God is a judge and will judge. However, God does not want anyone to perish. So he is putting off judgment in order to give sinners time to repent.

2 Peter is not, as our questioner thought, a letter in which the primary emphasis is punishment. Rather it is a letter in which the author tries to teach traditional truths in the face of scoffers. The

scoffers are wrong to dismiss the expectation of the parousia, thereby concluding that God will not come to judge. They are wrong to leave the paths of virtue and live sinful lives. The author of 2 Peter does not want his audience to do the same. "Therefore, beloved, since you wait for these (i.e. the time and circumstances of Christ's coming), be zealous to be found by him without spot or blemish, and at peace. And count the forbearance of our Lord as salvation" (2 Pet 3:14–15).

Scholars believe that 2 Peter is the last of the New Testament letters to be written. The author and audience share much with us. They are far enough removed from the saving events of Christ's life, death, and resurrection and far enough removed from the heavily charismatic early church that they must rely on the traditions as they have received them from those earlier Christians in order to have a knowledge of the historical Jesus and of the saving events which had occurred. The author is very concerned lest that knowledge be lost. As he closes he warns his audience, "Beware lest you be carried away with the error of lawless men and lose your own stability. But grow in the grace and knowledge of our Lord and savior Jesus Christ" (2 Pet 3:17–18).

We too are dependent on earlier inspired prophets and teachers who have faithfully handed on the tradition. Among those to whom we are indebted is the author of 2 Peter.

Review Questions

1. What are the scoffers asking? What conclusion are they drawing about the way they live?
2. How does the author defend the expectation of the second coming?
3. How does the author defend the idea that God does punish evil-doers?
4. Is the author stressing only that God punishes evil-doers? Explain.
5. How does the author explain why the parousia has not yet happened?
6. What do we have in common with the audience of 2 Peter?

Discussion Questions

1. Do we have scoffers in our society? What questions are they asking? What responses might we give?
2. Do you believe that God punishes evil and rewards good? On what do you base your belief?
3. Do you think God's ways can be explained? Why or why not?

Summation and Transition
from Letters to the Book of Revelation

When you began to read the New Testament letters you were fairly well equipped to understand what you were reading. After all, letters are a common literary form in our culture. The New Testament letters were far from the first letters you have ever read.

The same may not be true as you read the book of Revelation. You may be reading a kind of writing which you have never read before. You may be bringing to your reading some presumptions about the book of Revelation which are wrong and which may get you off on the wrong foot.

Nevertheless, do still start by reading the book of Revelation itself. You will probably be overwhelmed with questions. You will probably feel lost. This is fine. Just keep reading once through so you have a surface knowledge of the movement of the plot, a sense of the whole. As you read jot down questions. A great many of the questions which you ask will be answered in the following articles.

■ THE BOOK OF ■
■ REVELATION ■

ARTICLE 1

The Function of Prophecy

Question: "Is this book prophecy? I see the author calls it a 'prophetic message' (Rev 1:3) and says that it will show what's going to happen." (Rev 1:1; Rev 1:3; 10:11; 22:7 also discussed)

In terms of its literary form the book of Revelation is not primarily prophetic writing but apocalyptic writing. We will give a thorough explanation of apocalyptic writing in subsequent articles. But first we will respond to this question by explaining how the book of Revelation relates to prophecy.

The book of Revelation compares to prophetic writing in its function rather than in its form. So to understand the book of Revelation we need to understand the function of prophecy.

If you notice, our questioner assumes that the function of prophetic writing is to predict the future. The signal that this might be prophetic writing for our questioner was that it "will show what's going to happen." Actually, that is not the function of prophecy.

The function of prophecy in the Old Testament was to call people to be faithful to their covenant relationship with God. A prophet had a special spiritual gift, but that gift was not the ability to predict inevitable future events. In fact, fortune-telling was against the Jewish law.

Instead, the prophet's gift was the ability to understand covenant love and the ramifications of being in relationship with a loving God. The prophet's function was to call people to fidelity and to remind them of the ramifications of the fact that they are God's chosen people.

A prophet understood that a loving God insists on fidelity and insists that God's people treat each other lovingly. So when God's

219

BOOK OF REVELATION COMPARED TO PROPHECY

1. The book is referred to as "prophecy." "Blessed is the one who reads aloud the words of the prophecy" (Rev 1:1).

   "Blessed is the one who keeps the words of the prophecy of this book" (Rev 22:7).

2. The narrator is commissioned as a prophet. "You must again prophesy about many peoples and nations and tongues and kings" (Rev 10:11).

3. The book of Relevation has the same function as prophecy. It calls people to fidelity in covenant relationship. "Persevere and have hope. God will save."

---

people start to sin, to turn to other gods or to live in luxury and ignore the needs of the poor, the prophet understood the ramifications of this behavior and warned the people of trouble ahead. The message was not fortune-telling: "No matter what you do, such and such an event will occur." Rather, the message was a call to repentance: "You are sinning, and sin always leads to suffering. Repent!" So the prophet's role was to speak of the future, but not as a fortune-teller. Rather, the prophet spoke as a person who is capable of seeing the relationship between cause and effect. People called to covenant love cannot live in sin without bringing suffering on themselves and others.

Just as crucial to a prophet's role was to encourage those who are suffering that God will save them. Covenant love is permanent love. A loving God will save his people. So when people are living in distress or suffering persecution, the prophet would remind God's people that they have every reason to live in hope. No matter how bad things look now, they could depend on God's saving power and presence. God will save his people.

It is because one function of prophetic literature is to offer hope that the book of Revelation is referred to as prophecy. So each time the author of the book of Revelation refers to his work as "prophecy," this should be understood as a reference to the book's function of offering hope. In the introduction we read, ". . . blessed is the one who reads aloud the words of the prophecy . . ." (Rev 1:3 NRSV). Later the narrator is told, "You must again prophesy about many peoples and nations and tongues and kings" (Rev 10:11). As the book ends we read, "Blessed is the one who keeps the words of the prophecy of this book" (Rev 22:7 NRSV).

If one hopes to understand the book of Revelation it is very important to remember that the reason the book of Revelation is referred to as prophecy is that it offers words of hope to people who are suffering persecution. We will have many opportunities to see textual evidence of the truth of this statement. The audience is living near the end of the century, has already suffered persecution under Nero, is presently suffering under Domitian (d. 96 A.D.), and fears future persecutions as well.

Many readers of the book of Revelation misunderstand it because they presume the book is predicting future events, events which have not yet occurred. Acting on this false presumption, they try to decipher the symbols by equating them to modern-day people, nations, or institutions. Such an attempt is totally futile because it rests on a complete misunderstanding of the intent of the author.

The author of the book of Revelation is addressing his contemporaries. As you will discover, he wants them to know that God will save them through Jesus Christ, that their suffering will come to an end, and that this will happen very soon. As the author says, he is writing to show "his (Jesus Christ's) servants what must soon take place" (Rev 1:1).

Is the book of Revelation prophecy? If by "prophecy" one means "fortune-telling" the answer is "no." However, if one is referring to the function of prophecy one may accurately call the book of Revelation prophecy. This is true because the book of Revelation offers hope of God's saving power to God's covenant people.

Review Questions

1. In terms of its literary form, what kind of writing is the book of Revelation?
2. In what primary way does the book of Revelation compare to prophecy?
3. What is the function of prophecy?
4. What spiritual gift do prophets have?
5. Name two messages which prophets pass on to people.
6. Which of these two messages is the basic message of the book of Revelation?
7. Why is it futile to look for specific references to present-day events in the book of Revelation?

Discussion Questions

1. What acquaintance do you already have with the book of Revelation?
2. Have you thought that the book of Revelation is about our future? Why have you thought this?
3. Are you surprised to learn that fortune-telling was against the Jewish law? Why or why not?
4. Is it reasonable to offer hope to people devastated by persecution? Why? On what does hope rest?

ARTICLE 2

Some Conventions of Apocalyptic Literature

Question: "What does the author mean by 'revelation' when he says that this is the revelation which God gave Jesus Christ (Rev 1:1)? Why would the risen Christ need to be given a revelation?" (Rev 1:1–2; 1:9; 22:10)

When the author of the book of Revelation begins, "The revelation of Jesus Christ which God gave him to show his servants . . ." (Rev 1:1), the author is telling the reader that he or she is beginning to read a book of apocalyptic literature. Because "apocalyptic" literature is not used in our culture, a modern reader misunderstands the word "revelation" to mean "God's self-manifestation" rather than as the name of a literary form.

The Greek word *apokalypsis* is translated "revelation" in English. The word names a kind of writing which was common in the two hundred years before Jesus as well as in the following two hundred years. We have two examples of apocalyptic literature in the Bible, the book of Daniel in the Old Testament and the book of Revelation in the New Testament.

Apocalyptic writing is easily recognizable because it employs certain conventions. A convention is a characteristic of a given kind of writing, the conventional way of writing in that form. For instance, if I begin "Dear Emily," you know you are reading a letter because to begin with "dear" is a convention of letter writing. If I begin "Once upon a time," you are expecting a fairy tale because "Once upon a time" is a convention in telling fairy tales.

The conventions which are present in apocalyptic literature include claiming that the content of what is written is a hidden revelation which was known only to God, that an archangel gave this

223

CONVENTIONS OF APOCALYPTIC LITERATURE

1. The work contains a hidden revelation which was known only to God.

2. God or an angel gave the revelation to a person.

3. The person receives the revelation in a vision.

4. The revelation is in a sealed book.

5. The revelation is to be opened only at the end time.

6. The revelation is communicated through symbolic language and numbers.

7. The book is attributed to a venerated figure of a past generation.

8. The setting of the book is a past time, so past historic events are presented as though they will be future events.

---

hidden revelation to the author, that the author had a vision in which he received the revelation, and that the revelation is to be placed in a sealed book and read only at the end time.

As you can see, the author of the book of Revelation employs many of these conventions in his very first sentence. "The revelation of Jesus Christ, which God gave him to show his servants what must soon take place; and he made it known by sending his angel to his servant John, who bore witness to the word of God and to the testimony of Jesus Christ, even to all that he saw" (Rev 1:1–2).

Usually in apocalyptic literature the real author and the person who is said to have received the revelation are not the same person. The author attributes the work to a venerated person from a previous generation.

**WAYS IN WHICH THE BOOK OF REVELATION
DEPARTS FROM THE CONVENTIONS**

1. The work is attributed to a (then) present day author rather than a venerated figure from the past.

2. The setting is the (then) present rather than the past.

3. The book is not sealed since the (then) present time is understood to be the end time.

For instance, the book of Daniel is attributed to Daniel who lived at the time of the Babylonian exile (587 B.C.–537 B.C.). The author pictured Daniel as having been told to seal up the revelation since it could only be read at the end time. The book, of course, was read in the author's time. So the author was saying that the end time was the time of his contemporaries, for otherwise the revelation would still be sealed up.

The author of the book of Revelation departs from the usual convention when he says that he is John, a contemporary of the audience, in exile on the island of Patmos. "I, John, your brother, who share with you in Jesus the tribulation and the kingdom and the patient endurance, was on the island called Patmos on account of the word of God and the testimony of Jesus" (Rev 1:9).

Because the author chooses the present time for his setting, he can't use the convention of having the revelation sealed. Otherwise it would not be logical for his audience to be reading it. To solve this problem the author acknowledges the convention of the sealed book even as he departs from it. "And he (the angel) said to me, 'Do not seal up the words of the prophecy of this book, for the time is near' " (Rev 22:10). The message about the end time is obviously about the present time, the time in which the author is living, not some distant, far-off time, certainly not our time.

Is the John on the island of Patmos John the apostle? Is he the John who wrote the gospel? Some early tradition would have said "yes" to both questions. However, the present consensus is that the John of the book of Revelation is neither the apostle John nor the author of the gospel.

The John on Patmos never claims to be an apostle. The probable late date of the book makes it unlikely that Jesus' apostle John was still alive so late in the century.

Scholars are quite certain that the author of John's gospel and the author of the book of Revelation are not the same person. The style of the Greek is not at all the same in the two works.

So the author of the book of Revelation is otherwise unknown to us. However, we do know that he was well acquainted with apocalyptic literature and made good use of this well-known literary form to teach something true to his contemporary audience. As we read the book of Revelation we will discover just what truth has been recognized and treasured not only by John's original audience but by each succeeding generation, including our own.

Review Questions

1. What does "revelation" mean in, "This is the revelation which God gave . . ."?
2. What two examples of apocalyptic literature do we have in the Bible?
3. What is a literary "convention"? Give two examples.
4. Name four conventions of apocalyptic literature.
5. From what convention of apocalyptic writing does John depart? Explain.
6. Is the John who wrote the book of Revelation the apostle John? The author of John's gospel? Explain.

Discussion Questions

1. Do you have any previous acquaintance with apocalyptic writing? Explain.
2. What does the word "true" mean to you?
3. Can any literary form teach what is "true"? Why or why not?
4. Does it bother you to be told that the claim to have had a vision is a convention of apocalyptic writing? Why or why not?

ARTICLE 3

The Use of Symbols in Apocalyptic Literature

Question: "I don't understand the vision John has (Rev 1:12–16). Is the 'son of man' Jesus? Why does he have a sword in his mouth?" (Dan 7:9–10; 7:13–14 also discussed)

The reason our questioner does not understand John's vision is that she is not familiar with the way symbolic language is used in apocalyptic literature.

As was mentioned in the article on the function of prophecy, the book of Revelation is addressed to people who are suffering persecution. In order not to further endanger the audience, the author of apocalyptic literature writes his words of encouragement in symbolic language, in code, so that those who are persecuted will understand it while their persecutors will not. Otherwise the audience might be put in additional danger. This use of symbols is one more convention of apocalyptic literature.

We need only look at the passage in question to demonstrate the way in which symbols are used as a code in apocalyptic literature. "Then I turned to see the voice that was speaking to me, and on turning I saw seven golden lampstands, and in the midst of the lampstands one like a son of man, clothed with a long robe and with a golden girdle round his breast; his head and his hair were white as white wool, white as snow; his eyes were like a flame of fire, his feet were like burnished bronze, refined as in a furnace, and his voice was like the sound of many waters; in his right hand he held seven stars, from his mouth issued a sharp two-edged sword, and his face was like the sun shining in full strength" (Rev 1:12–16).

The reason this passage is so difficult for us to understand is that

227

we are not part of the "in group." The symbols are not familiar to us. When John's audience read this passage they would have immediately recognized the allusions to the other apocalyptic book in the Bible, the book of Daniel. We can acquaint ourselves with many of the traditional symbols which John employs by reading two passages from the book of Daniel.

In the book of Daniel, Daniel has a vision of the heavenly court. "As I looked, thrones were placed and one that was ancient of days took his seat; his raiment was white as snow, and the hair of his head like pure wool; the throne was fiery flames, its wheels were burning fire" (Dan 7:9).

This vision pictures God on his throne in heaven. Much of Daniel's symbolic description of God reappears in Revelation. As in Revelation, the figure in the heavenly court is dressed in white, his hair white as wool. In each vision fire symbolizes God's presence.

The second important passage from Daniel describes another figure approaching God on his throne. ". . . and behold, with the clouds of heaven there came one like a son of man, and he came to the Ancient of Days and was presented before him. And to him was given dominion and glory and kingdom, that all people, nations and languages should serve him; his dominion is an everlasting dominion, which shall not pass away, and his kingdom one that shall not be destroyed" (Dan 7:13–14).

In its original context this figure of a "son of man" was a messianic figure. The author of the book of Daniel was telling his persecuted audience that God would give someone, a "son of man," the power to save them from their enemies. God would save his people. By the time Revelation is written this "son of man" image has been associated with Jesus. In the synoptic gospels Jesus is regularly pictured as referring to himself as "the son of man."

Looking again at the vision in the book of Revelation we see that the author has combined the "son of man" figure who receives power and dominion with the figure of God himself. These two figures have become one and the same.

With this background we can see that the vision in the book of Revelation is teaching the audience something about Jesus Christ's nature and authority. By "translating" the symbols we will be able to understand what is being taught.

In the vision one like a son of man, who represents Christ, is clothed in a white robe and golden girdle. The long white robe symbolizes the priesthood, the golden girdle royal authority. His head and hair are white as wool. By taking the symbols which had been used to signify God's eternal wisdom and applying them to the "son of man," the author is teaching that the son of man is God. Jesus Christ is God. His eyes are like fire. Fire is a symbol of God's presence. (Remember the burning bush, the firebrand at the exodus, the tongues of fire at Pentecost.) Christ has "God's eyes" and so knows all things. His feet are bronze—sturdy and unchanging. His voice is like the ocean; it fills one with awe. In his right hand he holds seven stars. The Roman emperor was sometimes pictured as holding seven stars. To picture Christ holding seven stars is to say that Christ, not the emperor, holds ultimate authority. In his mouth is a sharp two-edged sword. Like a sword, God's word is powerful and effective.

Notice that in order to understand the symbols one must translate them into ideas rather than into visual pictures.

Through the symbols used the author is teaching his persecuted audience that the risen Christ is God and has power and authority far beyond the authority of the persecutor, the Roman emperor. The sword, representing God's word, will now go forth because John will be God's instrument in writing God's words to the churches.

Review Questions

1. Why does the author of apocalyptic literature write in code?
2. Why is it useful to be familiar with the symbols used in the book of Daniel in order to understand the book of Revelation?
3. What are some symbols which the two works share?
4. What is the author teaching by combining the figure of the one on the throne with the figure of the son of man?
5. What do the other symbols in the vision mean?
6. What is John teaching his audience through the vision?

Discussion Questions

1. What does this sentence mean: "In order to understand the symbols one must translate them into ideas rather than into visual pictures"?
2. Can you add your own ideas as to the meaning of the symbols? What are they?
3. In what way does the author say that Christ's authority is superior to the emperor's?
4. When you were little did you have any "codes"? Why?

ARTICLE 4

Letters to the Seven Churches

Question: "Is Jesus telling John to write letters to the church leaders? I don't understand what he means when he says to write to the 'angel' of the church (Rev 2:1). Also, what he is told to write isn't anything like Paul's letters." (Rev 1:4; 2:1; 2:8; 2:16; 2:27–29; 3:3; 3:21–22; 22:21 also discussed)

Remember that it is a convention of the form "apocalyptic literature" to say that the message to be delivered was received in a vision as a secret revelation. In this instance John claims that the message which he has for each church was given to him by the risen Christ.

In response to this statement students ask, "You mean Christ didn't really give John these messages? Then why is this book in the Bible?"

The book of Revelation is in the Bible not because the author claims to have had a vision. That is a convention in apocalyptic writing. The book is in the Bible because of the truth of its message. We will explore that truth as we come to understand what the author is saying.

So, within the context of the apocalyptic form, the risen Christ tells John to write to the "angel" or the "presiding spirit" of each of the seven churches. "The angel" is not an earthly church leader but a heavenly being. You might think of this angel as a "church guardian angel."

The questioner is right in noting that what follows isn't anything like Paul's letters. What follows takes the form of a prophecy more than of a letter. However, the seven messages are often referred to as letters to the seven churches because John first addresses the churches in a letter form.

231

Just before recounting the vision of Christ, John writes, "To the seven churches in the province of Asia: John wishes you grace and peace—from him who is and who was and who is to come . . ." (Rev 1:4).

We see here the conventional way of beginning a letter. The person/group to receive the letter is named, the sender is named, and a greeting is given. Next follows a doxology. (In Paul's letters a thanksgiving would have come next.)

As you will see, the convention of letter writing is utilized again as John concludes the book of Revelation. He ends with a conventional benediction: "The grace of the Lord Jesus be with you all. Amen" (Rev 22:21).

Even though the messages to the seven churches are framed by these conventions of letter writing, they do not each take the form of a letter. Rather, their form resembles prophetic literature.

Each message begins with a "commissioning," with Christ telling John to write. In prophetic literature such a commissioning might begin, "Go and tell my people this." Since John is in exile he pictures Christ telling him to write rather than to speak. However, those who receive the message are to understand that it comes from Christ.

That the message always comes from Christ is made clear because the speaker is described in images taken from the first vision. For instance, the speaker of the words to Ephesus is described as the one "who holds the seven stars in his right hand, who walks among the seven golden lampstands" (Rev 2:1). The speaker of the words to Smyrna is described as "The first and last, who died and came to life" (Rev 2:8). In each instance the reader knows the speaker is the Christ who appeared to John because the same images were used in the original vision.

Next the risen Christ is pictured as saying, "I know . . ." This "I know" introduces a section in each letter which functions as a prophetic oracle. An oracle traditionally began, "Yahweh says this." What followed would be God's message to the people. The message could be praise; it could be words of correction; it often called people to repentance and warned them of the ramifications

---

**THE FORM OF EACH OF THE "LETTERS"
TO THE SEVEN CHURCHES COMPARED
TO PROPHETIC WRITING**

- Each begins with a commissioning, with Christ telling John to write

- An "I know" section which functions as a prophetic oracle:
    - Praise
    - Correction
    - Call to repentance
    - Warning of ramifications of actions: punishment or salvation

- Conclusion: A promise of salvation and a command to listen

---

of their actions. Ramifications included a threat of God's judgment, but also a reminder of God's saving power.

In the messages to the seven churches these same elements occur. All but the church at Laodicea receive some praise. All but the churches at Smyrna and Philadelphia receive some rebuke. Those who are censured are also threatened. For instance, to the church at Pergamum Christ says, "Repent then! If not, I will come to you soon and war against them with the sword of my mouth" (Rev 2:16). To the church at Sardis Christ says, "Remember then what you received and heard; keep that, and repent. If you will not awake, I will come like a thief, and you will not know at what hour I will come upon you" (Rev 3:3).

Each of the seven messages ends with a promise of salvation and a command to listen. For instance, to the church at Thyatira Christ says, "To everyone who conquers and continues to do my works to the end, I will give authority over the nations . . . even as I also received authority from my Father; to the one who conquers I will also give the morning star. Let anyone who has an ear listen to what the Spirit is saying to the churches" (Rev 2:27–29 NRSV). To the church at Laodicea Christ says, "To the one who conquers, I will give a place with me on my throne, just as I myself conquered and sat down with my Father on his throne. Let anyone who has an ear listen to what the Spirit is saying to the churches" (Rev 3: 21–22 NRSV).

It is helpful to remember these traditional functions of prophetic oracles as you read the "letters" to the churches because it will enable you to get the general idea of a passage even if you don't get the precise meaning. Some censures are so cryptic that we do not know exactly who is being criticized and why. Some promises are expressed in images which are not familiar to us. However, without having the precise knowledge of the original audience we can still glean the general intent of the author.

In fact, the original audience may, to some extent, have shared our inability to understand every reference precisely. The seven churches addressed are seven communities located sequentially on one main road. As the book of Revelation was read in each community, a local church may have precisely understood those messages addressed specifically to that church but only generally those messages addressed to neighboring churches.

The "letters" never did exist as independent letters sent just to the one community as Paul's letters did. Rather, these "letters" were always part of a larger whole, the book of Revelation.

We, as did the original audience of the book of Revelation, can hear in these "letters" the prophetic mode: God speaking to his people through inspired human beings in order to call us to repentance and to promise salvation to those who remain faithful. This message of warning and hope is one which every generation needs to hear.

Review Questions

1. Why is the book of Revelation in the Bible?
2. What is the "angel" of the church?
3. Name four conventions of letter writing which John observes.
4. Do the individual "letters" take the form of a letter? What form do they take?

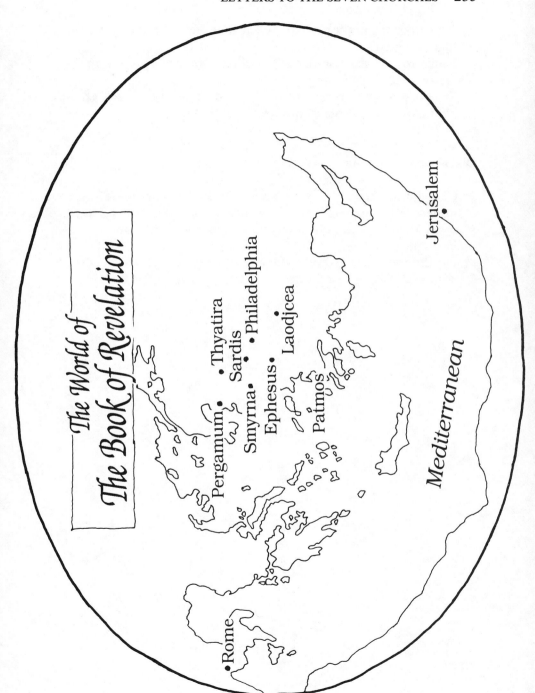

The World of
The Book of Revelation

Pergamum
Thyatira
Sardis
Smyrna
Philadelphia
Ephesus
Laodicea
Patmos
Rome
Jerusalem
Mediterranean

5. How does the author make it clear that the one giving the message is Christ?
6. Name four characteristics of prophecy which are present in the "letters" to the churches.
7. Why is it helpful to remember the traditional functions of prophetic oracles as you read the letters? Explain.

Discussion Questions

1. Can you understand the censures given to the churches? Do you understand the promises of reward? If you do not understand every detail, does that mean you miss the point completely? Explain.
2. Do the messages given to the churches have any relevance in your life? Why or why not?

ARTICLE 5

Moral Dilemmas and Cultural Assimilation

Question: "Who are the Nicolaitans? Why is the church in Ephesus commended for 'hating' their works?" (Rev 2:8; Rev 2:14; 2:15; 13:17; 14:9–10; Num 25:1–2 also discussed)

The Nicolaitans are mentioned in two of the "letters" to the churches. In the message to Ephesus we read, "Yet this you have, you hate the works of the Nicolaitans, which I also hate" (Rev 2:6). Again in the message to Pergamum we read, "So you also have some who hold the teaching of the Nicolaitans. Repent them . . ." (Rev 2:15). We don't know the exact identity of the Nicolaitans, but by looking at the context within which they are criticized we may be able to learn a little about them as well as a little about the moral dilemmas faced by Christians who lived in the Roman empire.

In the message to Pergamum the teachings of the Nicolaitans are mentioned along with the teachings of Balaam, "who taught Balak to put a stumbling block before the sons of Israel, that they might eat food sacrificed to idols and practice immorality" (Rev 2:14).

Balaam and Balak are people who appear in the book of Numbers. Balak was the king of Moab. He was afraid that the Israelites would defeat him, so he sent for Balaam to curse the Israelites (see Num 22–24). Evidently on Balaam's advice, Balak encouraged the sons of Israel to intermarry with the Moabite women and to join in worship to the Moabite gods. Numbers recounts, "While Israel dwelt in Shittim the people began to play the harlot with the daughters of Moab. These invited the people to the sacrifice of their gods, and the people ate, and bowed down to their gods" (Num 25:1–2).

237

Balak and Balaam are held up as examples of bad advisors who tempt you to make concessions to other cultures who have other gods. Perhaps the Nicolaitans were like Balak and Balaam, advising people that it is all right to "eat food sacrificed to idols" (Rev 2:14).

You may remember that Paul addressed the question of whether or not it was all right for Christians to eat food sacrificed to idols (see 1 Cor 8–10). Paul's judgment was that it was all right as long as one didn't scandalize a person of weak conscience who would misunderstand such an action. Paul reasoned that since no other gods exist, food isn't actually offered to other gods. A Christian knows this and is free to eat such meat, but love would demand that such freedom not be exercised at the cost of misleading and harming another person.

The author of the book of Revelation would have disagreed with Paul's reasoning. His audience was confronted with a number of situations that demanded a similar judgment call.

Since the time of Augustus (d. 14 A.D.) Roman emperors had been venerated in the same ways in which Roman gods were venerated.

Even if there were no persecution against those who did not participate in emperor worship, a Christian might well be motivated to "go along." If he did not he would be excluded not only from civic celebrations and games but from everyday business and social occasions. Should a Christian never participate in a business deal because it would be sealed with an oath to the emperor or to a pagan god? Should a Christian never go to a dinner party because a toast might be offered to the emperor or a pagan god? Just how much must a Christian withdraw?

Because the emperor controlled taxation, legal decisions, etc., emperor worship might be understood as political maneuvering rather than as idolatry by a Christian who knew perfectly well that the emperor was no god. Perhaps if the emperor were flattered and pleased he would grant a favor. For a Christian, going along with emperor worship might be rationalized as a social concession rather than an act of idolatry.

The author of the book of Revelation would adamantly disagree with this line of thought. John considered any involvement with emperor worship idolatrous. This will be very clear later in Revelation when he presents beasts who represent both the Roman empire and local officials who curry favor from the emperor through emperor worship. The beast is responsible for the fact that "no one can buy or sell unless he has the mark, that is, the name of the beast or the number of its name" (Rev 13:17).

Later in Revelation an angel announces, "Those who worship the beast and its image, and receive a mark on their foreheads or on their hands, they will also drink the wine of God's wrath, poured unmixed into the cup of his anger, and they will be tormented with fire and sulphur in the presence of the holy angels and in the presence of the Lamb" (Rev 14:9–14 NRSV).

For the author of the book of Revelation there is no compromise. One must not make concessions to emperor worship for business or social reasons. To do so is to choose "the beast" over "the lamb," to choose idolatry over Christianity. The author of Revelation hates the works of the Nicolaitans because they evidently advised people to make social and business concessions to emperor worship, advice which the author of the book of Revelation considers tantamount to turning people over to Satan.

Review Questions

1. Who is Balak? What bad advice did he receive from Balaam?
2. Who in Pergamum might be giving similar bad advice?
3. What advice did Paul give on eating food sacrificed to idols?
4. Would John have agreed with Paul's advice?
5. Why, even if there were no persecution, might a Christian be motivated to "go along" with "emperor worship"?
6. In John's eyes what does making concessions amount to?

7. What might be John's reason for hating the works of the Nicolaitans?

Discussion Questions

1. Do you think going along with the culture is contradictory to Christianity in our culture? How might it be?
2. If you were listening to Paul and John discuss the issue of eating food sacrificed to idols, with which would you agree? Why?
3. Could Paul and John both be right? Under what circumstances?

ARTICLE 6

The Martyrs and the Second Death

Question: "What is the second death?" (Rev 2:11; Rev 6:9–11; 7:9–17; 12:7–11; 14:1–5; 15:2–4; 19:9; 20:4–6; 20:13–14; 21:7–8 also discussed)

When John writes, "Whoever conquers will not be hurt by the second death" (Rev 2:11), he is assuring the church at Smyrna of eternal life.

The meaning of the phrase "second death" is clear in later passages. In chapter 20 you will read a highly symbolic description of judgment. All the dead come before the great white throne to be judged. "And the sea gave up the dead in it, Death and Hades gave up the dead in them, and all were judged by what they had done. Then Death and Hades were thrown into the lake of fire. This is the second death, the lake of fire; and if anyone's name was not found written in the book of life, he was thrown into the lake of fire" (Rev 20:13–14).

The second death is the death at judgment time, the death that is the opposite of that eternal life with Christ which is promised to those who remain faithful.

The same meaning is evident in chapter 21 when Christ is pictured as saying, "Those who conquer will inherit these things, and I will be their God and they shall be my children. But for the cowardly, the faithless, the polluted, the murderers, the fornicators, the sorcerers, the idolaters, and all liars, their place will be in the lake that burns with fire and sulphur, which is the second death" (Rev 21:7–8 NRSV).

A belief in the resurrection, that Christ rose from the dead and that those who remain faithful to Christ will join him in resurrec-

241

SOME PASSAGES IN THE BOOK OF REVELATION
ABOUT THE FATE OF THE MARTYRS

6:9–11	14:13
7:9–17	15:2–4
12:7–11	19:9
14:1–5	20:4–6
	20:12

---

tion, is always core to Christianity. However, it obviously receives a great deal of emphasis when the church faces persecution because it is this belief that makes martyrdom worthwhile. If life on earth is all there is, to choose martyrdom is ridiculous. Why give up the only life you have? But if life on earth is simply a preface to eternal life, everything is reversed. To choose life on earth rather than fidelity is to choose death, the second death. To choose death is to choose life.

The emphasis on life after death pervades the book of Revelation. In addition to a constant warning that the second death awaits those who are unfaithful, there is also a recurring picture of the fate of those who choose death on earth, thereby avoiding the second death. The reward received by the martyrs is life with the Lamb.

In chapter 6 we read, ". . . I saw under the altar the souls of those who had been slain for the word of God and for the witness they had borne; they cried out with a loud voice, 'O Sovereign Lord, holy and true, how long before thou wilt judge and avenge our blood on those who dwell upon the earth?' Then they were each given a white robe and told to rest a little longer, until the number of their fellow servants and their brethren should be complete, who were to be killed as they themselves had been" (Rev 6:9–11).

This passage causes many people problems because they see it as the martyrs calling for vengeance rather than as the martyrs being justified.

Imagine that you were living during the middle of a time of persecution. Good people are being killed. Evil people are thriving.

You have no idea when this will end. What is the use of remaining faithful? What is accomplished by dying? Where is God? Why doesn't God prevent such tragedies?

The question placed in the mouth of the martyrs is the question on the mind of John's audience. "How long, O Lord!" What good have the martyrs done? Nothing has changed. Maybe they didn't make the right choice after all. When will good triumph over evil?

John is assuring his audience that the martyrs did make the right choice, and that his audience would do better to make the same choice rather than turn away from Christ. The martyrs already are dressed in white. They are saved. True, the persecution is not yet over, but that does not mean that God has lost control of the course of human history. It may be that more people will die but they too will be saved. God's allowing this persecution to occur does not mean that the faithful are lost or that God has absented himself or lost power.

This preoccupation with the destiny of the martyrs continues throughout the book of Revelation (see Rev 7:9–17; 12:7–11; 14:1–5; 15:2–4; 19:9; 20:4–6; 20:12). As John constantly pictures the martyrs dressed in white in the presence of the Lamb in the heavenly court, he emphasizes for his audience the right choice which the martyrs have made.

If John's audience makes the same choice, they will help good triumph over evil. "Now the salvation and the power and the kingdom of our God and the authority of his Christ have come, for the accuser of our brethren has been thrown down, who accuses them day and night before our God. And they have conquered him by the blood of the Lamb and by the word of their testimony, for they loved not their lives even unto death" (Rev 12:10–11).

John wants his audience to know that martyrdom is preferable to infidelity. Evil does not triumph when martyrs die. In fact, martyrs defeat evil by choosing death. Those who have died live. They have nothing to fear in life after death, nothing to fear in judgment. The martyrs need not fear the second death.

Review Questions

1. What is the second death?
2. Why is the belief in the resurrection so extremely important in a church facing persecution?
3. What two important teachings, emphasized in the book of Revelation, depend on a belief in the resurrection?
4. Why does the picture of the martyrs in Revelation 6:9–11 cause some people a problem?
5. What is John teaching through this picture?
6. What does John want his audience to know?

Discussion Questions

1. Do you believe in life after death? Do you have any personal experience that has made the fact of life after death a matter of sure knowledge rather than a matter of faith?
2. How can this statement be true: "Because of the resurrection, to choose life is to choose death, to choose death is to choose life"?
3. If a belief in the resurrection really sunk in, do you think it would change your attitudes about life on earth? Your choices? Explain.

ARTICLE 7

Christ: Just Judge and Gentle Friend

Question: "The author of the book of Revelation makes Christ sound mean and vengeful. Whatever happened to Christ's love?" (Rev 2:20–23; Rev 3:20; 7:15–17 also discussed)

The passage which triggered this question appears in the "letter" to the church at Thyatira. Christ is pictured as saying, "I have this against you, that you tolerate the woman Jezebel, who calls herself a prophetess and is teaching and beguiling my servants to practice immorality and to eat food sacrificed to idols. I gave her time to repent of her immorality. Behold I will throw her on a sickbed, and those who commit adultery with her I will throw into great tribulation, unless they repent of her doings, and I will strike her children dead" (Rev 2:20–22).

In order to respond to the question we will first talk about the meaning of this particular passage. Then we will discuss the "punishing tone" in the book of Revelation.

Evidently a woman "prophetess" in Thyatira is teaching people to behave in much the same way that we read about in the letter to Pergamum. John once again uses an Old Testament type to refer to the woman. As we saw, in the letter to Pergamum he compared the advisor to the Old Testament character Balaam. Here he compares the "prophetess" to Jezebel.

Jezebel was the wife of King Ahab. She worshiped the god Baal and convinced her husband to worship Baal too (see 1 Kgs 16:31). So Jezebel is the "type" of a person who commits idolatry. To involve oneself in emperor worship was also to commit idolatry.

When John says that those who commit adultery with this Jezebel will receive great tribulation, he is using the word "adultery" as

245

SOME PASSAGES IN THE BOOK OF REVELATION
IN WHICH SEXUAL IMMORALITY (ADULTERY)
IS A SYMBOL FOR IDOLATRY

14:8	18:3
17:2	18:9
17:4	19:2

a metaphor for idolatry. He is saying that those who turn away from Christ will bring great tribulation upon themselves.

When John says that the children of this union will be struck dead, he is not talking about biological children but about those who adopt the beliefs of "Jezebel." Her followers are called her children.

You will understand the book of Revelation much better if you are able to interpret such symbolic language. The author of the book of Revelation consistently uses sexual immorality as a metaphor for idolatry (see 14:8; 17:2; 17:4; 18:3; 18:9; 19:2). So when you read of a great harlot you are reading of a person or nation who has committed idolatry. When you read that kings have committed fornication with her, you are being told that the kings were led into idolatry and failed to be faithful to Christ.

While this explanation somewhat softens the "mean and vengeful" tone of the passage in question, it remains true that terrible punishment and terrible sufferings are prevalent in the book of Revelation. To understand why this is true, we need to understand how these words would fall on the ears of the intended audience.

As you know, the audience is already familiar with suffering at the hands of the persecutors. It is to these innocent sufferers that John is writing. John's audience longs to be free of this suffering, but this can only be accomplished if their persecutors are somehow defeated.

So when John's audience reads about the punishments which

will be received, they do not fear that these punishments are meant for them. Rather they understand that this is what is in store for "the other guy," the "bad guy." It is as if a terrorist held an innocent person hostage. Both heard a voice say, "Evil will be punished. The good will be saved." Those words might strike fear into the heart of the terrorist but they would sound wonderful to the innocent hostage. The words would be a promise that suffering would soon end and that everything would turn out all right in the end.

While no one can deny the horror and gore in the imagery of the book of Revelation, it is also true that the passages offering hope are full of beauty and tenderness. For example, those who have survived the trial are promised, "He who sits upon the throne will shelter them with his presence. They will hunger no more, neither thirst any more; the sun shall not strike them, nor any scorching heat. For the Lamb in the midst of the throne will be their shepherd, and he will guide them to springs of living water; and God will wipe away every tear from their eyes" (Rev 7:15–17).

As you read the book of Revelation try to remember that, for the audience, the tribulations pictured are not possible future events but painful present events. The promise is not that these horrors might occur but that these horrors will end. Evil has no real grip. It will be defeated. Christ is not pictured as mean and vengeful in the book of Revelation. On the contrary, Christ is pictured as the just judge who will punish evil and reward good. For the good, Christ is pictured as a gentle friend. "Listen, I am standing at the door knocking; if you hear my voice and open the door, I will come in to you and eat with you, and you with me" (Rev 3:20 NRSV).

Review Questions

1. Who was Jezebel? What did she do?
2. What does John mean by "adultery"?
3. Who are "Jezebel's children"?
4. Why would the primary audience of the book of Revelation not find the threatened punishments frightening?
5. Is Christ pictured as mean and vengeful in the book of Revelation? Explain.

Discussion Questions

1. Have you ever been the victim of crime? Imagine that you have been. Would it be good or bad news to know that the criminal would be defeated?
2. Do you think adultery is a good metaphor for idolatry? Why or why not?
3. Did you think that Christ is pictured as being harsh in the book of Revelation? Why or why not?

ARTICLE 8

The Setting: The Heavenly Court

Question: "What are these four creatures in the room with the throne? This is a very strange scene." (Rev 4:6–8; Rev 1:9–20; 4:1–11; 8:2–5; 12:1–6; 14:1–15:41; 19:1–10; 21:1–18; Is 6:1–3; Ez 1:5, 10 also discussed)

For John's audience the vision of heaven's throne room would not have seemed as strange as it does to us, because the imagery which John uses was traditional imagery. In order to better understand why the images would have been familiar to the original audience we will look at two Old Testament passages which John has appropriated and adapted.

In the book of Isaiah we read, "I saw the Lord sitting upon a throne, high and lifted up; and his train filled the temple. Above him stood the seraphim; each had six wings: with two he covered his face, and with two he covered his feet, and with two he flew. And one called to another and said, 'Holy, holy, holy is the Lord of hosts; the whole earth is full of his glory' " (Is 6:1–3).

From this account John has adapted the basic setting—God's throne room—and the six winged attendants singing "Holy, holy, holy."

Ezekiel also has a description of the heavenly courtroom. In the throne room the prophet saw ". . . the likeness of four living creatures. And this was their appearance: they had the form of men but each had four faces, and each of them had four wings. . . . As for the likeness of their faces, each had the face of a man in front; the four had the face of a lion on the right side, the four had the face of an ox on the left side, and the four had the face of an eagle at the back . . ." (Ez 1:5, 10).

As you can see, John uses the same symbols of an ox, a lion, a man and an eagle, but he describes each creature as having one of these faces.

So John's audience, to some extent, was dealing with a familiar scene. However, they too would have had to ask, "What do the symbols in the scene mean?"

As you read the book of Revelation, remember to "translate" the symbols into ideas rather than visual pictures. The author is teaching the audience something he wants them to know.

The traditional symbols of ox, lion, man and eagle represent all that is beautiful and powerful in the created order. These creatures recognize their creator. "And whenever the living creatures give glory and honor and thanks to him who is seated on the throne, who lives for ever and ever, the twenty-four elders fall down before him who is seated on the throne and worship him who lives for ever and ever" (Rev 4:9–10).

The twenty-four elders are wearing white and crowned in gold. What do they represent? Some commentators suggest that they represent the twelve tribes of Israel and the twelve apostles. The church triumphant is seated in God's throne room. Other commentators suggest that the image is taken from astrology, that the twenty-four elders represent the twenty-four stars which the Babylonians referred to as "judges of the All."

If Babylonian astrology as well as the Old Testament is the source for some of John's imagery, three of the four beasts may be related to constellations which represent basic elements of the cosmos: the ox, Tarsus, represents earth; the lion, Leo, represents fire; and the man, Scorpio, represents water. The fourth creature, the eagle, would represent air.

Notice that without knowing about the Babylonian signs of the zodiac we said that the creatures represented all that is beautiful and powerful in creation. The more specific attribution to earth, air, fire, and water, the four basic elements of that creation, does not change our conclusion. Either way the beasts represent the created order.

As we said when discussing the promises of salvation made to the seven churches, it may be that you will not know the precise reference of an image but you will still be able to understand the general intent of the author. So do not demand a precise explanation for every image but let yourself get the overall impression and make whatever associations the images evoke for you. Otherwise you will get too bogged down in detail.

This vision of the throne room is the second heavenly vision we have had. We know the two visions are connected because the same voice is speaking. In the first vision John says, "I heard behind me a loud voice like a trumpet saying . . ." (Rev 1:10). The voice turned out to be the voice of the risen Christ. In this second vision John says, "And the first voice which I had heard speaking to me like a trumpet said . . ." (Rev 4:1).

As you continue to read the book of Revelation you will notice that the scene of the heavenly court recurs. In fact the setting for the book of Revelation becomes the heavenly court, and all the action and events proceed from there.

We have already seen that the sending of the seven letters proceeds from the first vision (Rev 1:9–20). The opening of the seven seals will proceed from this second vision (Rev 4:1–11). The blowing of the seven trumpets will proceed from the third vision (Rev 8:2–5). The battle between the devil and the woman will proceed from the fourth vision (Rev 12:1–6). The pouring of the seven bowls will proceed from the fifth vision (Rev 14:1–15:4). The word which goes forth to fight the final battles will proceed from the sixth vision (Rev 19:1–10). The final vision (Rev 21:1–8) will reveal the final victory of good over evil.

By making the heavenly court the setting for the book of Revelation John is saying that events are not out of God's hands, as they may appear to be to those who are suffering. All that exists and all that occurs is subject to Christ on his heavenly throne. That is why the twenty-four elders worship Christ saying, "Worthy art thou, our Lord and God, to receive glory and honor and power, for thou didst create all things and by thy will they existed and were created" (Rev 4:11).

Review Questions

1. Why would John's imagery have been familiar to his audience?
2. What did John appropriate from Isaiah?

BOOK OF REVELATION

Setting—Heavenly court.

Action, Events—The action and events proceed from the heavenly court.

Visions of the Heavenly Court:

1:9–20   The vision which begins here precipitates the sending of the seven letters.

4:1–11   The vision which begins here precipitates the opening of the seven seals.

8:2–5   The vision which begins here precipitates the blowing of the seven trumpets.

12:1–6   The vision which begins here precipitates the battle between the devil and the woman.

14:1–15:4   The vision which begins here precipitates the pouring out of the seven bowls.

19:1–10   In this vision the Word goes forth to fight the final battles.

21:1–8   This vision reveals the final victory of good over evil.

Conclusion: God has not lost control of events. Good will conquer evil.

3. What did John appropriate from Ezekiel?
4. What do the four creatures represent?
5. What do the twenty-four elders represent?
6. What source other than the Old Testament might John have used for his imagery?
7. What is the setting for the book of Revelation?
8. What is John teaching by making this the setting for the book of Revelation?

Discussion Questions

1. Do the four creatures or the twenty-four elders represent anything in your mind which we did not mention? What?
2. Have you ever felt that events were out of God's control? Explain.

ARTICLE 9

Why "Worthy" To Open the Seal?

Question: "Why is there such an emphasis on someone being 'worthy' to open the seal? Why couldn't anyone open it?" (Rev 5:2–5; Rev 5:6; 5:9–10; Gen 49:10; Is 5:3; 7:12; Ex 12 also discussed)

In apocalyptic literature a sealed scroll has a special significance. When we understand this significance we will understand why only Christ could open the scroll.

You may remember that in Article 2, when we were discussing the conventions of apocalyptic literature, we said that the revelation which is received is to be placed in a sealed book and read only at the end times.

So when a sealed scroll is present in the heavenly throne room we know that the scroll contains God's plan, God's revelation. To open the seal means that the end time is present; otherwise the seal would not be open.

So the question "Who is worthy to open the seal?" means, "Who is able to reveal God's plan and to initiate the events which will bring God's plan to fulfillment?"

The author of the book of Revelation is teaching his audience that only Jesus Christ can fulfill this role. Jesus is the revelation of the Father and the only one who has the power to bring God's plan for the human race to fulfillment.

The one who is worthy to open the seals is described by one of the elders as "the lion of the tribe of Judah" and "the root of David." Each of these titles is a messianic title, a title used to refer to the person whom God would send to save his people. The term "the lion from the tribe of Judah" refers to a passage in the book of

254

Genesis in which Jacob, the father of the twelve tribes of Israel, is telling each of his sons what will happen to them. Jacob describes Judah as a "lion" whose "hand shall be on the neck of your enemies." Jacob says, "The scepter shall not depart from Judah nor the ruler's staff from between his feet, until he comes to whom it belongs, and to him shall be the obedience of the peoples" (Gen 49:10).

The expected messiah is called "the root of David" because King David was the image of the kind of king who would save them. King David saved the Israelites from the Philistines and united the twelve tribes into one nation. He was the greatest king the Israelites had ever had.

While the elder uses two "great and glorious king" messiah images to refer to the one worthy to open the seal, John uses a "suffering servant" messiah image to refer to Christ. "And between the throne and the four living creatures and among the elders, I saw a Lamb standing, as though it had been slain, with seven horns and with seven eyes, which are the seven spirits of God sent out into all the earth" (Rev 5:6).

The image of Jesus as the slain Lamb refers to the slain passover lamb. During the time when Moses was trying to lead the Israelites out of Egypt and Pharaoh was refusing to let them go, a number of plagues occurred. The final plague was that "the angel of death" passed over and killed the Egyptian first-born sons (see Ex 12). Moses told the people to kill a lamb and put the blood of the lamb on the lintel so the angel of death would pass over their homes. The passover celebration, with its slain lamb, commemorates God's having saved the Israelites. It was at the passover meal that Jesus initiated the eucharist. Jesus' blood thus became the blood of the lamb that saves. However, Jesus' blood saves one from slavery to sin, not slavery to the Egyptians, and for eternal life, not merely for life on earth.

Jesus is also called the "Lamb" because this is the image which Isaiah used when he described the nation, Israel, whose suffering would result in new life for others. Isaiah says, "He (i.e. the nation personified) was oppressed, and he was afflicted, yet he opened not his mouth; like a lamb that is led to the slaughter, and like a sheep that before its shearers is dumb, so he opened not his mouth . . . yet

---

IMAGES OF CHRIST

- Great and Glorious King Images
  —The lion of the tribe of Judah
  —The root of David

- Suffering Servant Image
  —A lamb standing, as though it had been slain

---

he bore the sin of many, and made intercession for the transgressors" (Is 53:7, 12). Jesus became the Lamb who was slain, taking on the sins of many.

As the Lamb who was slain takes the scroll, the four creatures and the twenty-four elders sing a song which explains why Christ is the one who is "worthy" to open the scroll. "Worthy art thou to take the scroll and to open its seals, for thou wast slain, and by thy blood didst ransom men for God from every tribe and tongue and people and nation, and hast made them a kingdom and priests to our God, and they shall reign on earth" (Rev 5:9–10).

The reason the seals can be opened, the reason the end time is here and God's plan can be revealed, is that Christ has already defeated evil. The slain Lamb with seven horns (seven symbolizes perfection or completeness; horns symbolize power and authority) is already victorious and enthroned in heaven. The slain Lamb has already brought about universal salvation and has redeemed the human race into a kingdom of priests for God. Christ has accomplished those events which make it possible for God's plan to be revealed and for salvation history to come to completion. Because only Christ could and did accomplish redemption, only Christ is worthy to open the seal.

Review Questions

1. What is the meaning of opening a sealed scroll in apocalyptic literature?

2. Why can only Jesus open the scroll?
3. What two "great and glorious king" images are used to refer to Jesus?
4. What "suffering servant" image is used?
5. Name two reasons why Jesus is called "the Lamb of God."
6. Why can the seals be opened now?

Discussion Questions

1. When you think of Christ, do you think of a glorious king or a suffering servant? Are these two ideas compatible? Explain.
2. What does this sentence from the mass mean: "Behold the Lamb of God. Behold him who takes away the sin of the world"?
3. Can you think of anyone else who might be worthy to open the seals? Why or why not?

ARTICLE 10

The Opening of the Seven Seals

Question: "Why are the riders given permission to 'take peace from the earth' (Rev 6:4) and to kill a fourth of the earth (Rev 6:8)? It frightens me to think that all this is going to happen." (Rev 6:5–17; 9:13–21 also discussed)

Before we answer the question I want to comment on the statement, "It frightens me to think that all this is going to happen."

The person who made this comment has forgotten what we said about the function of apocalyptic literature, a function it shares with prophecy. Apocalyptic literature is speaking about the immediate future of the contemporary audience, not the future of an audience that lives two thousand years later. We can and should apply what the author tells his contemporaries to our own lives. But first we must understand the original message.

The riders to which the questioner refers are two of the four horsemen of the book of Revelation. The first horseman, on a white horse and with a bow and crown, would have reminded John's audience of the Parthians, Rome's greatest rival to the east. John apparently hoped that the Parthians would be the ones to defeat Rome (see Rev 9:13–21).

The second horseman, on a red horse and carrying a sword, represents war. The third horseman, carrying a scale, represents famine. (A denarius should purchase much more than a quart of wheat or three quarts of barley, life's staples.)

The fourth horseman, named Death, obviously represents the death that will come to many on earth.

Why would God allow death and suffering, especially of the innocent? When will God step in and save his people? This second

---

THE SEVEN SEALS SEQUENCE

First Seal: First horseman: white horse, bow and crown

Second Seal: Second horseman: red horse, sword

Third Seal: Third horseman: carrying scale

Fourth Seal: Fourth horseman: named death

Fifth Seal: Martyrs under altar

Sixth Seal: Earthquake

Two Inserted Visions
- 144,000 sealed
- Salvation of the multitude

Seventh Seal: Half hour silence and introduction of the seven trumpet sequence

---

question is the very question which, as we already noted, the martyrs ask after the fifth seal is opened. "O Sovereign Lord, holy and true, how long before thou wilt judge and avenge our blood on those who dwell upon the earth?" (Rev 6:10).

Next the sixth seal is opened, followed by an earthquake. "Vengeance" has begun. "Then the kings of the earth and the great men and the generals and the rich and the strong, and every one, slave and free, hid in the caves and among the rocks of the mountains and rocks" (Rev 6:15).

We will talk about "who can stand before it" in our next article. Notice that the ones who are doing the persecuting—the kings, great men, generals, the rich and strong—are the ones first mentioned as those who try to hide from the earthquake. However, an earthquake affects everyone, slave and free. The earthquake is understood as an expression of the Lamb's wrath.

The earthquake occurs at the opening of the sixth seal. Two scenes are inserted before the opening of the seventh seal which results in a half-hour of silence in heaven and the introduction of the seven trumpets.

With this quick overview of the seven seals in mind, how can we respond to the question, "Why are the riders given permission to harm the earth?"

Actually, the book of Revelation doesn't answer that question. To say that "Death has been given power over a fourth of the earth" is a picturesque way of describing experience. The people may not know *why* evil is prevailing but they do know *that* evil is prevailing. The questions which the book of Revelation addresses are the martyrs' question "How long, O Lord?" and the earthquake victims' question "Who can stand against it?"

Through the description of the opening of the seven seals the author is telling his audience that the persecution of the faithful is not yet over, but it will not last much longer. The martyrs already in heaven are told "to rest a little longer, until the number of their fellow servants and their brethren should be complete, who were to be killed as they themselves had been" (Rev 6:11).

In addition the author is assuring his audience that their persecutors will be judged. The persecutors do have something to fear from the wrath of the Lamb.

Finally the author assures his audience that the faithful who have already died are already saved. The faithful who will die will be saved. From the view of the heavenly court, it is the persecutors and not the faithful who have something to fear.

Review Questions

1. What is the function of apocalyptic literature?
2. What do the four horsemen represent?
3. What happens when the other three seals are opened?
4. What two questions does the book of Revelation address?
5. Name three ideas which the author teaches through the opening of the seven seals.

Discussion Questions

1. Do you believe martyrs have a special place in heaven? Why or why not?
2. Do you believe the end for those who do evil is different than the end for those who do good? Why?
3. Is it simply revenge that makes you want the good to have a different end than the evil? Explain.

ARTICLE 11

One Hundred Forty-Four Thousand
and Other Symbolic Numbers

Question: "Why are there only one hundred forty-four thousand redeemed from the earth (Rev 7:4; 14:3)? That doesn't seem like very many." (Rev 1:12; 1:16; 7:1–8; 7:9–12; 7:14; 14:1–5 also discussed)

There are not *only* one hundred forty-four thousand redeemed from the earth. The person who asked this question has based it on the scene in Revelation 7:4 in which one hundred forty-four thousand are sealed as the servants of God, and on a scene in chapter 14. In chapter 14 a new song is being sung in heaven. "No one could learn that song except the hundred and forty-four thousand who had been redeemed from the earth. It is these who have not defiled themselves with women, for they are chaste; it is these who follow the Lamb wherever he goes; these have been redeemed from mankind as first fruits for God and the Lamb, and in their mouth no lie was found, for they are spotless" (Rev 14:3–5).

We can say that there are not *only* one hundred forty-four thousand redeemed for two reasons. First, numbers in the book of Revelation are used symbolically. Second, the one hundred forty-four thousand do not represent all of the redeemed, as is clear from the second inserted vision (Rev 7:9–12) in which a "huge crowd which no one could count" (Rev 7:9) stands before the throne and the Lamb. Each of these reasons needs further explanation.

Numbers in the book of Revelation are used symbolically. These symbolic numbers fall into two categories: numbers which are on the side of good and represent wholeness and completeness, and

262

NUMBERS WHICH SYMBOLIZE COMPLETENESS

4   The whole world

7   Used in basic structure of book and of sequences

12   Completeness (tribes, apostles)

24   Tribes plus apostles

---

numbers which are on the side of evil and represent lack of wholeness, lack of completeness.

We see two examples of the symbolic use of numbers in the first inserted vision (Rev 7:1–8), both of which represent completeness. The first is the use of the number "four." "After this I saw four angels standing at the four corners of the earth, holding back the four winds of the earth, that no wind might blow on earth or sea or against any tree" (Rev 7:1). "Four corners of the earth" means the whole earth. "Four winds" means all the wind. Remember that the creatures in the throne room who represent all of creation number four creatures. "Four" always represents completeness.

The second symbolic number is one hundred forty-four thousand, which is $12 \times 12 \times 1,000$. Twelve and one thousand both represent completeness. Twelve, of course, recalls the twelve tribes, specifically named in this passage, as well as the twelve apostles. One thousand would represent magnitude, fullness. So $12 \times 12 \times 1,000$ (144,000) could be taken to mean the whole church. (You may remember that $12 + 12$ is the number of elders in the heavenly court.)

Another number which represents completeness is seven. This number is the most frequently used. We have already seen that the heavenly throne room has seven lampstands (Rev 1:12) and that Christ holds seven stars in his right hand (Rev 1:16). The seven lampstands represent the seven churches to which the letters are sent. There are seven visions of the heavenly court, seven seals on the scroll, seven "blowing of the trumpets," and seven bowls to be poured. In each case seven represents completeness.

Even though one hundred forty-four thousand is not meant to be taken literally, it does seem to represent a chosen group among the saved rather than all the saved. While the first vision pictures one hundred forty-four thousand saved, the second pictures a "great multitude which no man could number, from every nation, from all tribes and peoples and tongues . . ." (Rev 7:9). What is the difference between the one hundred forty-four thousand and all the saved?

The one hundred forty-four thousand are pictured as those who have "the seal of the servants of God upon their foreheads" (Rev 7:3). In chapter 14 we learn that the seal is the Lamb's name and the Father's name on their foreheads (Rev 14:1). These one hundred forty-four thousand have not committed idolatry. (Remember that adultery is an image for idolatry.) ". . . it is these who follow the Lamb wherever he goes; these have been redeemed from mankind as first fruits for God and the Lamb . . ." (Rev 14:4).

Scholars suggest that the one hundred forty-four thousand have followed the Lamb even to a martyr's death, and for this they are "first fruits" and have a special reward. As you will eventually see, they are pictured as sharing the thousand year reign with Christ. The multitude are those who "have come out of the great tribulation; they have washed their robes and made them white in the blood of the Lamb" (Rev 7:14).

To have washed your robes in the blood of the Lamb is to have turned from sin (dirty robes) to Christ. Conversion would have had to have been followed by perseverance because those who were Christians faced persecution.

Not just one hundred forty-four thousand are redeemed from the earth. A huge multitude from every nation is redeemed from the earth. However, the martyrs are a special group in that they have had the privilege of following the Lamb even through martyrdom. These triumphant martyrs have a special place in heaven.

Review Questions

1. Give two reasons why we can see that not just one hundred forty-four thousand will be saved.

2. Into what two categories do symbolic numbers fall?
3. What does the number four mean? Give some examples of its use.
4. What does one hundred forty-four thousand mean?
5. What does seven mean? Give several examples of its use.
6. What is the difference between the one hundred forty-four thousand and the great multitude which is also saved?

Discussion Questions

1. Do you think many people are saved or only a few? Why?
2. Do we use numbers symbolically in our culture? Can you think of any examples?
3. Why was it particularly important to John's audience to know that martyrs were already in heaven?

ARTICLE 12

The Word: Both Sweet and Sour

Question: "What is this about the prophet eating a scroll? Why will it be sour in his stomach but sweet in his mouth?" (Rev 10:9–10; Rev 8:7–12; 10:11; Ex 7–10 also discussed)

The scene of the prophet eating the scroll is an inserted vision in the sequence of the blowing of the 7 trumpets just as the sealing of the 144,000 was an inserted vision in the sequence of the opening of the 7 seals. In each sequence 6 seals are open or trumpets blown, 2 inserted visions appear, and then the seventh seal is opened or trumpet blown.

The disasters pictured as the result of the blowing of the trumpets allude to the plagues which Egypt suffered at the time of the exodus (see Ex 7–10). As in the case of Pharaoh, the "plagues" do not result in repentance on the part of the people but in the hardening of hearts.

After the sixth trumpet we read the passage in question in which John is told to take a little open scroll from the angel. "He (the angel) said to me, 'Take it and eat; it will be bitter to your stomach, but sweet as honey in your mouth' " (Rev 10:9).

Once more the author has taken his imagery from Ezekiel. As Ezekiel describes his call he says, "And he (God) said to me, 'Son of man, eat what is offered to you; eat this scroll, and go, speak to the house of Israel.' So I opened my mouth, and he gave me the scroll to eat. And he said to me, 'Son of man, eat this scroll that I give you and fill your stomach with it.' Then I ate it; and it was in my mouth as sweet as honey" (Ez 3:1–3).

The scroll is sweet in the mouth because it is God's word. It is sour in the stomach because the message is a message of woe rather

---

SEVEN TRUMPETS SEQUENCE

First Trumpet: Hail, fire, and blood

Second Trumpet: Mountain of flame thrown into sea

Third Trumpet: Star falls into rivers and springs

Fourth Trumpet: Sun, moon, and stars lose one-third of light

Fifth Trumpet: Locusts let out of abyss

Sixth Trumpet: Four angels from banks of Euphrates released to kill one-third of humankind

Two Inserted Visions
- The prophet eats the scroll
- The two witnesses

Seventh Trumpet: The Lamb victorious on his throne

---

than one of joy. Notice that the scroll is a little, open scroll, not sealed as is conventional in apocalyptic literature. In symbolic language this is saying that the end is near. John is told, "You must again prophesy about many peoples and nations and tongues and kings" (Rev 10:11). The prophet fulfills this new commission to prophesy in chapters 12–22 of the book of Revelation.

The sweet yet sour role of prophets is perfectly evident in the second inserted scene, the scene of the two witnesses. There two witnesses are commissioned to prophesy for 1,260 days. However, when their time of prophecy is over they will be conquered, killed and left unburied while all those who have failed to respond will mistakenly celebrate victory. Finally the two witnesses will be brought back to life, to the horror of the "conquerors."

The message is clear. For God's faithful witnesses there will be

---

NUMBERS WHICH SYMBOLIZE INCOMPLETENESS

$\frac{1}{4}$ of earth
$\frac{1}{3}$ of earth
Any fraction
$3\frac{1}{2}$ years
42 months (same as $3\frac{1}{2}$ years)
1,260 days (same as $3\frac{1}{2}$ years)
666 the superlative evil

---

pain and suffering before final victory. However, final victory is inevitable so no one should lose faith.

In our last article we mentioned the symbolic use of numbers and that they fall into two categories, those on the side of good which represent wholeness and those on the side of evil which represent incompleteness. Numbers in this second category are prevalent as we read about the blowing of the seven trumpets. With the blowing of the trumpets one-third of the land, sea, creatures, ships, rivers, springs, sun, moon, and stars are destroyed. To a modern day reader one-third may sound like a huge number. However, in apocalyptic literature fractions are used to show incompleteness. To say that one-third of something is destroyed is to say that the destroying force is internally flawed and will never be victorious. The destroyer's power is a temporary power. However, the prophet is still warning of terrible suffering because this one-third of everything destroyed is an escalation over the sequence of the opening of the seals in which only one-fourth was destroyed.

Three and a half years, another fraction, represents the duration of a situation that must end. In the book of Revelation three and a half years is a symbolic number used to refer to the time of persecution before the end. The same number is used in the other canonical book of apocalyptic literature, the book of Daniel, in the words "a time (i.e. a year), two times, and half a time" (Dan 12:7).

In the inserted vision of the two witnesses the holy city will be trampled by the nations for forty-two months. Forty-two months is three and a half years. The witnesses will prophesy for 1,260 days. These 1,260 days are also three and a half years. In both instances three and a half years is a symbolic number referring to the time of suffering before the end victory.

In addition to fractions, the number six represents incompleteness. Six is one less than seven, and half of twelve, both of which represent completeness. As you continue to read you will see how six is used to denote the opposite of good.

God's word in the little open scroll is both sweet and sour in the mouth of the prophet, but also in the mouth of all who receive it, for while it promises ultimate victory, it also promises severe suffering before that victory will be achieved.

Review Questions

1. To what do the disasters which resulted from the blowing of the trumpets allude?
2. From whom does John get the image of eating a scroll?
3. Why is the scroll sweet in the mouth and sour in the stomach?
4. What is meant symbolically by saying that the scroll is little and open?
5. What is being taught through the vision of the two witnesses?
6. What symbolic meaning do fractions have?
7. What does three and a half years represent? Name two other ways to say three and a half years.
8. What does six represent?

Discussion Questions

1. Do you find God's word both sweet and sour? Explain.
2. Do you think suffering is easier to take if you know it will end? Why or why not?
3. Does John tell his audience how long their suffering will last? Explain.

ARTICLE 13

Images: Both Archetypal and Specific

Question: "Is the woman in the sky Mary?" (Rev 12:1–2; Rev 12:5–14 also discussed)

To equate the woman in the sky with Mary is to give an archetypal image too narrow a meaning. Christians, of course, would see one of the meanings in the image of the woman as a reference to Mary because the child whom the woman bears is the messiah (see Rev 12:5). However, the woman in the sky also has a less distinct and less static meaning.

An archetypal image is an image which originates in the subconscious and relates to something common to the human experience. Myths, that kind of imaginative literature which deals with our origins and our orientation in a moral universe, use archetypal images to explore mysteries which are really beyond our comprehension. Among those mysteries is the battle between good and evil which is the common experience of all human beings.

As you know, John's audience is deeply involved in that mystery. They have embraced good, having been washed in the blood of the Lamb at baptism, yet evil, in the garb of the Roman empire, continues to have great power in their lives. How can this be? What does this experience mean?

In his scene of the woman and the dragon John uses archetypal images, mythic symbols to explore this battle between good and evil.

The woman represents good. In addition, while she could definitely be seen to represent Mary, she can also be understood as representing the nation Israel, which gave birth to the messiah. Eventually, as we will see, she comes to represent the church. This

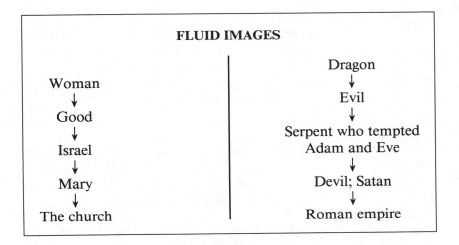

is evident as John says, "Then the dragon was angry with the woman, and went off to make war on the rest of her offspring, on those who keep the commandments of God and bear testimony to Jesus" (Rev 12:17).

In direct contrast to the woman, the dragon represents evil and the forces of evil. The dragon, too, is a fluid image and can legitimately be seen to have both mythic and specific meanings. Notice that originally the dragon is a huge beast in the sky whose tail sweeps down a third of the stars of heaven.

Later the dragon is specifically identified with the serpent who tempted Adam and Eve to eat the fruit of the tree of knowledge of good and evil. After the war in heaven in which the angel Michael defeats the dragon we read, "And the great dragon was thrown down, that ancient serpent, who is called the devil and Satan, the deceiver of the whole world—he was thrown down to earth, and his angels were thrown down with him" (Rev 12:9). Because the dragon has been cast out, victory has already been accomplished in heaven, but not on earth.

Next the dragon represents the Roman empire. The dragon is pictured as one who accuses the faithful. It is the Roman empire which accuses those followers of Christ who refuse to participate in emperor worship. "Now the salvation and the power and the kingdom of our God and the authority of his Christ have come, for the accuser of our brethren has been thrown down, who accused them day and night before our God. And they have conquered him by the blood of the Lamb and by the word of their testimony, for they loved not their lives even unto death. Rejoice then, O heaven and you that dwell therein! But woe to you, O earth and sea, for the devil has come down to you in great wrath, because he knows that his time is short" (Rev 12:10–12).

John is telling his audience that victory has already been accomplished through Christ. Those who have died martyrs' deaths already share in Christ's victory. However, those on earth still have to deal with evil for a short time before Christ's victory will be completely evident.

It is in the next section that the woman represents the church. God is protecting the church, "But the woman was given the two wings of the great eagle that she might fly from the serpent into the wilderness, to the place where she is to be nourished for a time, and times, and half a time" (Rev 12:14).

This is to say that the woman's time of trial, when she will continue to be pursued by the dragon will last three and a half years. As you already know, three and a half, because it is a fraction, represents incompleteness. Three and a half years is the length of time, a limited time, before the end time, the end of the church's present suffering.

You may notice that John's narrative operates much like a dream. In our dreams we use archetypal images to explore life's mysteries. The images can, at the same time, represent something common to the human race and something specific to our historical and personal situation. Our dream images are somewhat amorphous—images blend into each other; they change shape and meaning as the dream progresses.

Of course you do not control your dreams. They simply unfold. The more you can let the book of Revelation unfold in a similar manner, the more you will be able to experience as well as understand it.

The scene of the woman and the dragon is an example of a passage in which you need to let images work on your subconscious and evoke a number of meanings. The woman is Mary, but the woman is not just Mary. One cannot limit the meaning of an image to a single meaning if one hopes to understand the book of Revelation.

Review Questions

1. What is an archetypal image?
2. What is a myth? What is its function?
3. What mystery is being explored by John's audience?
4. Name four ideas/things which the woman represents.
5. Name three ideas/things which the dragon represents.
6. What is John teaching by saying that the woman's time of trial is three and a half years?
7. How might scenes in the book of Revelation be compared to dreams?

Discussion Questions

1. Is the battle between good and evil part of your experience? Explain.
2. What symbols would you use to represent good? To represent evil?
3. Do you remember your dreams? Are the images in your dreams fluid? Can you give any examples?
4. Why isn't John more specific in saying when the persecution will end?

ARTICLE 14

The Beasts from the Sea
and from the Earth

**Question: "Who are the beasts from the sea and from the earth?"
(Rev 13:1–18; Dan 7:4–7; Ex 15:11 also discussed)**

As was true with the dragon and the woman, the beast from the
sea represents both an archetypal image and a specific reference to
the historical situation.

As an archetypal image, the fact that the first beast comes from
the sea means that the beast represents primordial chaos and evil.
Notice that the beast has the authority of the dragon from the
previous scene (see Rev 13:5).

In describing the first beast John uses the imagery which appears
in the book of Daniel to describe not one but four beasts. "And four
great beasts came up out of the sea, different from one another. The
first was like a lion and had eagles' wings. . . . And behold, another
beast, a second one, like a bear . . . and lo another, like a leopard,
with four wings of a bird on its back; and the beast had four heads;
and behold a fourth beast, terrible and dreadful and exceedingly
strong . . . it had ten horns" (Dan 7:4, 5, 6, 7).

John's beast also has ten horns and a number of heads. It is like
a leopard with feet like a bear and a mouth like a lion (see
Rev 13:1–2).

In Daniel the four beasts represent four successive kings. In John
the beast from the sea represents the Roman empire. The individual heads of the beast represent individual emperors.

One of the heads of the beast "seemed to have a mortal wound,

274

but its mortal wound was healed . . ." (Rev 13:3). This is a reference to Nero Caesar. Nero committed suicide when he was still a young man. However, legends circulated that he was not dead but had joined the Parthians and would return with them to conquer Rome. The book of Revelation alludes to the idea that Nero is not dead (i.e. mortal wound now healed) but does not picture him as one who will save the people. Rather, Nero is linked with evil, with those who oppose God and will persecute God's people.

The second beast is also the Roman empire, but as its authority is wielded by local officials. "It (i.e. the second beast) used the authority of the first beast to promote its interests by making the whole world and all its inhabitants worship the first beast, whose mortal wound had been healed" (Rev 13:13). In an earlier article we discussed how local officials looking for political favors involved themselves and others in emperor worship.

John parodies the kind of "worship" given the beasts by describing it in such a way that it parallels the worship given to the Lamb. The mortal wound which healed on the head of the beast reminds one that the Lamb was once dead but now lives. The beast appears to receive universal acclamation on earth as the lamb receives universal acclamation in heaven. "In wonderment, the whole world followed after the beast. Men worshiped the dragon for giving his authority to the beast; they also worshiped the beast and said, 'Who can compare with the beast, or come forward to fight against it?' " (Rev 13:4).

At the time of the exodus, when the Israelites experienced God's saving power, they asked a similar question. "Who is like thee, O Lord, among the gods? Who is like thee, majestic in holiness, terrible in glorious deeds, doing wonders?" (Ex 15:11).

Because the dragon has already been defeated in the heavenly kingdom, John's audience knows who can come forward to fight the beast. They know that they themselves, as Christ's disciples, will eventually defeat the beast.

The parody of "worship" for the beast continues. The beast "forced all men, small and great, rich and poor, slave and free, to accept a stamped image on their right hand or their forehead" (Rev 13:16). This mark on the forehead clearly distinguishes the followers of the beast from the followers of the Lamb who have been

---

THE PARODY OF THE WORSHIP OF THE BEAST

- Nero might come and save us.

- "Who can compare with the beast?"

- Stamped image on right hand and forehead

- The Lamb lives and will save us.

- "Who is like thee, O Lord?"

- Baptism; 144,000 marked

- **Teaching through parody:**

- Emperors are not gods

- Those who challenge Christ are anti-Christs.

---

baptized, as well as from the 144,000 who have been marked with the Lamb's name and the name of the Father on their foreheads.

This parody in the description of the "worship" of the beast has two effects. First it criticizes the idea that the Roman empire and its emperors have a divine mandate to wield authority as they do, as well as the idea that the emperors are themselves divine. To treat the emperors as though they are divine is to become a worshiper of the beast.

In addition, the juxtaposition of the beast's worship to the Lamb's leads the reader to conclude that the Roman empire and those who wield authority in it are antichrists. They are the ones who challenge Christ's reign and persecute Christ's followers.

Who is the beast? The beast is Nero Caesar. When John says the number of the beast is 666, he is making a direct reference to Nero. Hebrew letters had quantitative value. The letters in Nero Caesar's name add up to 666.

However, the beast is also the Roman empire, primordial evil, and the antichrist. The number 666 also means "the greatest evil."

Six, as has already been explained, is a number on the side of evil. To repeat the 6 three times (completeness) is to make it "superlative": not just evil, not just more evil, but most evil. Only if we let the image remain fluid will we be able to glean all of its meanings.

Review Questions

1. As an archetypal image, what does the beast represent?
2. From what source does John appropriate imagery for the beast?
3. In an historical context, what does the beast represent? What do the heads on the beast represent?
4. To what legend about Nero does John refer?
5. What does the second beast represent?
6. How does John make a parody of the "worship" of the beast?
7. Name two effects of this parody.
8. Name two meanings of 666.

Discussion Questions

1. Did you think 666 was referring to a specific person to come in our future? Why or why not?
2. Do you think there are antichrist elements in our society? Have you had any contact with them? Explain.
3. Do you think people who "follow orders" are morally responsible for their actions? Explain.

ARTICLE 15

Good News: God's Judgment Is at Hand

Question: "John says that the first of the three angels (Rev 14:6–9) has 'an eternal gospel to proclaim' (Rev 14:6), but the message turns out to be 'Fear God' and everything that follows is blood and gore. This doesn't even sound Christian. How could this possibly give anyone hope?" (Rev 6:10; 14:7–12; 14:19–20; Jl 4:12–13 also discussed)

This question is similar to one addressed in relation to the opening of the fifth seal when the martyrs under the altar in heaven ask, "O Sovereign Lord, holy and true, how long before thou wilt judge and avenge our blood on those who dwell on the earth?" (Rev 6:10). In what way is the angels' news gospel, that is, good news?

The angels are announcing judgment. The idea of judgment is good news to innocent people who are suffering persecution from evil people.

The first angel says, "Fear God ("Honor God" in some translations) and give him glory, for the hour of his judgment has come; and worship him who made heaven and earth, the sea and the fountains of water" (Rev 14:7).

The second angel announces that Babylon has fallen. As we will see when we get to Article 17, Babylon stands for Rome. That Rome has fallen would certainly be good news for John's audience.

The third angel announces that anyone who has worshiped the beast will "drink the wine of God's wrath, poured unmixed into the cup of his anger, and he shall be tormented with fire and sulphur in the presence of the holy angels and in the presence of the Lamb. And the smoke of their torment goes up for ever and ever; and they have no rest, day or night, these worshipers of the beast and its image, and whoever receives the mark of its name" (Rev 14:10–11).

It is possible to read these lines and understand them as nothing but "blood and gore." It is also possible to hear them as comforting the faithful by suggesting that they will be pleased to know that their enemies will never stop suffering. Each of these interpretations misses the point. John is not promoting revenge but offering a motivation to remain faithful.

Remember that many in John's audience are questioning whether there isn't a middle ground. Wouldn't it be possible to be marked with the beast (i.e. use coins with the emperor's image on them? close a business deal with an oath to the emperor?) without actually worshiping the beast? Isn't there room for compromise? John's answer is "no." One must choose between the Lamb and the beast. To choose the Lamb is to choose eternal life. To choose the beast is to choose eternal death.

John explains that his motivation is to encourage people to fidelity when he says, "Here is a call for the endurance of the saints, those who keep the commandments of God and the faith of Jesus" (Rev 14:12).

John then goes on to use traditional imagery to describe the hour of judgment which had been announced by the first angel.

First a son of man seated on a cloud reaps the earth with a sickle. Scholars suggest that this "son of man" appears to be an angel rather than Jesus. The next angel who appears is called "another" angel, and this other angel gives directions to the angel holding the sickle.

The image of judgment being carried out as a reaping is found in the prophet Joel. When Joel describes the judgment of Judah's enemies he says, ". . . I will sit to judge all the nations round about. Put in the sickle, for the harvest is ripe. Go in, tread, for the wine press is full. The vats overflow, for their wickedness is great" (Jl 4:12–13).

In John's second image of judgment he uses Joel's image of a wine press to symbolize God's wrath. "So the angel swung his sickle on the earth and gathered the vintage of the earth, and threw it into the great wine press of the wrath of God; and the wine press was

---

THREE ANGELS AND TWO HARVESTS

1. *First Angel:* Herald of everlasting good news

2. *Second Angel:* Babylon has fallen

3. *Third Angel:* Those who worship the beast will suffer

1. *First Harvest Vision:* Son of man with sickle

2. *Second Harvest Vision:* Grapes gathered for wine press of God's wrath

---

trodden outside the city, and blood flowed from the wine press, as high as a horse's bridle, for one thousand six hundred stadia" (Rev 14:19–20). That blood flowed from the wine press suggests that this judgment would take place through a battle.

Scholars debate why the judgment seems to be in two steps: the reaping of the ripe harvest from all the earth and the gathering of the ripe grapes for the wine press. Is the first gathering a gathering of the just and the second the gathering of the wicked? Is the first the destruction of pagan nations and the second the destruction of the whole earth? Does the author simply use two images to describe the same idea so that there is no real distinction between them?

As we have seen, many of the sequences in the book of Revelation are not presenting new ideas but are presenting the same idea in a variety of images. Both "harvestings" are images of the good news which the first angel proclaimed, "Fear God and give him glory, for the hour of his judgment has come" (Rev 14:7).

Review Questions

1. In what way is the angel's news good news?
2. Is John promoting revenge? Explain.

3. Give some examples of being "marked with the beast" that might tempt John's audience.
4. What is John's motivation—that is, what is he trying to do?
5. From what source does John appropriate the images of the sickle and the wine press?
6. What might be meant by the two stages of judgment?

Discussion Questions

1. If you were to describe God's judging humankind, how would you describe it? What images would you use?
2. Do you think the ideas of God as merciful and God as judge are compatible? Explain.
3. Have you ever tried to help another person in terrible circumstances to persevere? What motivation could you offer such a person?

ARTICLE 16

The Pouring of the Seven Bowls

Question: "Are these plagues from the seven bowls (Rev 16:1–21) any different than the ones from the seven seals or the seven trumpets? All of this sounds repetitious to me." (Rev 2:5; 6:7; Jn 19:30; Mt 27:51 also discussed)

The book of Revelation is not like a story in which each new plot element adds something new to the story. Rather, the book of Revelation has one message, and this message is repeated over and over with a variety of images and a variety of emphases.

The sequence of the seven bowls does have a lot in common with the earlier sequences of the seven seals and the seven trumpets. All three sequences are assuring the audience that the end time is coming soon and that, when it comes, those faithful to the Lamb will be saved and those faithful to the beast will be destroyed. As with the sequence of the seven trumpets, the plagues are described in such a way that one is reminded of the plagues at the time of the exodus.

In the sequence of the seven seals we saw that the martyrs asked when they would be justified. In our last article we saw that the angel announced the good news of God's judgment. In this sequence the reader learns more about who will be the object of God's judgment and why God's judgments are just.

The first four bowls of wrath affect the whole world—earth, seas, rivers and sun. This is an escalation over the other sequences in which one-fourth and one-third of the earth were affected. Also, the object of God's wrath is more clearly delineated. The sores affect those "who bore the mark of the beast and worshiped its image" (Rev 16:2). The rivers become blood because people "have shed the blood of the saints and prophets . . ." (Rev 16:6).

282

```
┌─────────────────────────────────────────────────────────────┐
│                    SEVEN BOWLS SEQUENCE                       │
│                                                              │
│   1. First Bowl:    Boils                                    │
│                                                              │
│   2. Second Bowl:   Sun turns to blood                       │
│                                                              │
│   3. Third Bowl:    Rivers and springs turn to blood         │
│                                                              │
│   4. Fourth Bowl:   Sun scorches people                      │
│                                                              │
│   5. Fifth Bowl:    On throne of beast; kingdom in darkness  │
│                                                              │
│   6. Sixth Bowl:    Euphrates dries up; kings assemble for   │
│                     Armageddon                               │
│                                                              │
│   7. Seventh Bowl:  "It is finished"; earthquake; Babylon and│
│                     Gentile cities fall                      │
└─────────────────────────────────────────────────────────────┘
```

In addition, God's justice in meting out such punishment is upheld. The angels cry, "Just art thou in these judgments, thou who art and wast, O Holy One" (Rev 16:5). Then the altar cries, "Yea, Lord God the Almighty, true and just are thy judgments" (Rev 16:7). (Remember that the martyrs were earlier pictured under the altar.)

The reason God's judgments are just is that the sinners persevere in their sins. People "cursed the name of God who had power over these plagues, and they did not repent and give him glory" (Rev 16:8).

The remaining three scenes in the sequence continue the elaboration of the theme of God's just judgments, but they speak more directly to the political situation in which the people find themselves.

The fifth angel pours his bowl on the throne of the beast (the Roman empire). The sixth angel's bowl is poured on the Euphrates so that its waters dry up. This, of course, recalls the exodus experience. The underlying message in using the exodus imagery is that just as God saved his people at the time of the exodus, so will he save his people now.

With the drying up of the Euphrates the scene is laid for the gathering of evil forces for the final showdown at Armageddon.

The pouring of the seventh bowl precipitates an earthquake which causes the defeat of great Babylon (Rome).

Notice that in the description of the gathering of the forces at Armageddon, John says that they assemble "on the great day of God the Almighty" (Rev 16:14). In the sequence of the seals the same wording was used. "For the great day of their (i.e. the one on the throne and the Lamb's) wrath has come, and who can stand before it?" (Rev 6:7). The "great day" refers to the second coming of Christ, the "day of the Lord" with which we are familiar from Paul's letters. In Revelation, however, the coming of that day involves a great battle.

When the final bowl is poured the imagery calls to mind Jesus' crucifixion. The voice calling from the temple says, "It is done" (Rev 16:17), Jesus' words as he dies as told in John's gospel (see Jn 19:30). In addition, the earthquake which splits the city calls to mind that at Jesus' death the earth shook and rocks split (see Mt 27:51). This imagery reminds one that it is through Jesus' death that evil has been defeated.

Since this sequence has escalated the damage done from one-fourth to one-third of the whole earth one might well ask, "Will no one be spared?" Notice that those who are faithful are saved. They join the Lamb in his heavenly court. The enemies of the faithful are not saved because they fail to repent. This lack of repentance is mentioned three times (see Rev 16:9; 16:10–11; 16:21).

But what about those who are followers of the Lamb but were "marked with the sign of the beast" for political or economic motives and now are repentant? John is not addressing such a situation in this passage because he has already called people to repentance in the letters to the churches. "Remember then from what you have fallen, repent and do the works you did at first. If not, I will come to you and remove your lampstand from its place, unless you repent" (Rev 2:5).

Only those who fail to repent will suffer God's just wrath.

The plagues caused by the pouring of the seven bowls do recall the sequences of the seals and the trumpets. However, with the pouring of the bowls we can see the dramatic tension rising. The Lamb's enemies are named, God's justice is defended, and the day of the Lord appears to be even nearer.

Review Questions

1. What does the sequence of the seven bowls have in common with the sequences of the seven seals and the seven trumpets?
2. What special emphasis appears in the sequence of the seven bowls?
3. Why are God's judgments just?
4. What is the underlying message in using the exodus imagery?
5. What is "the great day"? What is unique about the coming of that day in the book of Revelation as compared to Paul's letters?
6. What is taught by using imagery reminiscent of the time of Jesus' death?
7. Will anyone be saved? Explain.

Discussion Questions

1. Have you had dreams in which the same scene appears and reappears but with added intensity? Explain. What does this question have to do with the book of Revelation?
2. Have you ever met a person who knows that he or she is doing wrong and yet refuses to repent? Do you know any way to bring such a person around?
3. What do you think God can do about a person who refuses to repent?
4. Do you like the image of a battle for the "great day"? Why or why not?

Babylon: A Type of Rome

Question: "I presume this woman on the beast is Rome and the Roman empire. Why is the name on her forehead 'Babylon'?" (Rev 17–18; Rev 14:8; 16:19 also discussed)

Babylon functions as a type for Rome in the book of Revelation. You may remember that Babylon was mentioned twice before. When the three angels announced God's judgment, the second angel said, "Fallen, fallen is Babylon the great, she who made all nations drink the wine of her impure passion" (Rev 14:8). Again, as the seventh bowl was poured, "The great city was split into three parts, and the cities of the nations fell and God remembered great Babylon, to make her drain the cup of the fury of his wrath" (Rev 16:19).

There can be no doubt that the woman and the beast represent Rome. This beast is the same as the dragon of chapter 12 and the two beasts of chapter 13. It has seven heads and ten horns and is full of blasphemy. The seven heads represent both seven mountains and seven kings. Rome is built on seven hills. The seven kings are thought to refer to Caligula, Claudius, Nero, Vespusian, Titus, Domitian, and one more who is yet to come. The "one to come" is probably a reference to Nero. As you know, legends questioned Nero's death and suggested that he might return with the Parthians to conquer Rome. Nero is referred to in the words, "it was and is not and is to come" (Rev 17:8).

Babylon functions as a type of Rome because Babylon conquered Jerusalem and destroyed both the city and the temple in 587 B.C. By the time the book of Revelation is being written, Rome has destroyed the rebuilt temple and is presently persecuting the

---

PLOT ELEMENTS IN JUDGMENT ON BABYLON
(Elaboration of Seventh Bowl)

- Harlot seated on beast (seven heads; ten horns)
- Harlot dressed luxuriously
- Explanation of meaning of woman (Babylon, i.e. Rome) and of beast (Roman empire)
- Other nations will defeat "Babylon"
- Angel announces Babylon's fall
- Laments by kings, merchants, and seamen

---

church, Christ's "temple." In addition, Babylon is a symbol of the abuse of political power, of decadence and of luxury.

Rome has wielded political power in a way that has brought terrible harm to followers of the Lamb. Babylon, the harlot, represents the idolatry which the Roman empire has caused by setting the emperor up as a god. Rome has "glorified" herself (Rev 18:7). Other kings and other citizens have been drawn into this idolatry: ". . . the great harlot . . . with whom the kings of the earth have committed fornication, and with the wine of whose fornication the dwellers on earth have become drunk" (Rev 17:2).

John suggests that the end of Rome's political power will come because Rome will be defeated by other nations (perhaps by Nero and the Parthians) who will unwittingly be carrying out God's will (Rev 17:16–17). The kings of these other nations will then be defeated by Christ.

The decadence and luxury of Rome is clearly pictured in the description of the harlot. "The woman was arrayed in purple and scarlet, and bedecked with gold and jewels and pearls, holding in her hand a golden cup full of abominations and the impurities of her fornication . . ." (Rev 17:4).

As the kings, the merchants and the seamen lament the fall of Babylon, we hear in their lament the reasons why Babylon/Rome must fall. The merchants participated in the luxurious decadence with their ". . . cargo of gold, silver, jewels and pearls, fine linen, purple, silk and scarlet, all kinds of scented wood, all articles of ivory, all articles of costly wood, bronze, iron and marble, cinnamon, spice, incense, myrrh, frankincense, wine, oil, fine flour and wheat, cattle and sheep, horses and chariots, and slaves, that is, human souls" (Rev 18:12–13).

Rome has loved luxury so much that it has become completely decadent and treats people as though they were of less importance than wealth.

In addition to its wielding of political power in such a way that it amounts to idolatry, and in addition to its luxuriant decadence, Rome has killed the followers of the Lamb. "And in her was found the blood of prophets and of saints, and of all who have been slain on earth" (Rev 18:24).

So, as the kings, merchants, and seamen lament her fall, heaven rejoices. "Rejoice over her, O heaven, O saints and apostles and prophets, for God has given judgment for you against her" (Rev 18:20).

Babylon is the type of Rome because Babylon stands for the same sins. Just as Babylon scourged God's people and destroyed God's temple in the Old Testament, so has Rome destroyed the temple and persecuted Christians, thus trying to destroy the new "temple," the church. However, Rome will not succeed. Rome will be destroyed, and the church, the followers of the Lamb, will triumph.

Review Questions

1. How do we know that the author is referring to Rome as he pictures the woman on the beast?
2. Why is Babylon a type for Rome?
3. How has Rome wielded political power?
4. What is it about pursuing luxury that leads to sin?
5. Why do the kings, merchants, and seamen lament?
6. Why does heaven rejoice?

Discussion Questions

1. Can you think of places that we use as types? What does "Waterloo" mean? "Watergate"? "Camelot"?
2. Do you think pursuing luxury inevitably leads to sin? Why or why not? Can you think of examples?
3. Do you think saints should rejoice when evil is conquered? Why or why not?

The Beast, the Dragon,
and the Thousand Year Reign

Question: "How could the dragon be released again after Christ has won victory and the birds have eaten the flesh of the defeated (Rev 19:11–20:14)? I don't understand this thousand year reign at all."

There are many unanswered questions raised by these scenes in the book of Revelation. To respond to the questioner we will first point out what is definitely a wrong interpretation. Next we will sort out what John actually pictures. Then we will try to explain what he might mean.

The wrong interpretation rests on a misunderstanding of the literary form of apocalyptic literature. Remember, the book of Revelation is not predicting specific events in our future. To presume that the thousand year reign is a particular identifiable event yet to occur is to misunderstand.

What does John actually picture? First John pictures the resurrected Christ on a white horse coming forth for victorious battle (Rev 19:11–16). Next, before the battle, there is a victory cry. Then "the beast was captured along with the false prophet. . . . Both were hurled down alive into the fiery pool of burning sulphur. The rest were slain by the sword . . ." (Rev 19:20–21). So the beast is not dead, but alive in the fiery pool. Next an angel chains up the dragon (Satan, the one who gave the beast power) for one thousand years. Next we see a scene of the heavenly throne room. Those who have died martyrs' deaths are alive. They reign with Christ for the thousand years. Other people, good or bad, do not come back to life for judgment until after the thousand years.

PLOT ELEMENTS SURROUNDING THE THOUSAND YEAR REIGN

- Christ comes forth for victorious battle.
- Victory cry precedes battle.
- Beast and false prophet are captured and thrown into burning sulphur. The rest are slain.
- Angel chains up Satan for one thousand years.
- Martyrs reign with Christ during the thousand year reign.
- Great battle takes place: Devil defeated. Beast, dragon and false prophet tortured forever.
- All come before God's throne for judgment. Good saved. Evil, along with death and nether world, hurled into fiery pond.

After the thousand years a great battle takes place in which the devil is defeated. The devil joins the beast and the false prophet in the fiery pool and is tortured forever.

Finally, all come before the throne of God for judgment. All those whose names are in the book of life are saved. Those others, along with death and the nether world, are hurled into the fiery pool.

What is John teaching through this array of images? The theme of persecution seems to have dropped out. In these scenes John is dealing with the themes of judgment and salvation.

Christ, the warrior on the white horse, is already victorious. He accomplished victory with his death on earth. That is why his cloak is bloody (see Rev 19:13). The victory cry precedes the battle. This is very important and teaches the same message which has been taught over and over by the choice of heaven as the setting for the book of Revelation. It is from heaven that all actions proceed. Victory is already won. The script is not all played out but it is already written. Christ has already conquered evil.

The beast is captured. The beast stands for Rome. John is assuring his audience that Rome will fall. They need not fear Rome;

certainly they need not take seriously the idea that the emperor is himself a god.

Now we move from the beast, Rome, to the dragon, Satan. Sometimes, since the beast is using the dragon's power, these two symbols are combined. Sometimes they remain separate, as they do here.

In moving from the beast (Rome) to the dragon (Satan) John moves from the specific political situation to a broader topic—the recurring battle of humankind with evil over the centuries. Evil sometimes seems to be conquered (the thousand year reign) but then it raises its ugly head again. Will evil never be defeated?

Through his imagery John acknowledges both the recurring nature of evil and the Christian hope in the face of this reoccurrence. Christianity has an answer to the question, "Will evil ever be defeated?" The answer is, "Yes."

The scene of the heavenly throne room in which the martyrs are already present, reigning with Christ for one thousand years, is part of John's constant assurance to his audience that the martyrs are already saved and have a special place in heaven. Even as John writes, the martyrs are already with Christ. They do not have to wait for a final judgment.

When evil does reappear it will be defeated. Because of Christ there is no other possible ending to the story. The final battle, whenever it comes, will see the victory of good over evil.

In addition, all will be judged. The good and the bad will come before the throne of God. "And I saw the dead, great and small, standing before the throne, and books were opened. . . . And the dead were judged by what they had done" (Rev 20:12). The good will be saved, the bad will be punished.

John uses mysterious imagery. Any interpretation is just that, an interpretation. Still, John's theme is clear. God judges and God saves. Do not fear evil because Christ has already overcome evil. Choose Christ and you will be saved.

Review Questions

1. What is a wrong interpretation of the "thousand year reign"?
2. Who reigns with Christ during the thousand year reign?

3. With what two themes is John now dealing?
4. What is taught by the fact that Christ's cloak is bloody?
5. What is taught by the fact that the victory cry precedes the battle?
6. How does John image the recurring nature of our experience with evil?
7. Will evil ever be defeated? Why?

Discussion Questions

1. Do you agree that, from the perspective of human beings, evil seems to be defeated and then reoccurrs? Explain.
2. If the book of Revelation were written today, who might have been the specific audience? Why?
3. Do you have any suggestions for how to interpret the thousand year reign? What are they?
4. Do you believe that from heaven's perspective evil has already been defeated? Why or why not?

ARTICLE 19

The New Jerusalem:
The Bride of the Lamb

Question: "Who is the woman who is the bride of the lamb?" (Rev 21:9; Rev 17:1; 21:3–4; 21:22; 21:24; 22:1–2; Ez 47:12; Gen 2:9 also discussed)

The woman who is the bride of the Lamb is the city, the new Jerusalem. The bride and Jerusalem are both images used to describe the eschatological union with Christ of those who have remained faithful to Christ.

The bride and Jerusalem are described so that they are the complete opposites of the harlot and Babylon. This is made obvious by the fact that as each scene is introduced reference is made to one of the angels who had the bowls of God's wrath. In the scene with the harlot we read, "Then one of the seven angels, who had the seven bowls, came and said to me, 'Come, I will show you the judgment of the great harlot who is seated upon many waters . . .' " (Rev 17:1). In this scene we read, "Then came one of the seven angels who had the seven bowls full of the seven last plagues, and spoke to me, saying, 'Come, I will show you the Bride, the wife of the lamb' " (Rev 21:9).

As we saw in earlier descriptions, John uses traditional imagery from Ezekiel and Isaiah as he describes the appearance of Jerusalem and of God's presence in it (see Ez 40–48; Is 60:1–20). The gates of the city have on them the names of the twelve tribes; the foundations of the walls have on them the names of the twelve apostles. Clearly the whole picture is an array of images that describes not a thing but a people in relationship, the people who have remained faithful to the Lamb.

Unlike Ezekiel's description of the holy city, the new Jerusalem does not have a temple. "And I saw no temple in the city, for its temple is the Lord God the Almighty and the Lamb" (Rev 21:22). Again, it is clear that John is describing the relationship between God and his people.

In the city there is a river. "Then he showed me the river of the water of life, bright as crystal, flowing from the throne of God and of the Lamb through the middle of the street of the city; also on either side of the river, the tree of life with its twelve kinds of fruit, yielding its fruit each month; and the leaves of the trees were for the healing of the nations" (Rev 22:1–2).

This image of the river is also present in Ezekiel (see Ez 47:1–12). Ezekiel pictures a steadily rising river coming from below the threshold of the temple and going to the Dead Sea where it turns salt water into fresh water so that life abounds. Ezekiel's message is that the presence of God gives life to his people.

On the banks of the river Ezekiel describes trees. "And on the banks, on both sides of the river, there will grow all kinds of trees for food. Their leaves will not wither nor their fruit fail, but they will bear fresh fruit every month, because the water for them flows from the sanctuary. Their fruit will be for food, and their leaves for healing" (Ez 47:12).

John takes this beautiful image and associates it with the trees in the garden of Eden. In Genesis we read, "And out of the ground the Lord God made to grow every tree that is pleasant to the sight and good for food, the tree of life also in the midst of the garden . . ." (Gen 2:9).

So the trees that grow by the river in the new Jerusalem are the trees of life whose leaves heal nations. If one eats from the tree of life one will live forever. Salvation is extended to all nations.

An earlier beautiful image, taken from Isaiah, also includes all nations in God's saving power. The holy city has no sun or moon, for the glory of God is its light. "By its light shall the nations walk; and the kings of the earth shall bring their glory into it" (Rev 21:24).

The truths of Christianity can be taught through a variety of images. To teach that Christ is our strength, our sustenance, our source of life, we could say, "Jesus is the bread of life," or we could say, "The river that flows from the throne of the Lamb waters the tree of life. Come and eat." To teach that Christ's truth is a light to all nations we could say that three kings brought gifts to the manger, or we could say, "The leaves of the tree of life heal all nations." A variety of images can be used to teach one truth.

John uses the image of a bride dressed for her bridegroom and the image of the new Jerusalem filled with the glory of God to teach his audience the truth of their final union with Christ. As the voice from the throne says, "See, the home of God is among mortals. He will dwell with them as their God; they will be his people, and God himself will be with them; he will wipe every tear from their eyes . . ." (Rev 21:3–4 NRSV).

Review Questions

1. Who is the bride of the Lamb?
2. What are the images of the bride and Jerusalem used to describe?
3. How do the bride and Jerusalem contrast with the harlot and Babylon?
4. From what sources does John appropriate his imagery for the city of Jerusalem?
5. Why does the new Jerusalem not have a temple?
6. Is the description of the new Jerusalem describing a place? What is it describing?
7. What is John teaching by saying that the leaves of the tree of life heal nations?

Discussion Questions

1. What does this sentence mean: "The truths of Christianity can be taught through a variety of images"? Do you understand the two examples given? Can you give examples of your own? What are they?
2. Do you prefer John's image of the bride or his image of the city

to describe one's final union with Christ? Why? Does each image teach something which the other image fails to teach? What?

3. If you wanted to describe our final union with Christ, what images would you use? Why?

ARTICLE 20

Can Apocalyptic Writing Be True?

Question: "In the epilogue (Rev 22:6–21) Jesus tells John that 'these words are trustworthy and true' (Rev 22:6), and John says, 'I, John, am he who heard and saw these things' (Rev 22:8). Yet you say that the visions were not really visions but conventions of apocalyptic literature and that the book isn't about events in our future at all. If you are right, then I don't see why the book of Revelation is in the canon. Why is it?"

The book of Revelation is in the canon because it teaches the truth about Christianity. We can see these teachings, which are "trustworthy and true," reiterated in the epilogue, although they have been taught throughout the book. The author, John, "heard and saw these things," in the sense that he is an inspired author and so "saw" the truth of Christianity in circumstances that had blinded many to that truth. The gift which John received was not the gift of prognostication but the gift of spiritual insight. Like all prophets, John was able to see the ramifications of covenant love.

What are these eternal truths which are found in the book of Revelation, truths which are just as valuable for us today as they were for the original audience?

First, the author emphasizes that only God should be worshiped. In the epilogue he reiterates this truth by saying, "I fell down to worship at the feet of the angel who showed them to me; but he said to me, 'You must not do that! I am a fellow servant with you and your brethren the prophets, and with those who keep the words of this book. Worship God' " (Rev 22:8–9). As you know, we have seen constant warnings throughout the book of Revelation against

298

worshiping the beast or worshiping anyone or anything that tempts people to fail to worship the one true God.

Next, as has also been true throughout the book of Revelation, the author identifies the risen Christ with God and recognizes that Christ has a cosmic role. Jesus says, "I am the Alpha and the Omega, the first and the last, the beginning and the end" (Rev 22:13). The present dreadful circumstances of the audience do not put them outside of Christ's power, outside of God's provident plan for God's people.

The author also reminds his audience that the effect of Jesus' passion and death is salvation for those who follow Christ. "Blessed are those who wash their robes (i.e. in the blood of the Lamb) that they may have the right to the tree of life and that they may enter the city (i.e. the new Jerusalem) by the gates" (Rev 22:14).

The risen Christ is judge. The good will be rewarded; the evil will be punished. "See, I am coming soon, my reward is with me, to repay according to every one's works" (Rev 22:12).

Since Christ has saved and is judge, people suffering persecution need only persevere. The time of continued suffering will be short. "The time is near. Let the . . . righteous still do right, and the holy still be holy" (Rev 22:11).

John realizes that many who have chosen evil will not heed the words of this prophecy. However, those who have strayed from the right path are still called to repentance. "The Spirit and the Bride say, 'Come,' And let everyone who hears say, 'Come,' And let everyone who is thirsty come, let anyone who wishes take the water of life as a gift" (Rev 22:17 NRSV).

Even as John reiterates all of these core truths in his epilogue, he still acknowledges the conventions of the form of apocalyptic literature in which he has chosen to write. We still see the frame of a special revelation, known only to God, passed on by an angel to the prophet. In this epilogue it is sometimes Jesus who is the speaker, sometimes the angel, and sometimes John.

The angel in an apocalypse would usually tell the recipient of the vision to seal up the revelation until the end time. However, John has the angel say, "Do not seal up the words of the prophecy of this book, for the time is near" (Rev 22:10). The reason for this direc-

---

**ETERNAL TRUTHS TAUGHT IN THE BOOK
OF REVELATION**

- Only God should be worshiped.
- The risen Christ is God. Christ has a cosmic role.
- Through his passion, death and resurrection Christ has re-deemed humankind.
- The risen Christ is judge. Good will be rewarded. Evil will be punished.
- The martyrs are already with Christ in heaven.
- Those suffering persecution should persevere in hope. To choose "death" is to choose life. Christ will save.

---

tion is that John is telling his audience that the end time is their time. The end of their present suffering is near.

So there is something incompatible about thinking of the book of Revelation as a book predicting events which are yet to occur and at the same time saying that the book is an example of apocalyptic literature. Once one understands the conventions and purposes of apocalyptic literature, one realizes that it is simply a mistake to think that John was a fortune-teller looking into our future.

But there is nothing incompatible about thinking of the book of Revelation as an inspired book which teaches the truth and belongs in the canon, and at the same time realizing that it is written in the form of apocalyptic literature.

A work written in the form of apocalyptic literature could be true and revelatory, or it could fail to be true and revelatory, depending on what it teaches.

The book of Revelation teaches that Christ is God, that Christ has saved those who are his disciples, and that no evil, certainly not the Roman empire, can undo God's saving acts on behalf of God's people. Christians need only persevere and they will join Christ, as well as those who have already been martyred, in heaven. The end of the story has already been written, and it is a happy ending.

Review Questions

1. Why is the book of Revelation in the canon?
2. In what sense did John "hear and see these things"?
3. What was John's spiritual gift?
4. Name six teachings basic to Christianity taught by the book of Revelation and reiterated in the epilogue.
5. What conventions of apocalyptic literature appear in the epilogue?
6. What is the significance of not sealing up the book?
7. Are these two ideas compatible? "The book of Revelation is about specific events which have not yet occurred." "The book of Revelation is an example of apocalyptic literature." Why or why not?
8. Are these two ideas compatible? "The book of Revelation is written by an inspired author and it teaches truth." "The book of Revelation is an example of apocalyptic literature." Why or why not?

Discussion Questions

1. Did you like the book of Revelation? Why or why not?
2. Do you think you basically understand the book? Why or why not?
3. What still most puzzles you about this book? Why? Where might you find more information?
4. Do you think the book of Revelation is misunderstood and/or abused in our society? Why or why not?
5. For you personally what is the most important truth taught by the book of Revelation? Why?

Endnote

You have now read the Acts of the Apostles, a selection of New Testament letters, and the book of Revelation. As you have seen, these represent very different kinds of writing, written in different contexts to a variety of audiences. As a reader you needed to have a different mind-set as you read each in order to understand what the author was saying to his audience.

While each of these works differs one from another, as a group they have a great deal in common with each other. In each instance we have an inspired author, an author who has the spiritual insight to see the ramifications of events, to see that events are the result of God acting in the lives of God's people. God's presence and activity did not stop when the historical Jesus was no longer present on earth. The ramification of the resurrection is that Christ lives and so is still present and active in the lives of his people.

In each of these New Testament writings we could see the Holy Spirit bringing about the growth of the church. Those who had faith in Christ had a close bond with each other. How was their life in Christ to be nurtured? How would the truth be maintained? What structures would be developed? How would leadership be chosen? Who would decide differences? Who would correct wrong-doers? Who would urge others on to faith at times of persecution? Who would continue to reach out to others with the good news?

The story of the first century church is the story of God's providing for God's people by dwelling in their midst. The story unfolds: the church, God's people, is born, grows, responds, and changes under the guidance of the Spirit, just as the church is doing today.

When we read the New Testament we are reading our own history. We are reading a story which is not yet over and in which we

302

are characters. We, at this time, under the influence of the Holy Spirit, are writing the history, the tradition of the church, for the generations who will come after us.

The New Testament is church tradition, first century church tradition. The New Testament is not a box in which we are enclosed, beyond which we cannot grow. Rather it is roots to which we must always stay connected and be faithful. Each century, connected to these roots and to the growth of intervening centuries, produces new growth.

In each century the core truth remains the same, but that core truth must be interpreted in the context of each century's new knowledge and new challenges. This process of interpretation has been present from the beginning and will always be present.

It is our responsibility, as the church of this century, to learn to love and understand our roots so that we can be an outgrowth of them. To become the church of our century it is essential that we read and understand the Acts of the Apostles, the New Testament letters, and the book of Revelation.

Glossary

Ahab: King of Israel from 869–850 B.C. Married to Jezebel.

Allegory: The name of a literary form (a kind of writing). An allegory has two levels of meaning: a literal level and an intentional level. To understand the author's intent one must figure out what the literal or surface level "stands for." The real topic is on the intentional level.

Analogy: A correspondence between two things. Often an analogy is used as part of an explanation; something unknown is compared to something similar which is already known.

Ananias: The Jewish Christian to whom Paul went immediately after his conversion experience. Ananias restored Paul's sight.

Ananias: The Jewish Christian in Jerusalem who pretended to give more than he did give and suddenly died.

Angel: The word means "messenger." The word refers to a heavenly spirit.

Antioch: Antioch was in Syria and was a province under Roman rule. The Christian community in Antioch was founded by fugitives who fled from religious persecution in Jerusalem after Stephen's martyrdom. Paul was sent on his missionary journeys from Antioch.

Apocalyptic: The word means "revelation." Apocalyptic litera-ture is a kind of writing which uses code to give hope to people facing persecution. Its message is that the "end" (of the time of suffering) is near.

Apocalyptic Images: An "image is a mental representation of something not present to the senses. An apocalyptic image is an image used in conceptualizing and describing the end times.

Apollos: A Jew from Alexandria who may have been influenced by Philo. He taught in Corinth (Acts 18:24). Some preferred him to Paul (1 Cor 3:6).

Apologia: A formal justification or defense.

Apostolic Authority: This concept has broadened to include more than direct authorship. A work may be considered to have apostolic authorship if it is guided by the apostolic truth and spirit, i.e. written by a disciple of the apostles.

Appropriate: This verb means to take something and make it your own. To appropriate a story would be to retell an existing story in such a way that you give it your own emphasis.

Archetypal Image: An image which has its origin in the subcon-scious and deals with experiences common to the whole human race. A beast or dragon is an archetypal image of evil or chaos.

Athens: The Greek city where Paul argued with the Epicureans and the Stoics (see Acts 17:10–34).

Augustus: Ruled Rome from 32 B.C.–14 A.D. Jesus was born during his reign. The emperors who succeeded Augustus used the name as a title.

Baal: A way of referring to a god worshiped under a number of titles in Canaan.

Babylon: A city on the bank of the Euphrates to which the Israelites were moved after the Babylonians defeated the Israelites and destroyed their city and temple (587 B.C.).

Balaam: A seer who was asked to curse the Israelites by Balak, the king of Moab (Num 22:51).

Balak: The king of Moab who asked Balaam to curse the Israelites (Num 2:2ff).

Barnabas: The Christian of the Jerusalem church sent to investigate the church in Antioch. He summoned Paul to Antioch and accompanied Paul on his first missionary journey. Later he went with Mark.

Bible: The word means "a collection of books." The Bible includes the Old Testament (the Hebrew scripture) and the New Testament (the Greek scripture).

Brothers: In the Greek New Testament this word has a less precise meaning than it has in English. Jesus' "brothers" could be relatives, close friends, or followers.

Canon: A "canon" is an instrument by which something is measured. In the context of the Bible the canon refers to the books which are considered revelation and inspired and are therefore in the Bible. These books are the "rule" of faith.

Category of Thought: A familiar way to conceptualize something. As a category of thought, "miracle" was a much broader category in pre-scientific times than it is now. In our day, the category "art" is being debated. What is art? When people first heard of Christianity they would try to associate it with categories of thought which they already had. For instance, Christ would be compared to the Greek idea of Logos.

Catholic Epistles: James, 1 and 2 Peter, 1, 2, 3 John and Jude are called the Catholic epistles.

Cephas: Cephas means "the rock." It is the name given Peter by Jesus. Cephas is an Aramaic name, Peter a Greek name.

Christ: The word "Christ" means "anointed." The word is a messianic title, applied to those whom the Jews understood to be God's instruments to save them. To apply the word to Jesus is to claim that Jesus is the messiah.

Christological: Centers on christology. Christology studies Jesus, his nature, and his function.

Church: The word means "the assembly of ones called out." In the New Testament context "church" refers to the Christian community—those who are united with Jesus Christ.

Circumcision: The removal of the loose fold of skin that covers the tip of the penis. Circumcision was required by the Jewish law.

Claudius: Emperor of Rome from 41–54. He expelled the Jews from Rome (Acts 18:2).

Coliseum: An amphitheater in Rome in which many Christians died.

Collate: To gather and arrange in a particular order.

Context: That which surrounds a word or passage. The context within which something is said or written affects its meaning.

Contextualist: A person who reads in context. In relation to the Bible, a contextualist would ask, "What is the literary form of the book? What were the beliefs of the people of the time? How does this fit into the process of revelation?"

Convention: A literary convention is an accepted way of writing in a particular form. For instance, to begin a letter with "Dear" is a convention in letter writing.

Cornelius: The centurion who was directed by an angel to summon Peter. Cornelius and all his household received the gifts of the Holy Spirit and were then baptized.

Corpus: A collection of writings. Paul's corpus refers to the collected letters known to have been written by Paul.

David: Succeeded Saul as king (ca. 1010–970 B.C.). He united the twelve tribes and defeated the Philistines. David was seen as an ideal ruler. People expected the messiah to be one like David.

Deacons: The word deacon means "one who serves at table." The word is used in reference to the seven chosen to see that Greek-speaking Christians were served equitably (see Acts 6:1–6). Deacons had a defined function in the early church and were installed through a laying on of hands.

Deutero-Pauline Letters: Colossians, Ephesians, 2 Thessalonians. These letters have been attributed to Paul but are believed to have been written by a disciple of Paul's.

Dialogical: A dialogical argument is one that seems to include a dialogue. One learns both points of view as the opponent's thoughts are presented in order to be refuted.

Elders: Jewish elders belonged to the sanhedrin. Christian elders had a position of authority in the church. They were appointed to head local communities.

Ephesus: The capital of the Roman province of Asia, a wealthy port and marketplace. Paul preached in Ephesus on both his second and third journeys. Ephesus is one of the seven churches addressed in the book of Revelation.

Epicureans: Followers of Epicurus who did not believe in an afterlife or that the gods influenced human affairs.

Esau: Eldest son of Isaac and Rebekah. Twin of Jacob. He sold Jacob his rights as first-born (Gen 25:27).

Eschatology: The word means "study of last things." When Jesus speaks of the end times his words are about "eschatology."

Etiology: A story that describes the origin of a place, institution, name, etc.

Eunuch: A man with undeveloped or castrated testes. Philip converted an Ethiopian eunuch (Acts 8:26–40).

Exodus: The core experience of Jewish salvation history when God led his people out of Egypt and through the desert to the holy land ca. 1250 B.C.

Ezekiel: A prophet deported to Babylon (593–571 B.C.).

Form: The shape of something. In literature the form is the kind of writing, or the "shape" of the whole piece. Is it a poem? a letter? a legend? One cannot understand the author's intent unless one understands the literary form in which the author is writing.

Freedman: An ex-slave.

Function: The use to which something is put, or its role. In literature different kinds of writing have different functions. An editorial has a different function than a straight news story or a feature article.

Galatia: Galatia has two meanings: (1) The plateau of central Anatolia (northern Galatia) near Pontua and Bithynia. (2) The province of Galatia which included Derbe and Lystra (southern Galatia). Scholars argue over which community received the letter to the Galatians.

Gamaliel: Paul's teacher and the member of the council who advised that the council leave Peter and the apostles alone, not knowing if their work was of God or not. Time would tell.

Gentile: Any non-Jew. A Gentile is a "foreigner" from the point of view of the Jews.

Glossolalia: "The gift of tongues"—a form of charismatic prayer experienced as part of the outpouring of the Holy Spirit. It is unintelligible and needs to be interpreted. It is a sign for unbelievers of the presence of the Spirit.

Hellenism: The influence of the Greek culture on the eastern Mediterranean world which began with Alexander the Great (356–323 B.C.) but continued long after his death.

Hellenists: Those who spoke Greek. In Acts 6:1 the Hellenists are Greek-speaking Christians as compared to those who spoke Hebrew.

Hierarchy: A group organized according to their authority or rank.

Image: A mental conceptualization of something not present to the senses. A concrete way of thinking about an abstract concept.

Inspire: To affect by divine influence. When we say that the Bible is inspired we mean that God affected the human authors.

Interpolation: A part of a text which has been inserted into a pre-existent text.

Isaiah: The prophet after whom the book of Isaiah is named. He was a prophet in Jerusalem from 742–701 B.C. The book of Isaiah is a prophetic book which contains writings from three distinct historical times: First Isaiah (chapters 1–39, ca. 742 B.C.); Second Isaiah (chapters 40–55, after 587 B.C.); Third Isaiah (chapters 56–66, 520 B.C.).

Jacob: Son of Isaac, twin of Esau, father of the twelve tribes of Israel.

James: Head of the early church community in Jerusalem (Acts 12:17).

Jerusalem Council: The council held in approximately 49 A.D. at which it was decided that Gentile Christians need not be circumcised.

Jew: Used to name the Israelites in both an ethnic and a religious sense.

Jezebel: Queen of King Ahab of Israel (1 Kgs 16:31). She promoted the worship of the god Baal.

Joel: The name of a post-exilic book of prophecy. Some imagery from Joel is appropriated by John in the book of Revelation.

Kerygma: A form of early Christian preaching which included the core truths of Christianity.

Legend: An imaginative and symbolic story with an historical core.

Lintel: The horizontal beam on the upper part of a window or door.

Literary Form: The kind of writing. Examples are poetry, fable, myth, history, biography, science fiction, etc. In order to understand any book you need to know its literary form.

Literary Technique: A systematic way of accomplishing something in a written work. Luke uses a trip as a literary technique around which to organize his gospel.

Logos: In Greek philosophy Logos was the source of order and intelligibility, a kind of cosmic reason. In the New Testament this idea becomes associated with Christian concepts. Logos is associated with the Word which became flesh.

Luke: A companion and fellow worker of Paul's. The authorship of the gospel according to Luke and the Acts of the Apostles is attributed to him.

Matthias: Matthias was chosen by lot to take the place of Judas (Acts 1:23–26).

Messiah: Hebrew for "anointed one." "Messiah" and "Christ" are synonyms. Both are used to name the person whom God would send to save his people.

Messianic Title: A title which names Jesus as the expected messiah (i.e. "Christ," "Son of David," "Son of Man").

Metaphor: A metaphor is a comparison that does not use "like" or "as." A comparison which does use "like" or "as" is a simile. Example: Simile—"The nurse is like an angel." Metaphor—"The nurse is an angel."

Miracle Story: A story which reveals God's saving power. It usually includes: an introduction that presents the situation; a request for help; an account of help given; the result of the help; the reaction of the spectators.

Moses: The great leader of the Israelites who led them out of slavery under the Egyptians (ca. 1250 B.C.).

Narrative: The act, technique, or way of telling a story.

Narrator: The "voice" telling the story. The narrator cannot always be equated with the author. The author may create a character who tells the story and is thus the narrative voice.

Nero: Emperor of Rome (54–68 A.D.). He was emperor when Paul wished to be tried (Acts 25:11). Legend held that after his death he would return and defeat the Romans.

Nicolaitans: A group rebuked twice in the letters to the churches in the book of Revelation. We do not know specifically who they were or what they taught.

Occasional Letter: A letter written for or in response to a particular occasion. Obviously it is best understood in the context of that occasion.

Onesimus: The slave who belonged to Philemon, ran away, and was converted to Christianity by Paul. The letter to Philemon is about Onesimus.

Oral Tradition: The traditions of the community handed on by word of mouth.

Overseers: See Elders

Pagan: A person who has no religion, or who is neither Christian, Moslem, nor Jew.

Palestine: The strip of land bordering the eastern side of the Mediterranean Sea.

Passover: The Jewish festival that celebrates the escape of the Jews from Egypt.

Pastoral Letters: 1 and 2 Timothy and Titus as a group are called the pastoral letters. The letters are addressed to the pastors of Christian communities and deal with church life and practice.

Paul: Paul is the Greek name used by Saul of Tarsus. He was converted on the road to Damascus and became a great missionary.

Pentateuch: The first five books of the Old Testament. Also referred to as the law.

Pentecost: "The fiftieth day." Originally an agricultural feast of the Israelites. Later a celebration of the giving of the law to Moses. In Acts Pentecost is "the birthday of the church," the day on which the apostles received the outpouring of the Holy Spirit.

Pharisees: Members of a leading religious sect in Judaism that stressed scrupulous observance of the law.

Philemon: A Christian slave owner who had been converted by Paul. Paul asked him to accept Onesimus back without punishment.

Philip: One of the seven chosen as deacons in Acts 6:1–6. He was the first to preach the gospel in Samaria.

Philo: A Hellenized Jew from Alexandria who tried to explain the torah in Greek categories of thought. His thinking influenced the Corinthians.

Polemic: An argument designed to refute an opinion or doctrine.

Post-Exilic Period: The period after the Babylonian exile (587–537 B.C.) when the Jews were returning to the holy land and rebuilding.

Proof Texting: To misuse biblical passages by taking them out of context and using them to "prove" the truth of a statement which the biblical passages are not addressing.

Prophet: One who speaks for another. In the context of scripture—one who speaks for God and who constantly reminds the people of the ramifications of living in covenant love.

Pseudonymous: A pseudonymous letter is one whose author attributes his or her work to someone else. The author takes on another persona and writes from that person's point of view.

Rhetorical Device: A rhetorical device is a method that enables an author to say something that he wants his audience to understand. For instance, an author can have one character question another character. The composed answer enables the author to teach the audience. Rhetorical devices can also be used to improve the style of writing or speaking, to make it more interesting or attractive.

Sadducees: A Jewish sect. They were extremely conservative aristocrats who accepted only the torah. Their disagreements with the Pharisees included the fact that they did not believe in the resurrection. In Acts the Sadducees are the apostles' adversaries.

Sanhedrin: The council of the Jews which included elders, high priests and scribes. It had authority over Jewish matters and functioned as a local court.

Sapphira: The wife of Ananias who, along with her husband, pretended to give more than she did give to the church in Jerusalem and then died suddenly.

Saul: Saul was Paul's Jewish name. Paul is called Saul during his first appearances in Acts (see Acts 7:58–13:9).

Simon the Magician: A magician in Samaria who tried to buy the power of the Spirit which he witnessed in the apostles (Acts 8:9–24).

Simony: Purchasing spiritual things. For instance, trying to buy indulgences or absolution. This sin was named after Simon the magician who tried to buy spiritual power from Peter.

Son of Man: Son of Man is usually a messianic title, a reference to the book of Daniel in which a "Son of Man" receives power over the nations. This is the messianic title which appears on Jesus' lips in the synoptic gospels. In the book of Revelation "Son of Man" may, at least in one instance, refer to an angel rather than to Christ.

Spirit People: The Corinthians, influenced by Philo, were called Spirit people because they valued the spiritual to the point of practically dismissing the material, including the body.

Stephen: A Jew living in Jerusalem who became a Christian, a deacon (Acts 6:1–6) and a martyr (Acts 6:8–7:60).

Stoics: Members of a Greek school of philosophy founded by Zeno. They taught that human beings should be free from passion and accept all that happens with "apatheia," because all is directed by a divine force. Paul ran into Stoics in Athens (Acts 17:18–34).

Synonym: A word which has the same meaning as another word.

Synoptic Gospels: The gospels of Mark, Matthew, and Luke are called synoptic gospels because they have many similarities and can be seen as one.

Temple: The temple in Jerusalem was the only authorized center for sacrifice and for the worship of Yahweh. The first temple was destroyed in 587 B.C. The magnificent temple which existed during Jesus' life was destroyed in 70 A.D.

Testament, New: Testament means covenant. The New Testament is the collection of Christian Greek scriptures.

Testament, Old: Testament means covenant. The Old Testament is the collection of Jewish Hebrew scriptures.

Theme: The main idea or perception expanded upon in a larger work.

Theophilus: The person addressed as the recipient of Luke's gospel and of the Acts of the Apostles.

Titus: One of Paul's fellow workers. He was Paul's emissary to the Corinthians between the time when Paul wrote 1 Corinthians and 2 Corinthians.

Type: An "image," "model," or "example." An Old Testament person, event, that is used as a model or pre-figurement of a New Testament person or event.

Typology: Presenting people, institutions or events in the Old Testament as "types" of people, events or institutions in the New

Testament. For example, Moses is a type of Christ. Moses prefigures Christ in that many parallels can be drawn between them.

Yahweh: A translation of the name of God as revealed to Moses. Many scholars believe the name is derived from the Hebrew verb "to be" and means "He is."

Index of Biblical References